EURI...

THE WAR PLAYS

IPHIGENIA AT AULIS,
THE WOMEN OF TROY,
HELEN

TRANSLATED AND INTRODUCED BY DON TAYLOR

methuen

Euripides
The War Plays

Iphigenia at Aulis, The Women of Troy, Helen

In these plays, written during the Peloponnesian War, Euripides voices his most complete condemnation of the brutality of war. Don Taylor, through his powerful and compelling translations, conveys with equal clarity the bitterness and violence of *Iphigenia at Aulis* and *The Women of Troy*, and the subtle irony of *Helen*. Don Taylor directed *Iphigenia at Aulis* for a BBC TV production broadcast in summer 1990. The cast included Roy Marsden as Agamemnon and Fiona Shaw as Clytemnestra.

Euripides was born near Athens between 485 and 480 BC and grew up during the years of Athenian recovery after the Persian Wars. His first play was presented in 455 BC but he failed to win the first prize for tragedy until 441 and rarely afterwards. Despite this, nineteen of his plays survive, a greater number than those of Aeschylus and Sophocles combined. He wrote a substantial number of plays on the subject of war, including The Children of Heracles, Andromache *and* Hecuba. *His later plays, of which* Iphigenia at Aulis *is one, are marked by a sense of bitterness and disillusion at man's propensity for slaughtering his fellow man. A year or two before his death, Euripides left Athens to live in exile at the court of King Archelaus of Macedonia, where he died in 406 BC.*

The translator, Don Taylor, was born in London in 1936. He graduated from Oxford University and spent a short time in the theatre before joining BBC TV. He became a leading drama director and worked exclusively on new plays, including early work by David Mercer, Hugh Whitemore and David Turner. He became a freelance in 1964, and since then has directed plays for television and theatre. His first stage play was presented at the Edinburgh Traverse Theatre in 1967 and he has continued to write many plays for TV, among them Dad, Flayed, When the Actors Come, In Hiding *and* The Testament of John, *and for the theatre, including* The Roses of Eyam, The Exorcism *and* Brotherhood. *With works for radio, he has written more than fifty plays and films, including three verse plays. In 1986 his translations of Sophocles* The Theban Plays, *which he directed for a BBC TV production the same year, were published by Methuen Drama. His autobiography,* Days of Vision, *was published by Methuen Drama in 1990.*

EURIPIDES

The War Plays

Iphigenia at Aulis
The Women of Troy
Helen

Translated and introduced by
Don Taylor

Methuen Drama

METHUEN'S WORLD DRAMATISTS

These translations first published in Great Britain in 1990 by
Methuen Drama, Michelin House, 81 Fulham Road,
London SW3 6RB and distributed in the United States of America
by HEB Inc, 361 Hanover Street, Portsmouth, New Hampshire
03801

The front cover shows a detail from 'Soldiers at Rye' by Edward
Burra from the Tate Gallery (Reproduced by permission of the
Lefèvre Gallery; photograph © The Bridgeman Art Library.) The
back cover shows Euripides and is reproduced by courtesy of the
Trustees of the British Museum.

A CIP catalogue record for this book is available from the British
Library

ISBN 0 413 64250 X

Printed and bound in Great Britain
by Cox & Wyman Ltd, Cardiff Road, Reading

CONTENTS

INTRODUCTION

A good translation of a play presupposes a production. The practical necessity of preparing a text for performance imposes disciplines which can only bring the translator nearer to the origin of the text he is attempting to translate. As he writes, he becomes himself the playwright, hearing his words spoken, seeing the actors move in the theatre of his mind.

In making texts for performance of plays as old as these, the discipline is even more beneficial. In matters of textual criticism and interpretation, crucially difficult in many places in the three plays in this volume, the scholar poet can afford the luxury of an open mind. The director poet must make decisions, and make sure that those decisions will stand up to the rigorous examination of actors' rehearsal and public performance. In that respect he finds himself in a similar position to that occupied by the poet director who made these plays in the fifth century BC.

The sense of theatrical logic applied by good modern actors to the exercise of their trade is particularly useful. In the contemporary theatre, actors perform a continuous act of literary criticism upon the texts they work with, simply to make it possible to bring them to life at all. There is no skating over the sonorous surface of verse these days. Actors must dig into a text, to find the different layers of meaning within it; like Theseus, they must find the line or thread that leads them through the labyrinth of the play, so that a journey that starts at the beginning will carry them logically and convincingly through to the end. There can be no fudging in the process of discovering that journey. Only bad actors fudge, and their fudging is quite obvious, when the clear line of dramatic action is obscured. The process of translation is not only the process of rendering the words and images of one ancient language into another modern one. It is the uncovering, the making plain, of that clear line of action. If the translation is good, it will choose words and images that preserve the dramatic logic, the subtext of the piece, even if that concept is one that a classical dramatist would hardly have recognised. The fact is that the classical texts do contain this inner dramatic logic. It is one of the qualities that has enabled them to survive as performances, rather than mere literary texts, for two and a half thousand years.

The actor's necessity to find this thread, this subtextual logic, is the greatest possible aid to the translator. Again and again in directing Sophocles' Theban plays and *Iphigenia at Aulis*, I found actors' instincts slightly ill at ease with what I had written. They couldn't find the thread, the dramatic logic was somehow eluding them: and again and again I returned to my study, and found the slightest of mis-emphases in my translation, the choosing of just the wrong word, an image that was slightly off-centre: and the closer I managed to get to what I understood the Greek to mean, the happier the actors invariably were, the more truthful they found the development of the dramatic logic within the words. Of all the practical disciplines imposed on the director-translator, this I have found to be the most exciting and rewarding.

I made these three translations with a specific production plan in mind. The intention was, and is, to create a trilogy of Euripides' plays to be performed in my own productions on BBC Television, and then to be of general use in the theatre. I made no textual or structural concessions to the Television medium. These plays are far too good to be tampered with merely for the sake of setting up a few clever camera angles or tracking shots, and what Euripides has to say is too complex and subtle to be interpreted merely visually, without the richness of his words and structure. I believe Classical Greek plays must be translated for our generation within the language and style of the modern theatre, as a living part of contemporary drama, not as an act of archaeological rediscovery, or as a presentation of ancient modes of drama that have not survived into modern practice. There are no masks in my productions, no formalised dancing, and the language I have used, within the limits of my own ability, is the poetic speech of the present age. The central truths contained within Euripides' plays seem to me to be almost shockingly contemporary, and nowhere more so than in his plays about war. I have therefore translated him as though he were a living dramatist, not a dead one, the sort of fellow playwright you might bump into in the crowded foyer at the Royal Court, or with whom you might share a drink at the National Theatre bar.

Why 'The War Plays'? What war are we talking about and what plays do we mean? Euripides left no collection of plays with that title, and it has not been deemed necessary to issue volumes of his plays under a generic title before.

It is a matter of the profoundest regret that we have no complete trilogy of play by Euripides or by Sophocles. It is known that tragedies were presented in competition at the Athenian City Dionysia in the spring, and that the terms of the competition required the playwright to enter four plays, three tragedies, and a satyr play, the latter a low comic piece to send the audience home amused, and to celebrate the unity of Athenian culture. Whether the satyr plays, with their probable celebration of the universal pleasures of physical existence and the instinctive wisdom of the common man, had any thematic or artistic relation to the three preceding tragedies, we have no means of knowing. Only one satyr play, *Cyclops* by Euripides, has survived complete, and we have no knowledge of the subject matter of the tragedies that played with it. Perhaps we should really think in terms of tetrologies, rather than trilogies, and try to assimilate the rude comedy that followed the great draining tragedies into our view of the Greek theatrical experience? I suspect that we should, and that if we could consult them the classical playwrights would be amazed and shocked that we have come to think of their tragic confrontations without the comic celebration that followed them. But the brute fact is, we can't. The Dark Ages' destruction of the classical texts, from the burning of the library of Alexandria by the Islamic armies in the seventh century to the capture and sack of Constantinople by the Turks in 1453, slams like a door in our face. We don't know, and short of some extraordinary miracle, the recovery from the desert sands of a whole library of lost Greek texts, we never will.

Only one complete trilogy survives, without its satyr play, the *Oresteia* of Aeschylus. From that we learn that three plays can be related to form a grand and satisfying whole. But it is also clear from other archaeological and literary evidence that the unity of the three plays was by no means always the playwright's aim.

Aeschylus' trilogy demonstrates the simplest of unities, both a developing story and a growing theme, but it is clear that playwrights often presented three plays that had no story connection at all. Whether they had thematic connections remains a matter of guesswork, without any complete trilogies against which to test the question. We know that Euripides' *Iphigenia at Aulis* and *The Bacchae* were presented on the same bill with a lost *Alcmaeon*, and it is quite clear that the two plays that have survived have almost nothing in common. But these plays were presented after Euripides' death, and their lack of relationship with each other might have been untypical, simply because with the playwright dead that was the only way his last plays could be presented.

Of the other plays in this volume, the history of *The Women of Troy* is the most frustrating. We know that it was the third play of a trilogy, which began with an *Alexander*, and had a *Palamedes* as the second play, with a *Sisyphus* satyr play rounding off the entertainment. Alexander is the second name of Paris, whose judgement between the three goddesses and subsequent rape of Helen started the Trojan War, and Palamedes is one of the Greek heroes who died at Troy, stoned to death after having been falsely accused of treason by Odysseus: so it seems likely that what we have lost here is a full Euripidean trilogy on the subject of the Trojan War, related both as a developing story, and by theme. The one play we do have, *The Women of Troy*, is the most shattering and complete condemnation of the atrocities of war in any language, and arguably the greatest play on the subject of war ever written. It was created when Euripides was at the height of his powers, and when he had a particularly harsh and uncompromising message to deliver to his Athenian compatriots, as they began the last stage of the war with Sparta with an act of *hybris* that, to a tragedian, might seem certain to lead to catastrophe. Greek scholars have tended to assert, with desperate optimism, that the best plays from the Greek age have been the ones that survived, on the principle that the best plays would have been copied in MSS most often. Some of the texts that have survived seem to be set book copies, for the use of students, and though we might agree that set books are likely to contain a fair sprinkling of great works, a glance at our own lists will only confirm that a good many great titles don't appear.

Scholarly optimism also seems in danger of confusing greatness with popularity. Euripides eventually left his native city, and spent the last years of his life in exile, and though we do not know why he did that, he would hardly have done so if he had been the favourite dramatist of the age. The subject-matter of his last plays suggests that they might have made him powerful political enemies, and Aristophanes' picture of him, although we have no grounds for believing it is at all accurate, at least makes it clear that he was a controversial figure. We do know for certain that the trilogy that ended with *The Women of Troy* did not win the first prize in 415 BC, and there are good historical reasons for suspecting that it was particularly unpopular, at least in some political quarters. Whatever the truth of what is always doomed to be a speculative matter, it seems likely that in the loss of this Euripidean Trojan War trilogy (he almost certainly wrote more than one) we have lost two-thirds – perhaps one should say three-quarters – of one of the greatest works of dramatic literature.

But however sad it is, the fact remains that there is no surviving Euripidean trilogy, nor even a synthetic trilogy – plays that follow each other as a simple narrative, but weren't actually written as a trilogy – like Sophocles' Theban Plays, which, though they are often discussed and published and performed under that title, were produced separately by Sophocles over a period of about thirty-five years.

After the success of my translations and productions of the Theban Plays in 1986, I was very keen to complete a similar project with Euripides, a writer I had always particularly loved. When I first proposed that I should do a Greek play on television, it was the *The Women of Troy* I suggested, not the Theban Plays. The problem was how to find in Euripides three plays that would tell a developing story and explore a central theme, among the nineteen plays of his that survive from a writing life that must have lasted more than fifty years.

There are almost three times as many plays surviving by Euripides as by either of the other two great tragedians. Compared with the seven plays each by Aeschylus and Sophocles, nineteen plays have been ascribed to Euripides' name, still barely a quarter of his estimated output of about eighty. Of these, at least eight can be described as having war as their principal subject, either in its immediate effects, or its aftermath. Three of them, *The Children of Heracles*, *Andromache* and *Hecuba*, seem to have been written between 430 and 425 BC, when Euripides was in his early fifties, one, *The Suppliant Women*, around 420, and the remaining four, *The Women of Troy*, *Helen*, *The Phoenician Women* and *Iphigenia at Aulis*, between 415 and Euripides death in 406, the decade of his late sixties and seventies. For most of the last ten years of his life, at least as far as the surviving plays are concerned, war was at the forefront of his mind, its horrors, moral and physical, its essential pointlessness, and the ethical price it exacts from individuals and states who wage it. During that last period he created, in addition to his spiritual masterpiece, *The Bacchae*, his two most powerful statements on the subject of war, *The Women of Troy*, and *Iphigenia at Aulis*.

It was obvious that if a performable Euripidean trilogy was to be constructed, war, and specifically the Trojan War, would have to be its subject. His greatest plays that do not deal with the Trojan War, *Medea*, *Hippolytus* and *The Bacchae*, could not be made to tell a coherent story, and though there are thematic links to be observed, to do with the power of instinct and the qualities of tragic women, they are tenuous, and would certainly be tendentious as a basis for performance.

It was clear that *The Women of Troy* would have to be the centre of such a created trilogy, and having made that decision the choice of *Iphigenia at Aulis* as the first play was obvious enough. We would then begin with a play about the ominous beginning of the Greek expedition against Troy, and continue with a second play about its disastrous ending. After a great deal of thought and discussion at the BBC between myself, Louis Marks the Producer, and his assistant Paul Marcus, we decided to choose *Helen* for the third play, so that the final part of the story would be the very much lighter tale of how Menelaus finally rescued Helen from Egypt and took her home to Sparta seven years after the war had ended. Not the tale as any of the Greek masters would have told it, certainly, but a convincing story, how the war began, how it ended, and its aftermath, with one character, Menelaus, in all three plays, and Helen herself in the second and third, and brooding like a malign force over the first. The project was agreed, and I was commissioned to make new translations of all three plays, for eventual performance as a connected trilogy, on BBC TV.

The reason for Euripides' concern with war stares at us from the face of history. From 431 to 404 Athens was engaged in a war against Sparta and her allies, waged inconclusively during the earlier years, which became in the ten years following 413 a life and death struggle that ended in the total defeat of Athens by the militaristic Spartan Oligarchy. Thucydides, its great historian, called this Peloponnesian War the greatest war the people of Hellas had ever known, and it was certain that the city states of Greece had never experienced anything like it, not even during the great Persian invasions of some two generations earlier. In a sense the war was even greater than Thucydides himself knew. After the Spartan defeat and occupation of Athens, there was very little peace between the Greek city states. Thebes, Sparta, Corinth, and Athens herself, which recovered surprisingly quickly from the disaster of 404, observed and occasionally assisted by the Persian Empire, conducted a fifty year struggle between themselves, which left them so weakened that they were no match for the combination of the Macedonian Phalanx and King Philip's diplomacy which swept down upon them from the north in the 350s. No Greek state ever again attained the political dominance and the cultural glory of the Athenian Empire in the last days of the Periclean democracy, the years immediately before the war began. Thucydides was right to point out the war's great importance. Over a period of years it slowly undermined and weakened the foundations of Classical Greece in an endless round of battles, massacres, revolutions, oligarchic and democratic coups, executions and murders. Thucydides and, to a lesser extent, Xenophon are the great chroniclers of that slow destruction, and Euripides is its principal dramatic poet, speaking to us clearly on our own stage with all the pain and despair with which he warned the no doubt unheeding Athenian statesmen who were bringing their city to the dust, and dishonouring its democratic ideals.

The first group of plays to have war as their subject, *The Children of Heracles*, *Andromache* and *Hecuba*, seem to have been written in the first six or seven years of the war. The most remarkable of them is *Hecuba*, which in its horror, violence and cynicism we might otherwise be tempted to place in the late group of war plays, in which Euripides' disillusion seems to be complete. *Hecuba's* bloody revenge on the children of Polymestor, and the prophecy of her own transformation into a dog, is a clear prefiguring of what the poet reveals in *Orestes*, some twenty years later, that total war can only lead to a total destruction of all moral values, in the defeated as well as in the victorious. The Hecuba who suffers from the atrocity of the murder of the boy Astyanax in *The Women of Troy*, commits in the earlier play a similar, even worse atrocity on the sons of Polymestor, with no better motive than a scarcely sane desire for revenge for the deaths of her own children. It is no accident that it is prophesied that she will turn into an animal. On the stage in front of our eyes she has already become one.

It is extraordinary that Euripides should have written a play of such moral war-weariness so early in the great conflict. By the time he wrote his late group of war plays, twenty years had passed, and the poet had been reduced to something that seems very like despair. Athens too had been brought to the very edge of defeat, a defeat that with resourcefulness and luck she staved off for a further ten years, but which when it came was total.

The Peloponnesian War was an odd affair. From the beginning the Spartans and their allies had the dominance in land warfare. The Spartan military machine, based upon a totalitarian political system, and an almost religious idealisation of military virtues, although it was defeated on land by the Athenians and their allies on more than one occasion, was always dominant. The Athenian Empire was a sea-based power, relying upon the fleet that since the battle of Salamis had always been dominant in the Aegean. The Athenians relied upon corn coming through the Hellespont for their survival, and on money from the Aegean islands and Greek cities of Asia Minor, over whom their fleet gave them dominance, for their military and economic power: and Sparta and her allies relied upon their hoplite armies – heavy armed infantry – to prevent Athens dominating the whole of the Peloponnese, fear of which had started the war in the first place. Thus an element of stalemate was built into the conflict. The Athenians could only win by a total and overwhelming defeat of the Spartans and their allies on land. The Spartans could only win by destroying Athenian sea power, and following that up with a blockade that would starve Athens into submission. Neither side seemed likely to achieve this aim for many years, which is why the war, hot and cold from year to year, lasted for such a very long time.

In 416-15 the Athenian leaders, and principally Alcibiades, dreamed up one of those maniacally ambitious schemes that to the hindsight of history seems certain to lead to disaster, like Napoleon's or Hitler's invasion of Russia. They decided to mount a huge expeditionary force against Sicily, ostensibly to aid an allied city there, but with dreams of total conquest not far below the surface. Certainly if the Sicilian venture had succeeded, Athens would have become unstoppably powerful in the Mediterranean. There were already strategists in Athens who were looking to the next step beyond the Sicilian victory, the conquest of Carthage and Greek Italy. Equally certainly, with a war having raged on their own doorstep for sixteen years – even if they were having the best of it in the Peloponnese in 415 – and with their control of sea power in the Aegean vital to their survival, it was a foolhardy thing to attempt, the opening of a second front with a vengeance.

Sicily, for Athenian triremes, was a very long way away, and certainly a very large country to be invaded and dominated by armies the size of those employed in this conflict. The expedition was the most massive ever assembled by a Hellenic state, with more than a hundred ships, more than five thousand hoplites – and large numbers of light armed skirmishers. The whole project had disaster written all over it. There was impassioned debate in Athens as to whether it should sail at all, and its Commander-in-Chief, Nicias, was the leader of the opposition to the whole venture. Nevertheless he was preserved in command, with an old soldier named Lamachus, and the untrustworthy, charismatic and fatally arrogant Alcibiades as co commanders. Very little went right from the beginning. The wrong decisions were made, both militarily and politically, and during 413, the whole task force, in spite of reinforcements almost equal to the original expedition, slid towards disaster. When it came, in 413, the disaster was complete. The whole fleet was lost and every man was either killed, or enslaved, or reduced to desperate escape under cover through the Sicilian countryside. Very few of the thousands who left ever returned to Athens. It was the most complete disaster in Hellenic history, and left Athens with no significant fleet, and a whole army destroyed, at the mercy of her enemies. That the city didn't fall at once was due to its own resourcefulness in providing a new fleet very quickly, and a lack of ships, and cash and dash on the part of Sparta and her allies.

Of the three plays in this volume, *The Women of Troy* was presented in 415, when the Sicilian expeditionary force was assembling in the harbour of Piraeus, and *Helen* in 412, at the first Dionysia after the news of its total destruction got back to Athens. *Iphigenia at Aulis* was probably presented in 406, two years before the city's fall, shortly after Euripides' death, and the likelihood is that it was written in 408-7, when the poet was living at the court of King Archelaus of Macedonia. All through these last years Euripides seems to have been following the advice of a later war poet, 'all a poet can do today is warn', with increasing intensity and increasing despair at the chances of being heeded. All three plays are, it seems to me, passionately related to the historical circumstances that produced them, and though the detail of those circumstances and the precise political resonances within the plays are irrecoverably lost, the tone of voice, and the warning note, sounds remarkably clear and relevant across the centuries.

In order to make a translation of any work, the translator needs to have a clear idea of what sort of work he is dealing with. This seems too obvious to be worth stating, but with two of the plays in this volume it is an essential precondition to translating a word. In the case of *Iphigenia at Aulis*, and *Helen*, there is no agreement among scholars as to what sort of plays they are at all, nor is there sufficient evidence to enable a final decision on the question ever to be made, one way or another. It is part of scholarly discipline that when a question cannot truthfully be closed, it must remain forever open, but that is an option that is not available for the translator who is preparing his own production, nor for anyone else whose love for Euripides takes the practical form of wishing him to stay alive on the stage he has graced for two thousand years. To perform a play you must know what kind of play you are performing, and even if the evidence is inadequate, you must make a decision upon what there is. That you will be recreating Euripides to some degree in your own image is therefore inevitable: but the art of idiomatic dramatic translation presupposes that recreation anyway. The decisions forced upon the director-poet by the state of scholarship and the lack of evidence are of the same kind as face any translator, only pushed a good deal further.

What sort of play is *Iphigenia at Aulis*? And at a tangent to that simple question, an even simpler one: who wrote it?

Scholars have decided that the text of the play is a mess. It has been asserted that Euripides left it unfinished at his death, that it was finished by his son, also named Euripides, that the last section after Iphigenia's exit is an obvious Renaissance forgery, that it has two beginnings, and that it is full of actors' interpolations. In addition, a few lines have been discovered which have been argued to be from another, possibly original Euripidean ending, which seem to be spoken by the goddess Artemis: not in itself unlikely, as Euripides very often chooses to end his plays with a god or goddess from the machine.

I can't claim much interest in textual criticism, and I have even less training or skill, but it seems to me that two things emerge from this scholarly bog of claim and counterclaim. The first is that the play *was* performed, probably soon after it was written, and that it was well known among the author's works. Aristotle refers to it, disparagingly, in the *Poetics*, establishing himself not only as the first dramatic critic, but also the first to get it wrong, by diametrically misunderstanding what the playwright has put before his eyes. Aristotle would not have referred to the play as an example if it were not likely to be well known among his students. So whatever the scholars assert about the state of the text now, there was a text that was considered finished enough to become part of the fourth-century repertoire, nor did Aristotle suggest that it was not written by the author whose name is associated with it.

The second point is that when I read the play, in other peoples' editions, it made sense to me as drama only in its complete version. Texts following the Gilbert Murray line, like the Greene and Lattimore Chicago edition, translated by Charles R. Walker, which relegates the messenger speech and the last scene to an appendix, left me with a stunted and essentially unperformable play. To end the play with Iphigenia's heroic exit makes nonsense of all the cynicism that has preceded it. If that was Euripides' intention, then he was incompetent as a playwright: which we know he was not. In the complete version of the play I sensed a wholeness of artistic purpose, a work that hung together both dramatically and thematically. Whatever the provenance of the text, the complete version worked as a play and spoke very clearly to our age, and the truncated version did neither. My intention was to test the scholars' assertions in the only arena that matters for a play, rehearsal and performance. If I became conscious of interpolations, lines that obstructed the flow of the drama, or sections of the play that seemed at odds with the dramatic and artistic direction, I could easily remove them: and if the play did hang together as an artistic unit, I would feel that as clearly as I would feel the presence of unnecessary or alien material. I couldn't by that method discover who wrote the lines, but I could find out whether they cohered artistically. And if I found that they did, I would feel I had in my hands a weapon at least as powerful as the scholars' tools of textual analysis.

Accepting the complete text doesn't solve the problem of what sort of play it is. Euripides tells the traditional story. The Greek expeditionary force against Troy is becalmed at Aulis. Calchas the prophet tells Agamemnon that only the sacrifice of his eldest child, Iphigenia, to the goddess Artemis, will cause the wind to change. Agamemnon is put in a tragic dilemma. Clytemnestra his wife, and Iphigenia herself, plead that he should not go through with the sacrifice. Agamemnon puts his duty as leader of the expedition before family feeling, and sacrifices the girl. But at the altar a miracle occurs. The girl is whisked up to heaven, and a deer is slaughtered in her place.

We have here a traditional story, very much older than Classical Greece, and common to several cultures. The Hebraic version, Abraham and Isaac, comes to a similar conclusion, though interestingly it omits the women's roles. At a mythical level, the story dramatises a crucial moment in the early history of civilised development, when semi-civilised tribes substituted animal for human sacrifice to the gods they had created. It seems likely that the Greek myths, like myths in other cultures, dramatise all kinds of significant watersheds in early human development, in the Greek case principally the movement from matriarchy to patriarchy, female to male gods, when hunter-gatherers set down their nomadic herds of people to form farms and settlements, and the ability to fight for and defend what you had got became, for the first time in human history, more important than the bearing of children.

We have enough Greek tragedies to know by the time the great tragedians were flourishing, in the last thirty years of the fifth century, these stories were treated with great artistic sophistication. The Electra plays of all three tragedians, and the Antigone plays of Sophocles and Euripides, make it clear, even with such limited evidence, that the playwrights, while keeping to the broad outlines of the traditional stories, could interpret them to suit what they wished to say, and that the same story could easily be slanted to say quite different things.

What did Euripides, probably in the last year of a long life, want to say by choosing the story of the sacrifice of Iphigenia? For eight years, taking only the evidence of the plays that survive, he had been saying almost the same thing, telling the Athenians that nothing good could come from the continuation of the war, and that their values as well as their economic and political fortunes were being undermined by the endless fighting and opportunistic politics. The last play we have before *Iphigenia*, *Orestes*, performed in 408, while not directly about war, shows that the compulsion to revenge his mother's crimes has turned the hero into a psychopathic maniac. There is nothing that can be called heroic in any of these late war-inspired plays, only a despair that the endless slaughter should be continuing. We know that in Athens after the Sicilian disaster, when the immediate danger was over, a pro-war party arose which created a kind of war hysteria in 409-8, and that several possibilities of peace were rejected by the Athenians. It is more than likely that Euripides wrote his play about a navy waiting to sail just as the Athenians were financing and crewing a new battle fleet, which was shortly to be successful in the Battle of Arginusae. We also know that Euripides, when an extremely old man, chose to leave his native city at the invitation of King Archelaus, to live in exile. However favourable the terms, and however honoured he was at the King's court, it must have been a shattering decision for any Athenian, particularly we might imagine, for one in the eighth decade of his life. In deciding whether the play before us describes an heroic miracle or a cynical waste, the evidence of the master's other plays, and the times he lived in, must be crucial.

It all hangs on the last section of the play, the suspect and much disputed text. When the messenger comes back and tells his miraculous tale, are we meant to believe him? Is he describing exactly what happened, the enacting of a miracle, before the significantly lowered eyes of the whole Greek army – only Calchas, it seems, was actually watching – or is he telling the public relations version, the official story issued to save Agamemnon's face, the Big Political Lie? Certainly the messenger makes very heavy weather of pointing out how fortunate Agamemnon has been, and by implication Clytemnestra too, in being chosen by the gods for this signal honour, and how Clytemnestra, far from being angry with her husband, should share his joy. Equally certainly Clytemnestra, almost as her last utterance, asks the messenger if he expects her to believe this story, which is only told for her comfort.

Before we make interpretative judgements about the last section of the play, it is reasonable to look at the earlier scenes. What sort of play do they present? The answer is clear. In the first episodes, Euripides does the biggest demolition job on the Homeric heroes before Shakespeare put them to the sword in *Troilus and Cressida*. Even Shakespeare doesn't have such obvious contempt for his 'heroes' as Euripides does. There is a kind of weight in Shakespeare's Ulysses and Agamemnon, even if Thersites does reduce them all to boils and pustules, and a certain dangerous brutality in Achilles. But what can be said for Euripides' Homeric leaders? Agamemnon is a completely third rate politician, with no moral sense at all, prepared to lie to his wife, manipulate his colleagues and murder his daughter in order to keep command of the Greek Force against Troy. Certainly his wily instinct tells him that the Greek soldiers are so brutally determined to get their hands on the plunder of Troy that if he seems to be standing in their way, they will not scruple to murder him, his wife and his children, but there is not the slightest sense in Agamemnon of any desire to stand up against this force, even if he could. He weeps bitterly at the intractability of his dilemma, but he is no tragic hero who will go down defending the moral right, as Antigone does. He is the worst kind of greasy political compromiser, utterly without moral feeling, utterly determined to stay top of the pile whatever it costs him, or his family, or his country: the kind of politician, we might be tempted to say, that Euripides would have had plenty of opportunity to observe at close quarters during the years of Athens' decline. Indeed, some commentators have associated the portrait of Agamemnon with Theramenes, a political operator who suffered the common fate of such people during the tyranny of the fifty after the city fell.

Menelaus is as unprincipled as Agamemnon, but utterly brainless into the bargain. He too is completely self-interested, but is so stupid as to think that his blatant manoeuvres to gain his own ends are not immediately obvious to everyone. When he asserts that he has changed his mind purely out of love for his brother, he naively seems to think that Agamemnon will believe him: whereas Agamemnon knows perfectly well that Menelaus can now afford to put on an appearance of generosity, and plead for Iphigenia's life, because he is well aware that the situation that has arisen with the army makes that tactic for Agamemnon a political impossibility. He is all bluster and transparent cunning, a fatally stupid man who thinks himself wonderfully clever, the kind of officer that is a deadly liability to any army, and Agamemnon contemptuously treats him as such.

Perhaps we learn most about Agamemnon's character by the fact that he has chosen to lure his wife and daughter to the camp for the sacrifice, by promising that Iphigenia is to marry Achilles, the greatest soldier in Greece. That Agamemnon thinks he might get away with this is perhaps the richest comment, both on his relationship with his family, and on his skill as a political leader, but it is when the great hero himself, Achilles, comes on to the stage that Euripides' political cynicism and despair rises to the summit of bitter comedy. Achilles is a prancing idiot, stupid beyond comprehension, and so intoxicated with self-love as to be almost incoherent. When Clytemnestra pleads for his help to save Iphigenia, his only thought is for his image, how he will appear as the girl's saviour, and the one thing that really sparks his anger is the thought that Agamemnon's machinations are an insult to his grandeur and an undervaluing of his power. He is completely unaware of any moral dimension to the dilemma, and the richest moment of comedy comes when he blusters that if the Greeks had *asked his permission* to sacrifice Iphigenia, he certainly wouldn't have withheld it. All that is at stake for him is his own reputation. Whether the girl lives or dies means nothing, and that the question has moral parameters never at any point crosses his mind. When Clytemnestra offers her naked heart's blood, and reveals her pain like a wounded animal, he replies with rodomontade and bluster, booming away about how much greater his family is than Agamemnon's, and swearing that he will save Iphigenia's life at all costs, while at the same time suggesting cowardly strategies that will keep his name out of the action at all. The scene is funny and terrifying at the same time: funny because Achilles is such a fool, sicker of self-love even than Malvolio: terrifying when we realise that this hero with feet of plasticine is Clytemnestra's only hope.

More than one commentator has suggested that Achilles is Euripides' damning portrait of Alcibiades. If so, he certainly knew how to put the knife in; and reading Alcibiades' speech to the Athenians, as attributed to him, not without some creative licence no doubt, by Thucydides, in which the hero modestly tells his fellow citizens what a tremendous fellow he is, and how he won four medals in the chariot race at the Olympics, and how great men like him always attract envy, we feel that Euripides could well be pillorying the same man.

The Chorus, when they arrive, rubbernecking tourists from Chalcis across the strait, serve to intensify the power of the playwright's vision of pygmies who think they are gods. In their entry song, they are awestruck to be in the presence of all the great heroes whose names they have often heard, but whom they have never seen before. Excitedly, they repeat their catalogue of what ships and commanders they have spotted, in the process employing a conventional poetic device, the Homeric list of ships, as a powerful starting point of the ironic drama to come, emphasising the godlike qualities of heroes who are soon to be revealed as men of straw. By the first Ode they are very disturbed by what they have seen, assuming that love is the cause of the devastating quarrel between the two sons of Atreus, and asserting that only by hanging on to the simple tenets of traditional morality can anyone be safe. The second Ode is a terrifyingly vivid description of what will happen when Troy falls, of the rape, destruction and murder visited upon a sacked city, which must have been particularly disturbing to the Athenians, with a humiliating, if not immediately threatening, Spartan army camped at Decelea, within sight of the Athenian walls, and the possibility of defeat and the destruction of their own city always at the back of their minds. In the third Ode, after a desperate attempt to keep their spirits up by remembering the marriage of Peleus and Thetis, and the prophecy of Achilles' greatness – immediately after we have seen his idiocy demonstrated – they become obsessed with the brutal fact of Iphigenia's coming sacrificial murder, and end with a strophe which memorably defines Euripides' despair at the moral through his society has fallen into:

Crimson the face of shame,
Can goodness prevail, can virtue prevail?
A godless generation is in power.
Where is decency, who speaks her name?
Stifled, choked by the stinking breath
Of self-interest, in this darkest hour
When the fear of god is dead, brotherhood gone rotten,
And the vengeance the jealous gods exact from men forgotten.

From that point on the Chorus are helpless witnesses of the ritual of Iphigenia's slaying. At the end of the play they can say nothing, except to utter ridiculously inappropriate best wishes for Agamemnon's trip to Troy, a last cry of patriotism in a scene too dark to tolerate such facile optimism. The tourists have learned a lot during their day in Aulis. The optimistic holiday mood of their arrival is completely lost as they drift sadly away from an expedition and a family already doomed by self-interest and moral illiteracy.

Into this corrupting atmosphere of self-seeking and brooding violence Euripides brings his two great ladies from Argos, who come expecting a wedding, not a human sacrifice. Surely, in the spectacle of the mother fighting for her child's life, and the child herself, innocently dying to save her country, we shall see the true stuff of heroic tragedy, admirable characters overcome by the force of unyielding circumstance? Euripides begins by making it clear they shouldn't be here at all. This is an army camp, full of brutal and undisciplined soldiery, and no place for women, least of all women of the breeding of Clytemnestra and Iphigenia. What sort of marriage can be celebrated in such an unpropitious place?

In Clytemnestra the poet gives us one of his great female characters, worthy to stand with Medea, Phaedra and Hecuba in the gallery of wonderful female roles he has bequeathed to the repertoire. She enters as the perfect wife, charming, gracious, a mistress of public relations, as the wife of a great leader should be; but by the end of the first scene, it is clear that her marriage to Agamemnon is no genuine companionship, something already made plain in Agamemnon's comments about the need to deceive her. It looks much more like a battleground, with man and wife defining and fighting for the area of territory that belongs to them. When she learns of her husband's murderous plan, she becomes a raging fury, fighting like an animal to defend her young, frightening in the power and range of her emotions, and prepared to use every subterfuge, even flattering the ridiculous Achilles, to save her child's life. In the central confrontation with Agamemnon we see the full falsity of her marriage, based on the murder of her first husband, Tantalus, and her own rape, by the man who became her second. That second husband, who now stands before her, has already been guilty of the murder of Tantalus' child, by bashing its brains out on the ground. There was nothing that compelled Euripides to introduce this horrific imagery at this point in the play: there is plenty of material for the central debate without it. He chose to – and dramatically it seems an utterly convincing choice, though some scholars have argued that it is an interpolation

– so that the moral darkness of the world he is representing should be painted in the most frighteningly vivid colours. By the end of the scene, Agamemnon has been left in no doubt of the quality and power of the enemy he has made of his wife. It is quite clear who is the superior human being, and who from the second drawer. It is the very force of her personality that makes her the more dangerous when injured. By the time her daughter has been slain, she has been through all the stages of her personal *Via Dolorosa*, desperate defence, anguished mother's suffering, even to howling animal agony, and has finally become a stony avenging fury, fully prepared to initiate the terrible events of the *Oresteia*. We see within the confines of the play the transformation of a sophisticated worldly woman, with a conventional political marriage, into a destructive monster, capable of committing one of the great crimes of mythological antiquity. She begins the play as a victim, the woman to whom a great evil has been done, but who has risen above it, to become a model wife. When a second even greater evil is done to her, in the dark world of the army camp where violence and moral savagery are the ruling values, she doesn't rise above the evil that surrounds her, to subdue it with the power of her own tragic virtue. She accepts the world that has punished her, makes its values her own, becomes a greater slayer than any of the men. The darkness of the story, the bleak tale that Euripides is telling us, is unrelieved.

And what of the child, Iphigenia? Euripides milks her youth and innocence for every drop of pathos and tragic irony his mastery can squeeze out, creating her as the suffering victim till two-thirds of the way through the play, the point where we would expect a peripeteia, a sudden reversal of expectation, from a Greek tragic master. And what a peripeteia it is! The savage atmosphere suddenly has its effect on the girl too, she becomes intoxicated with her own role, and the power it gives her to stir the men. She realises she is going to die, and becomes possessed by the brutality and violence of the soldiery, exuding like the smell of sweat from the camp all round her. In a moment of inspired realisation she offers herself as a patriotic icon, and spurred on by the situation, and the soldiers' approval, makes crudely rabble-rousing speeches full of lines reminiscent of the kind of things Hitler said at Nuremburg, when he was working his audience up to the heights of war hysteria by scapegoating the Jews. She tells her mother she didn't bear her child only for herself, but for the Fatherland, that Greeks must always dominate barbarians, and that the best consolation she can have for her own denial of marriage and children is that Troy will be reduced to a ruin. In performance the speech is genuinely frightening, seeing the young girl transforming herself before our eyes into a fascist poster, or a Nazi statue of German womanhood sacrificed for the greater Reich.

Is this an accident on Euripides' part, incompetence – did the old fellow not know what he was doing in his seventies, had he turned into an Athenian pro-war patriot in his old age? Or is it the most savage of ironies, created by the master ironist of theatre history? Surely he knows exactly what he is doing. Had he not seen this all round him in Athens, as the extremists tried to whip up the young fighters into a new frenzy against Sparta? And this master stroke of characterisation is what the first of dramatic critics, Aristotle, setting the standards for his less distinguished descendants, no doubt, failed to comprehend! He uses Iphigenia as an example of an inconsistent character, because she changes her mind, is initially terrified of dying, and then finds herself uttering heroic sacrificial speeches. In fact, one of the most striking features of the characterisation in this play is precisely this sudden changing of mind. Agamemnon, Menelaus and Achilles all change their positions with great suddenness, Agamemnon in particular going through the most extraordinary series of political U-turns. It is this structural device as much as anything that gives the play its particular feeling of dry-mouthed cynicism. We feel we are in a world in which people have no values beyond the exploitation of the moment, and will do anything for short term advantage. It is extraordinary that the great critic and theorist failed to see this, or in the case of Iphigenia, to see what Euripides had seen, that in war it is always the young who suffer and die, and vulgar rhetoric encourages them to do so with flags in their hands and tunes of glory on their lips. What we have seen in the play is the corruption of two potentially heroic women by the degraded atmosphere of the army camp, a world in which morality has disappeared and self interest and violence rule. The two women arrive in this military world, and they are destroyed by it, Clytemnestra being transformed into an avenging fury, and Iphigenia becoming that most tragic of spectacles, an innocent allowing herself to be used as an icon of vulgar patriotism and destruction.

What more natural in such a world than that the messenger speech should be a pack of lies, a public relations man's gloss on a scene too horrific to contemplate, the slitting of a young girl's throat at the command of her father, in order that a city should be sacked? Whoever wrote the play, however many hands are present, the whole thing hangs together as an artistic statement of relentless integrity. It couldn't be better structured, or more rancidly satisfying, if it had been put together by a great master at the height of his powers: as I suspect it was. Even the famous double beginning doesn't feel like repetition in performance, and in fact, nothing is repeated. We begin with a scene quite unlike any other in the Greek canon, an atmosphere piece about the brooding tragedy to come, more naturalistic in mood than any other scene in the repertoire, and follow it with what seems like the usual Euripidean expositional prologue. Why should not this be simply a new way of beginning, a development of the playwright's usual practice, an experiment full of potential for the future of drama? The fact is, in performance it works, and gives no feeling at all of two beginnings. Either section of the opening would be fatally weakened by the omission of the other, and simply playing the scene makes it quite clear they belong together. In my production none of the passages usually scored out by scholars were omitted, and all seemed to earn their place in the play. Only two tiny cuts were made in the text here printed, the omission of one strophe in the Homeric list of ships in the Chorus' entry song, where we felt we had heard rather more of the participants in the Trojan expedition than we needed, and the reference to the horses that pull Clytemnestra's chariot, hardly practical in a television studio, or the modern theatre. The fact is, in this translation the piece plays magnificently as it stands, both convincing as drama, and coherent as a statement. Whoever wrote it, the thing is a masterpiece, and is best left alone to perform its magic, without allowing academic surgeons to cut it about, and probably kill it on the table.

Overall broods Euripides' bitter message to his countrymen about the disasters of war, and his central metaphor is as telling now as it was when he first set pen to papyrus. In all wars the old sacrifice the young to preserve their own power, and in far too many the young are willing participants in their own destruction. We remember the generation of 1914, rushing to the glory of war 'like swimmers into cleanness leaping', and then, only a few years later, Wilfred Owen's anguished comment in his own Abraham and Isaac poem, where he shakes hands with Euripides across sixty generations:

> But the old man would not so, but slew his son
> And half the seed of Europe one by one.

That metaphor, to our shame, is never out of date. It lives as fearfully as ever in the modern world, and not only in the performance of the play.

A few days before we began rehearsing, the old men of China sacrificed their children in Tiananmen Square, to preserve their own power.

There has scarcely been any doubt what sort of play *The Women of Troy* is, nor of its central place in the repertoire as one of the masterpieces of Mediterranean civilisation. There are moments in the play which are almost unendurable to read, and must in the playing touch on emotions and levels of experience we would all rather not contemplate. One is reminded at times of the memoirs, on film and in print, of Auschwitz survivors, and the strangely compelled sense of horror that keeps us watching and reading.

The play's performance history is precise. Aelian, in *Varia Historia*, written at the beginning of the third century AD, says, 'In the first year of the ninety-first Olympiad (415 BC) Xenocles and Euripides competed against each other. Xenocles, whoever he may have been, won the first prize, with *Oedipus, Lycaon, Bacchae* and a satyr play *Athanas*. Euripides was second with *Alexander, Palamedes, The Women of Troy* and the satyr play *Sisyphus*.'

In the winter of 416-15, a few months before the play was presented, the Athenians had committed one of the many atrocities which disfigured the Peloponnesian War. They had laid siege to the Island of Melos, which had refused to join the Athenian alliance, and when the defenders capitulated, the Athenians murdered all the men of military age, down to boys of fifteen, and enslaved all the women. It has always been assumed that *The Women of Troy* is Euripides' attack on his fellow citizens for that dreadful act, and no doubt the assumption is correct. Certainly it must have been a subversive work, not only for its comment on the Melian massacre, but also for its implied criticism of the Sicilian invasion. The great fleet was assembling as Euripides' play was presented, and the prophecy of disaster on the Greek fleet returning from Troy, because they had dishonoured the gods' temples in sacking the city, must have seemed the worst possible omen for the Sicilian expedition. Everybody knew the Homeric story, that the returning Greek fleet was scattered in a storm, that most were drowned and many of the rest never reached their homes for many years, and in his opening scene Euripides strongly emphasises this aspect of the story. It really isn't surprising that he came second to Xenocles in those circumstances. We might be tempted to think it even more surprising that his play was accepted at all. Of course, there is no way of knowing where the Archon's sympathies lay when he accepted Euripides' trilogy, nor that he saw how politically relevant the piece might seem in performance: though the Chorus's praise of the men of Sicily for their bravery and their integrity can hardly have been misinterpreted. It is as clear a warning as the Athenians were likely to get from one of their tragedians.

But the fact is that it didn't need the Melian massacre to inspire the play. The history of the war had been full of such atrocities: the execution of the Plataean conspirators after they had surrendered on terms in 431 at the very beginning of the conflict; the slaughter of the whole Plataean garrison, followed by the enslaving of the women and reducing the city to ashes when it finally fell to the Thebans and Spartans in 427; the murder of a thousand prisoners at Mitylene; also in 427, the slaughter of the whole male population of Scione in 421, the list goes on and on. It was a war conducted with little mercy on either side, and considering the small forces involved, with much bloodshed. Thucydides makes it clear Euripides' warning voice was not heard. In 413, a party of Thracians, arriving too late to join the reinforcement convoy for

Sicily, were sent back home, under an Athenian commander, with instructions to do as much damage as possible. They sailed up the Euripes, murdering and laying waste to Euboea as they went, and then crossed over into Boeotia to the city of Mycalessus where they 'sacked the houses and temples, and butchered the inhabitants, sparing neither the young nor the old, but methodically killing everyone they met, women and children alike, and even the farm animals, and every living thing they saw . . . Among other things they broke into a boys' school, the largest in the place, into which the children had just entered, and killed every one of them.' No doubt the Melos massacre was in the front of Euripides' mind, but what he was describing was behaviour that was commonplace, not exceptional.

Without the other two tragedies that comprised the trilogy we can't be sure, but it seems likely that Euripides composed a powerful protest cycle, probably with a quite clear political purpose. There was an impassioned debate in Athens about the wisdom of the Sicilian expedition, which was not only foolhardy in itself, but a stepping up of the war, which had lain mostly dormant for about five years. What could be more likely than that Euripides was one of those Athenians who were against restarting the war, and against the Sicilian expedition, and that he used the horror and guilt that must have existed in some men's minds about the recent slaughter on Melos as a powerful reminder of what war really meant in human terms? There is no evidence at all as to what part political influence played in the presentation of plays at the City Dionysia, but the plays deal so regularly with the ethical questions that are the basis of political decisions that it must have been considerable. The comedies of Aristophanes are openly political, even naming names, and it seems likely that the tragedies too, in their serious manner, considered political issues and perhaps even glanced at political personalities. More than one scholar has suggested that Sophocles' Oedipus might be a portrait of Pericles, and other similar attributions have been guessed at from time to time. Certainly it is inconceivable that Euripides could have presented such a subversive play, one likely to cause such fury among the supporters of a renewed war, off his own bat. He must have had powerful friends, beyond the producer who financed him, who were able to get the Archon's ear to ensure that Euripides' project was selected out of the doubtless many others presented. And the debate in Athens must have been reasonably evenly balanced too. If the anti-war party were in a small minority, would the play have been allowed, when the likelihood was that it would offend the majority of the audience? As with so many fascinating questions about Greek drama, we simply don't know. All we do know is that it was presented, so the Archon must have thought it, for whatever reasons, suitable material for the Dionysiac festival: and that it didn't win.

Whatever the truth of that, I suspect a good many people got more than they bargained for. There is a relentless quality, a harshness in *The Women of Troy* that leaves no room for compromise. The play's principal subject is the agony of war, the fact that it causes mass death, separation of loved ones, slavery and suffering. Euripides confronts us mercilessly with this unavoidable truth. There is hardly a word anywhere in the play about the glories of war, the manliness of conquest, still a genuine ideal in the Classical Age, only a eulogy of the dead Hector, as an attempt by the defeated Trojans to grasp some shred of dignity out of their disaster. Beyond that, the whole play is a heightened lament, the death song of a city, a culture, a whole population. Troy clearly stands in for all of us. It is civilisation that is going down in blood and fire, not just a city.

It is significant that the play has no messenger speech: but what is there to report? The catastrophe is being enacted in front of our eyes, not offstage. For a great master at the height of his powers, form is a servant not a master, a way of enabling him to express what has to be expressed, a structure that liberates rather than restricts.

Within the general picture of the horrors of war, there are three moments of unflinching precision, things which we know are part of human experience when men get weapons in their hands, but which in the normal run of things we prefer not to confront. The first is the dragging out of the incoherent prophetess Cassandra, the sanctified virgin whom even the god Apollo won't touch, to be Agamemnon's whore. Euripides spares us nothing here, not even the sexual perversity that we might think is our particular modern subject. Agamemnon is hot for Cassandra because she *is* a sanctified virgin. It is the very fact that she is forbidden that makes him desperate to have her, liberating the dark sexual fantasy that makes men want to rape nuns. In Greek Classical culture the symbol is even more powerful, a blasphemy that dares to sully what the gods have decreed pure. It stands in for all the shameful desires that are unloosed when men let their savage fantasies usurp reason, and become creatures of appetite. We already know what this will cost Agamemnon. The two gods at the beginning of the play have sworn vengeance on the Greeks for precisely this reason, the dishonouring of their temples, and all the varieties of degraded behaviour that symbol represents. The inspired, raving Cassandra, after her grotesque parody of a marriage hymn, prophesies the horrors that will fall on the House of Atreus as a result of Agamemnon's blasphemy, but in truth we hardly need to be told that no good will come of it. An action beyond the bounds of decent human behaviour is being enacted before our eyes, and we are in no doubt that retribution will follow.

The second precisely delineated moment of horror is the tearing of the child Astyanax from his mother's bosom. In production, this almost goes beyond the bounds of the bearable, and a passionate actress playing Andromache can create a moment of horror as powerful as the blinding of Gloucester in *King Lear*, or the stoning of the baby in *Saved*. As we might expect, the officer in charge is a decent enough fellow, disgusted by the job he has been given to do. Talthybius is a very recognisable chap, with a suburban semi, no doubt, and two point five children, kind to his friends, who wouldn't hurt a fly. They always are. He hates what he has to do, he says so, and we believe him. But he does it. Talthybius is a very twentieth-century-seeming character, and in a sense, without thinking too deeply about it, we have come to assume men like him are our age's particular creation. The family man who runs a concentration camp, the state torturer who goes home at six and plays with his children, the policeman who beats up his victims to extract false confessions and then goes for a relaxing pint in the local, all these figures we claim as our own, together with the murderers who defend themselves by saying that they were only obeying the orders of their superiors. But Euripides was there a long way before us. It is his very decency that makes Talthybius such a powerful creation. He is like us, he knows these things are wrong and should not be happening. Yet it is he who commands the party that seizes Cassandra and drags her off to Agamemnon, shaking his head in disapproval all the while; it is he who orders his guards to tear the boy Astyanax by force from his mother's arms, and supervises his killing: and it is he who brings the dead boy back on Hector's shield, having washed the blood from his shattered body. He is a kind-hearted fellow, does everything he can to ease the women's grief for the boy, arranges a decent burial, no doubt wipes away a tear or two himself. But what he actually *does* is to allow himself to be the instrument that enacts the play's two principal atrocities. He truly is the man who wipes away the blood, who tries to make the crime look decent, who hides the wounds.

When he leaves Hecuba with her dead grandson, cradled in her dead son's shield, the play lifts off into immortality. Hecuba's lament is the greatest speech in the whole canon of Greek tragedy, its power surviving every kind of translation, from the most clumsy or old fashioned to the most prosaically modern. Confronting it, every translator feels the presence of its author very near, and is tempted to say, 'Dear old friend, I'll do the best I can for you, but I need to be Shakespeare!' The part is one of the great peaks of the female repertoire. Any actress who can get anywhere near the summit of Hecuba is by definition one of the mistresses of her craft, and it is this heartrending speech, this third moment of horror precisely delineated, that is the greatest test and the greatest opportunity. In it, Hecuba speaks for every woman in history who has ever lost a loved one in war, and particularly for the unnatural sorrow of an old woman grieving for a young life destroyed before it has had the opportunity to live. Even beyond that, she speaks for all of us, regardless of sex, as Lear does, protesting against the pain and injustice of existence, and the agony of the suffering that human beings inflict upon their own kind. Reading her grief is like standing at the Nations' memorial at Auschwitz, confronting the grave slabs all carrying the same message in so many languages, listening to the wind jangling the ropes on the metal flagpole. It is to bear witness at the graveyard of the human spirit, head bowed in apology.

The play is a sustained lyrical poem of grief, a dark cloud heightened by stabs of terrifying lightning; but as you would expect with Euripides, savage irony is present too. In the debate that invariably constitutes the central section of a play by Euripides, Menelaus comes to seize Helen, the woman who caused the war, and who is in that sense the author of all the suffering we are witnessing. Euripides gives us a masterly character-study as well as an exercise in forensic rhetoric, as Helen argues for her life. When Menelaus enters, he intends to kill her on the spot. Helen too is scared, seeing summary execution very close at hand. By the end of the scene Helen has not only managed to persuade him to put off all punishment till they arrive in Sparta, she has gone half way to convincing him of her own innocence. Menelaus, prompted by Hecuba, who has seen Helen at work many times before, has at least agreed that they shall sail back to Sparta in different ships, but how long do we believe that arrangement will last? Between the ruins and the beach Helen will surely wheedle him into letting her share his vessel, and eventually his bed. Even before the scene has ended it is clear that he is lost, as much her sexual slave as he was ten years before, when he called up his Greek compatriots and launched a war for her sake. The power of Helen verges on the awesome, the divine. She is destructive Aphrodite in human form, and men will kill, torture, destroy and abase themselves for the chance to kiss her skirt hem.

The destructive power of instinct is one of Euripides' central themes. In the rational Greek world, he was the great affirmer of the power of the irrational, and he wrote two of his greatest plays, *Hippolytus* and *The Bacchae*, to dramatise its destructive force. In this play too, it is clear that the goddess Helen/Aphrodite is going to have her way, but that is not the central matter being considered here. Euripides did not need to include a scene with Helen, or any of this material. He chose to do so, not simply to dramatise the irrational power of sexual love, but to demonstrate the essential pointlessness of all the suffering we have seen enacted and heard described in the play. Helen will not be punished, she and Menelaus will live in Sparta as before. So the war's great end has apparently been accomplished. But was it worth it? Is that why all those men, a whole civilisation, died? So that Helen can twist Menelaus round her little finger, just as she has done before our eyes? Euripides not only confronts us with the suffering, but also with a question. If this is what we do to each other, and for this reason, can it possibly be worth it?

It is a question that must have echoed in a good many Athenian minds as they went down between the Long Walls to Piraeus and saw the great Sicilian task force assembling in the bay.

The decision to include *Helen* as the third play of a created Euripidean trilogy was a purely theatrical one, with scholarly considerations playing little or no part. The first plan was that the third play should be *Hecuba*, showing the consequence of the war in the destruction of Hecuba's moral character by her obsessional drive for revenge. But this initial decision was problematic. The thematic connection within a project entitled 'The War Plays' was tenuous, to put it kindly, and there was also a narrative problem, in that Hecuba is told of Polyxena's death in *The Women of Troy*, and learns the same information only half way through *Hecuba*. What finally weighed the scale against *Hecuba* was the feeling that it was impossible to follow *The Women of Troy* with another tragedy. That play seemed such a peak, that a third tragedy could only be at best an equal, and more likely an anti-climactic experience. In Euripides' original scheme *The Women of Troy* was the climactic tragedy, followed by the broad comedy of the satyr play. To conclude with *Helen* would create a change of mood which would surprise and delight the modern audience, while making an ironic comment on the whole business of the war fought to rescue Helen from Troy: which would be good theatre, and not wholly remote from the original Euripidean experience. As I began to study the play in greater detail for translation, this decision seemed more interesting and more justified. By the time I had assimilated the possible meaning of the date of the play's first production, I had become convinced that *Helen* was a positive and creative choice, and indeed the best conclusion for a Euripidean trilogy on the subject of war: that conviction had also indicated to me very clearly how I should translate the play.

Even more than with *Iphigenia at Aulis* the decision as to what kind of play *Helen* is, is crucial to the chances of making a workable translation. The play bristles with scholarly problems, never likely to be finally resolved, short of discovery of a new text, complete with footnotes! Almost all these problems reflect upon the question of what style of dramatic English should be used to render the play's meaning. The director-poet cannot afford the luxury of scholarly detachment, least of all in this play. He must decide, firmly and clearly, what kind of a play he thinks it is, and solve all the problems of text and tone as they arise, in the light of that decision. That way, though he might find gangs of angry Greek scholars beating on his doors, breaking his windows and burning him in effigy, he will at least end up with a highly entertaining and performable play, indeed, a Euripidean masterpiece.

We have to begin with the evidence, what we know about the play with any degree of certainty, and we start with the hard fact that it was performed in the spring of 412. Almost certainly an *Andromeda* was performed with it, but no evidence has come down to us to identify the third play or the satyr play, or to tell us how the whole work was placed in the competition. Further external evidence comes from Aristophanes' *Thezmophoriazusae*, produced in the year immediately following *Helen*, which contains a parody of the recognition scene between Helen and Menelaus, as well as parodies of Euripides' lost *Andromeda*. As *Helen* is an example of the rescue or escape genre, as *Andromeda* by the very fact of its story must also have been – they may be the first representatives of that long and distinguished tradition that includes *The Abduction from the Seraglio* and *Fidelio* – there is every chance that they belonged together.

Further complexities arise from Euripides' own work. Scholars have detected in the earlier scenes of *Helen* an element of self-parody, reflections of speeches and situations from *Andromache* and *Hippolytus* and what might be reminiscences of actual lines from *Iphigenia among the Taurians*. The latter play also bears some relationship to *Helen*, though precisely what is by no means clear. The story of Iphigenia's rescue by Orestes from the clutches of the evil Thoas is essentially the same as the story of Helen's rescue by

Menelaus from the clutches of the ridiculous Theoclymenus, but the Iphigenia play is much darker in tone, with the possibility of a savagely tragic outcome only narrowly averted by the intervention of Athene, and it lacks any of the pantomime quality never far from the surface in *Helen*. The relationship is so close that some scholars have assumed that *Helen* is in fact a parody of *Iphigenia among the Taurians*, and that the one was written immediately after the other. But the arguments offered don't really convince. To a playwright it seems inconceivable to write two plays so very alike within months of each other, other than as a joke or squib, and although there is a great deal of comedy and parody in *Helen*, it has a serious dimension too that makes it clear that it is a major work written with serious intent, not a sketch to amuse people at the author's own expense; and if *Helen* were known as Euripidean self-parody of *Iphigenia among the Taurians*, wouldn't there be some reference to the fact in *Thezmophoriazusae*, where the parody of the previous year's play is so clear and open? Why should Euripides *want* to parody himself anyway, either in the whole structure of the play, or within detailed speeches? What point would he be making by doing such a thing, and how can it help us to elucidate the overall purpose of the play, the dramatic gesture it makes as a statement by a great playwright at a particular time? The fact is that the external and internal literary evidence is thought-provoking but maddeningly incomplete. We will not learn what kind of play *Helen* is, and how we should read the lines the text hands down to us, from the hard evidence or the conjectured evidence alone.

A consideration of history might help us to understand something of the situation in Athens when the play was performed. Thucydides, though he is not precise about the time of the year, suggests that the news of the destruction of the Sicilian expedition must have arrived some time in the autumn of 413. Certainly a great many events happened in 413, from the Athenian defeat in the great harbour of Syracuse, the defeat of Epipolae, and again at sea, through to the final destruction of the whole force, so that the dreadful tidings must have reached Athens later in the year rather than sooner, certainly after the summer. What Thucydides does describe memorably is the panic that occurred when the news did arrive. He roundly states that for a long time the Athenians simply couldn't believe what they were told, even when the story was related by men who had seen it with their own eyes. He then tells us of the despair that ensued, the sense of the great loss of so many ships and men, and the feeling that the city was left naked to her enemies, and could expect a final assault at any moment. Finally he tells us that the city, like all democracies, was galvanised into action by the disaster, and moved quickly to attempt to defend itself, by providing new ships and men. He doesn't tell us of the great grief that must have swept Athens, but he hardly needs to. At least ten thousand men went on the Sicilian expedition, and though a good many of them were from allied cities and states, there can hardly have been a household in Athens, still a city with a small population in the late fifth century, that wasn't grieving for an immediate member of the family, or close friend. After a period of peace, fathers, brothers and sons had been wrenched away in a completely unexpected disaster, and, to the city's shame, all three of its generals who led the expedition had died, two of them by execution at the hands of the Syracusans. The city must have been paralysed with grief and fear: and it was to these shattered, traumatised people that Euripides presented his *Helen*, probably within six months of the dreadful news arriving.

During that six months the Spartans and their allies began an active campaign to persuade all Athens' allied states in the Aegean and Ionia to revolt, as they could now afford too, Athens not having enough ships to send punitive expeditions against them. The Spartans themselves began to think of bringing their own navy up to strength, building new ships and training new crews, and to assist them in this task they made overtures to the Great King of Persia, in the persons of his satraps on the western coast of Ionia, Pharnabazus and Tissaphernes. It was obviously in Persian interests to help destroy Imperial Athens, Persia's great competitor in the Aegean and along the Ionian seaboard, and to keep the Greeks fighting each other, and from this time onwards the Persian presence, in terms of money and ships, was a permanent factor in the politics of the Greek city states, till Alexander's armies removed the Persian state from the political map completely, some eighty years later. It must have seemed a disgraceful thing to some of the Athenians, this negotiating with barbarians, bringing them in to fight against fellow Greeks. There won't have been too many men left alive who remembered the great Patriotic War against the Persian invasion and the heroic victories of Marathon, Salamis and Plataea, but they will all have heard the stories from their fathers and grandfathers. It had become the national myth, Aeschylus himself asking to be memorialised on his tomb not as a playwright, but as one who fought at Marathon, and to see the Spartans beginning to deal with the historic old enemy, the same enemy that had wiped out their heroic Spartan grandfathers at Thermopylae, must have been very shocking. Within a very few years the Athenians themselves joined enthusiastically in the game of playing the Persian card, but to some at least in 412 it must have seemed a pretty disgraceful development.

What sort of play did Euripides create for this shell-shocked audience, still choking back tears of grief for the men they had lost, and trying to master their fears for the uncertain future? Three years earlier, in 415, he had spoken to them with an uncompromising directness, even, through the mouths of Poseidon and Athene, prophesying disaster; but now the disaster had come, perhaps even more completely than it had in his imagination. It might be only a few months before the Women of Athens found themselves in the same position as the Women of Troy. This was not the time to rub salt in their wounds, and indeed, we would expect a man who had lived in his native city all his life, and spoken to its people so passionately, to share in its suffering and express some solidarity with its grief. He may have had good cause to share their feelings himself, and if he hadn't suffered any personal loss, he must have known good friends and acquaintances who had. It would not be many years before he would be confronting his fellow citizens, with the harsh truths of *Orestes* and *Iphigenia at Aulis*, but it would have taken a particular kind of unfeeling sadism to do so in the spring of 412. How could he speak to his audience honestly about the war, and the feelings they all shared, without whipping open wounds, and without compromising the truth of his own experience?

He turned to a comic and face-saving story he found in Herodotus, not entirely unlike the story of Iphigenia at Aulis he was to use five years later. That story, showing how Agamemnon's face is saved by the gods from the ignominy of murdering his daughter, could have been written in a lighter manner than it is, if he had wanted it to be. The miracle could have been emphasised, not the cynicism of the self-interested slaughter, just as the Helen story could have been treated more seriously than it is, with more emphasis on the tragic past and less on the comedy of recognition and escape.

What he gives us is an essentially light-hearted piece, describing how Menelaus comes to Egypt in his wanderings, and finds Helen there, who asserts that she has been in Egypt all the time, and never went to Troy at all. What went to Troy was a wraith, a false Helen, no more than a mist in the air, created by the goddess Hera, to spite Aphrodite for beating her to the beauty prize in the judgement of Paris. The play is genuinely funny. It makes fun of Spartans, who are not to be taken seriously, demonstrates a lofty Greek contempt for barbarians, and is an escape story, which shows its hero and heroine wriggling out of a tight spot by the use of intelligence, energetic resource and courage.

It has the happiest of happy endings, with two people, who emphasise again and again what a rough time they have had, and how weary they are of their sufferings, coming to a safe harbour at last, and even being blessed by the gods and promised a continuation of good fortune, as far as divinity for Helen, and an eternity in the Islands of the Blessed for Menelaus. It must have been an excruciating illusory comfort to those whose sons and husbands had disappeared across the sea, to watch this story of a soldier coming safe home after many adventures and seven years of wandering. 'If Menelaus can make it, so can my son,' must have been a thought that passed through many a desperate mother's mind. A very well thought-out and psychologically satisfying scenario, we might think, by a playwright who is well aware that his audience is in a very fragile state, and badly needs some comfort and a stiffening of morale.

All pure speculation of course, but compatible with what the historians tell us, and with the play that has survived. Nothing in Thucydides' and Plutarch's accounts, or in Euripides' text, is fundamentally incompatible with such a pattern of events, and there is much in the play that begins to make a very particular kind of sense when viewed in that light.

That the play *is* a comedy, and a very funny one, seems certain. Helen herself is a wonderfully rich creation, beautiful, witty, intelligent and resourceful, and determined to survive at all costs. She reminds us of nothing so much as one of Shaw's life-force girls, an Anne Whitefield or Lady Cecily Waynflete, or Major Barbara. Like them she is all wit and charm, and at the same time the motive energy of the plot. It is she at every stage who runs the show, sorting out the confused Menelaus, persuading Theonoe to help them, working out the escape plan, and being the chief actor in getting it underway. Only when brute force and ignorance are required does she yield place to Menelaus, to do his Boys-own-Paper Bulldog-Drummond stuff.

Menelaus himself is an utter blockhead, as he invariably is in Euripides, but this time his stupidity is raised to such heights as to make him one of the great comic creations. To watch his tiny brain coping with the idea that there might be two Helens, two Spartas, two Troys and even two Zeuses is to witness a moment of sublime comedy, and a scene which seems created to inspire the invention of our greatest comic actors. The mighty hero enters from the sea, bearded and in rags, looking like a kind of half-witted Robinson Crusoe, or Michael Palin in the opening titles of *Monty Python's Flying Circus*, and can't even stand up to the rough tongue of a fearsome old concièrge, a character that reminds us of Giles' ferocious cartoon Grandma, or almost any character performance by Patricia Hayes. When Helen explains her escape plan, he is so thick that he simply cannot understand it until she spells it out in words of one syllable, and the pompous idiocy of his speech to Theonoe, in which he threatens to kill himself and Helen on her father's tomb rather than lose his dear wife, makes it one of those scenes good comic actors would give their right arms to play. If Helen is an Anne Whitefield, within the same tradition Menelaus is an English silly arse, one of Pinero's gloriously rigid officers, or a P.G. Wodehouse chump. The rest of the characters exist in the same world, the splendidly irrelevant officer-type Teucer – just passing through – the overblown Theonoe, the heavy villain Theoclymenus, perhaps the first of a long line stretching right down to the heavies of the Buster Keaton and Chaplin films, and two ludicrously frivolous Heavenly Twins, as morally and philosophically empty a pair of immortals as even Euripides ever created.

Of course, we must admit the possibility that over two and a half thousand years, and within an unimaginably different social situation, we may misread Euripides' characters, and see in them comic traits which he intended should be taken seriously. Of course that is possible. But what it is impossible to misread, especially for any regular theatre worker, is the play's structure, which is inescapably comic. The central truth about the theatre in Aristotle's Poetics is that the most important constituent of a play is its action. Whatever the words say, however many beautiful or tragic speeches you make, the audience's reaction will be principally determined by the action they see played out in front of them, what things happen and in what order. Creating that dramatic structure is the most crucial imaginative task that confronts the playwright, and getting it wrong is the most certain harbinger of failure. The situation that Euripides creates is entirely comic. 'It wasn't me,' cries Helen, like a rumbled schoolboy, or an old lag caught with his finger in the till. The woman who in every other Euripides play about Troy is always the principal source of guilt, and vilified by everyone, protests her innocence with the most unlikely of alibis, and that in itself is comic. So is her whole situation with Theoclymenus, and her painful sexual frustration, after seventeen years of enforced chastity. She is more than interested in every man who appears, even keeping the ghastly Theoclymenus at the back of her mind as a last possibility if all else fails, and the conflict between fastidiousness and rampant desire at the appearance of her hirsute, ragged and stinking husband can't fail to amuse the audience. The recognition scene, the planning of the escape, and the way in which Helen persuades the heavy villain to provide all the necessities of their escape himself, all create structurally comic situations which determine the audience's reactions almost regardless of the words. If Euripides had wanted to create a serious work, he would have been very pushed to have pulled it off with the scenario he has created in *Helen*. If he had clothed the bones of the plot with a body of his most lofty and glorious verse, the likely effect would have been bathos, not sublimity. We would probably have laughed all the more. I can't believe that Euripides could have been that incompetent. I cannot believe that he would have created such a pattern of events if he didn't intend that we should be amused by them.

So, is the play merely an escapist comedy, a delightfully amusing romp to salve the bruises of the battered Athenians, and to make no greater demands of them than that they should laugh away their worries for two hours, and be charmed and amused enough to forget their griefs and fear? A lesser playwright might have done such a thing, and indeed many lesser playwrights have done, down the centuries. But we are talking about Euripides, the master dramatic ironist, who has no equal in any period in the art of twisting the knife in the wound, even if, in this case, he twists it rather gently, so that it won't hurt too much. If in *Helen* he creates a new genre of play, it is not the frothy Shaftesbury Avenue light comedy, whose bubbles pop harmlessly before disappearing for ever, but a tragi-comic mixture of farce, character comedy, and, at moments, great poetry, brittle as a mouthful of broken glass, or like a celebration on a frozen lake, where the dark waters of intellectual despair can be clearly seen swirling beneath the ice.

Hunting through Greek tragedies for topical or political references is a largely fruitless game, which nevertheless remains fascinating because we are quite convinced that such allusions are present even if we can't be sure we have pinned them down. Nevertheless, there are references in this play that can't have failed to contact the first audience with great force.

Most obviously, they were presented with the spectacle of an impoverished and shipwrecked Spartan King tricking a barbarian King into giving him the most up-to-date naval resources, the very latest design of Phoenician galley, together with the money and material to crew it. These barbarians, what's more, are under orders to kill all Greeks on sight, are all the slaves of one man, and are to be despised for their lack of freedom, but can easily be outwitted with a little intelligence and courage. The reference to current Spartan policy must have been obvious to every spectator, who would nevertheless have been encouraged to feel that barbarians were nothing much to be feared any more than Spartans were. The most striking and unmistakable of the contemporary references would certainly have been the sailor's speech attacking oracles. All the oracles and soothsayers had prophesied a successful outcome for the Sicilian expedition, and Thucydides reports how much anger was directed at them in Athens when the news of the disaster arrived. It is perhaps difficult for us to understand just how large a part soothsaying and divination played in the lives of the supposedly rational Greeks. Before every action, large or small, their soothsayers would consult oracles, or more often sacrifice animals to particular gods, seeking favourable omens. The most striking example is reported by Plutarch in his life of Aristides, describing the battle of Plataea, the climax of the struggle against the Persian invasion, when both armies were drawn up in force, ready to fight. Sacrifice after sacrifice turned out badly, and the Greek army waited and waited till the omens should be favourable. Indeed, the stoical Spartans sat with their shields on the ground allowing themselves to be shot down by the Persian archers till the sacrifice could be read in an optimistic way. Only then did the Greeks attack and carry the day. In more than one play Euripides reveals his contempt for this aspect of Greek religion, and nowhere more intensely than in the sailor's words. The speech is certainly longer than the context requires, indeed the sailor does a false exit, and comes back to make his point, as if he can't leave without having his say. His attack on soothsayers is very direct, and must have reflected a powerful feeling in the audience of the day. We can easily imagine angry cries of agreement as some members of that audience rose tearfully from their seats to support the shipwrecked sailor, remembering their own shipwrecked friends and loved ones who would never come back. When I saw the first production of *Oh What a Lovely War* at Stratford East in 1963, an old man with silver hair stood up in the audience when the cast sang 'We've seen them, We've seen them, Hanging on the old barbed wire,' and shouted out, 'Yes, I seen 'em an' all, mate.' It was one of the most moving things I have ever seen in a theatre, and, interestingly, in a performance of a war play that similarly employs a comic way of dealing with an unbearably tragic situation. Perhaps the feeling of that old man, who had personal experience of what the Great War meant, gives some indication of what the feeling of Euripides' audience might have been, when his bitter comedy was enacted in front of them.

At the very centre of the play there does indeed lie a harsh bitterness and an irony as savage as any Euripides created, even if this time he indicates it with the lightest of touches. Behind every joke there lurks the same subversive question: if Helen never was at Troy, and the Helen that appeared in Paris' arms was no more than a wraith, a cloud, an illusion, then why did all those men die, what was the purpose of the war? Was a whole generation murdered, a whole civilisation destroyed, for the sake of a puff of smoke? This sentiment emerges into speech on several occasions during the play, but Euripides doesn't harp upon it. It would have been far too painful for his scarred audience to keep hammering home that all the sufferings of both Greeks and Trojans, and by implication, of the Athenians themselves, were for nothing, for an illusion, and that all those lives had been sacrificed quite pointlessly. It was

> Merely to dispense with
> So much superfluous humanity, I suppose,
> To rid mother earth of the weight of so many
> Useless human beings,

says Helen, with her most winning smile, and a chilling prevision of one of the stated Nazi motives for the Holocaust. 'Zeus has it all planned,' intone the glittering and inhuman Dioscuri, at the very end of the play, as a final comment in a work which reveals the gods, as Euripides' plays invariably do, to be utterly empty, utterly self-centred, morally vacuous beings, to whom pride and petty insults are far more important than justice or the sufferings of the human race. This fearful image, of the complete pointlessness of the Trojan War, and the meaninglessness of all the deaths and destruction it caused, is too savage to hold in the mind for long, and Euripides keeps it in the background, but it is always there, at the centre of the play, like ice in the heart: the *casus belli* that was no more than an illusion, the woman whose mere shadow caused a whole generation to die. Euripides is saying the same things to the generation who had created and lived through the Peloponnesian War as he had always said: the game is not worth the candle, all the men and women are dying for nothing. He says it gently, quietly, behind a façade of wit and charm and good humour, but he says it none the less.

On two occasions the play's darker depths flow up to the surface. In the so called Nightingale Chorus – the nightingale being a harbinger of death in Greek culture – while Helen is offstage preparing to make a pretence of grief for her dead husband, who is actually alive and at her side, the Chorus sings a genuine lament for the dead Trojans, full of the intensity Euripides displays in similar anti-war Choruses in *Hecuba* and *Iphigenia at Aulis*. In the last strophe the lament rises to a denunciation of all war, and of the very idea that anything can be settled among civilised men by bloodshed, which resonates powerfully in our own ears:

> Lunatics, all of you, who see it as an instance
> Of your manhood with spear thrust or sword cut
> To end some poor devil's life, what ignorance,
> What savagery! If bloodshed
> Is to be the only arbiter of the rights
> Of human conflict, mankind
> Will never see an end to war, or cities at peace.

Later, in the Demeter Ode, Euripides probes even more interesting depths of thought and feeling, going so deep that he seems to have left a good many scholars and critics behind him. 'Why the story of Demeter here?' they cry, forgetting that it is poetry we are dealing with, not a scholarly dissertation, and that poets can convey subtleties of experience by association and suggestion rather than by statement. The Ode tells the story of how Demeter, the goddess of growth and fecundity, when her daughter was kidnapped by the god of the underworld, in rage and despair wreaked her vengeance on the human race and the gods. Nothing grew on earth and both gods and men were wasted by starvation. To remedy a desperate situation, Zeus sent Aphrodite and Dionysus to the weeping Demeter, and they soothed her grief by incorporating her into their mysterious dance, the dance of regeneration and rebirth in which love and ecstasy play so crucial a part. Euripides is almost certainly making a reference to the Eleusinian rites here, still as mysterious to us as they were to non-initiates in the poet's own day. Helen, the Ode tells us, had no experience of those Eleusinian Mysteries of death and rebirth – as a Spartan she could not have, because only Athenians were admitted to the ceremonies. But she, like the god Dionysus and his followers, like Aphrodite, enshrines irrational powers of destruction and regeneration *in herself*. Helen, the semi-divine being, fathered by a god, who will on her death be transported to the stars like her brothers, embodies powerful forces that can kill or cure. Like Demeter, she has within herself the ability to sustain or destroy the human race, the ultimate power of godhead. The war, like all wars, has been fought in pursuit of an illusion, and yet Euripides had seen enough of men's behaviour, in his seventy-third year, to know that certain illusions have great creative and destructive powers, and will draw men on to kill for them again and again, and that Helen/Aphrodite is perhaps the most powerful and dangerous illusion of them all. Demeter is the most natural analogy to draw, for like Helen/Aphrodite, she is the source of all life, the yearly cycle of rebirth – as Helen/Aphrodite represents the force that will ultimately draw men to reproduce themselves – and her myth tells how the destructive powers of her grief, the yearly carnage of winter, were incorporated into the dance of regeneration. It is not without significance that this Ode is delivered while Menelaus and Helen are offstage making love, enacting the rite of Aphrodite, in which the rites of Demeter are also bound up and symbolised, or that at the end of the Ode it is the curative and regenerative qualities of Helen/Aphrodite that are emphasised. This play, unlike *Hippolytus*, is to end happily, with sexual love binding up all wounds and healing all bruises. But the power is godlike, and that power, illusion or not, broods over the whole play. The exit immediately before the Demeter Chorus, with the two frustrated lovers barely able to keep their hands off each other for one moment longer, is the purest comedy, and it is juxtaposed at once with an Ode of the profoundest seriousness and poetic subtlety. It is the definitive moment of this comic masterpiece, which without disturbing the essentially comic flow, deals with bitter and painful aspects of the war, and digs as deep as any into the mysterious springs of action that make men fight each other in the first place, and can eventually hope to bring them into brotherhood and regeneration.

Just in case we haven't got the point, Euripides makes it quite explicit, when the two lovers are just about to put their dangerous escape plan into action, and immediately before the Nightingale Chorus, which describes the disasters of war. Praying to Aphrodite – who else? – for success in their plan, Helen cries:

> Are you never satisfied
> At the sufferings you inflict on human beings?
> Your weapons are lust, and deceit, every sort
> Of intrigue and manipulation, even potions and poison
> And bloodshed within families. If only your power
> Could be restrained! For what other goddess
> Has given mankind gifts as sweet as yours!

Short of spelling it out for us a syllable at a time, Euripides could hardly make it clearer.

The play makes a striking and thought-provoking third part of a created Euripidean trilogy of war plays, not only because it was written at a crucial time during the war, and is historically so closely related to *The Women of Troy*, both being Sicilian expedition plays, but also because its underlying subject is war and the futility of war just as completely as the other two plays in this volume. I can only see it as being a comic offspring of that same tragic disaster, against which the earlier play sounded its grim warning, and therefore all my translation decisions, as to tone of voice, and English style, and even individual choice of words, have been coloured by that initial perception. I have sought a unity of style, an overall dramatic and linguistic gesture, that can convey the rich comedy, the irony, the bitterness and the poetry of this marvellous work. It is up to others, and most of all, the test of public performance, to judge how far I have succeeded.

I owe my thanks to Geoffrey Lewis, of the Department of Classics at Edinburgh University, as completely as ever, not only for his meticulous literal translation, which is no mere version, but which tries to suggest associations and alternative meanings in the Greek which must greatly help to bring me closer to Euripides' original. In addition, he has initiated me into some of the textual problems which bedevil such ancient plays, and given me the benefit of the latest research in the most modern editions. In particular, his close professional knowledge has been particularly helpful in an understanding of the history of the later years of the Peloponnesian War, and we have had many fruitful discussions, on the phone and face to face, on all aspects of Greek history, art and culture, which have been most stimulating, and have contributed greatly to this present work. His comments on my first versions have been unrelentingly strict, allowing me to get away with nothing, particularly when I have taken wing on an imaginative flight of my own and drifted rather far from Euripides. On every such occasion, he has led me firmly back to the text, much to the benefit of the final version. In the case of *Iphigenia at Aulis*, as formerly in *The Theban Plays* of Sophocles, he has been at my elbow in rehearsal, and we have both enjoyed the rich pleasure of correcting the translation in the light of the crucial insights into dramatic line good actors can give.

All the decisions about text, translation and interpretation have been mine, and when they go against modern thinking in the matter of interpolations and textual confusions, or at times against Geoffrey Lewis's knowledgeable advice, that has been because I have put my own dramatic instinct before scholarly conclusions. In every case where the text is in question, I have followed my own judgement as a playwright, creating a version that seems to me dramatic and playable, even if, as in a few cases, I have gone against most recent opinion. In the case of the choral dialogue between Hecuba and Andromache in *The Women of Troy*, where the distribution of the lines has been much questioned, I have based my distribution upon a poetic form of my own, a pattern of repetitions that needed to be worked through, though one not without some scholarly justification; and in the lines at the end of *Helen* which may be given to a slave who has never previously appeared, or to the Chorus, I have opted for the Chorus, for the simple reason that no theatrical producer is going to employ another speaking actor for so small a part, and it is much more theatrically satisfying that the Chorus, whom we know, and whom we know to be on Helen's side, should participate in a small way in the action. Sophocles certainly allowed his Chorus to participate in

Oedipus at Colonus, when they bar Creon's escape, so why should not Euripides have had the same idea a few years earlier – even if he does refer to the slave in the masculine gender! Let the scholars decide what seems correct to them, as they must if they are to be any use to me or anyone else. It is only their meticulous work that gives us the opportunity to make creative decisions.

These plays were originally translated, during 1987 and 1988, to be presented on BBC television as a complete trilogy. Only one of them has been recorded at the moment of writing – Spring 1990 – and the other two may or may not find their way on to the screen, depending upon the vagaries of internal BBC politics. Whatever the outcome of that, I look forward to seeing the whole trilogy performed in its natural home, the theatre.

IPHIGENIA AT AULIS

Characters

AGAMEMNON, Commander in Chief of the Greek army
OLD MAN, servant of Agamemnon
MENELAUS, brother of Agamemnon, husband of Helen
CLYTEMNESTRA, wife of Agamemnon
IPHIGENIA, their daughter
ACHILLES, a Greek hero
FIRST MESSENGER, from the guard party bringing
  Clytemnestra and Iphigenia to Aulis
SECOND MESSENGER, from the sacrifice
CHORUS of women from Chalcis
SECONDARY CHORUS of soldiers
PRIESTS AND PRIESTESSES, ATTENDANTS, ORESTES'
  NURSE, ARMOUR BEARERS

This translation was commissioned by BBC Televison and first produced in the summer of 1989, with the following cast:

AGAMEMNON	Roy Marsden
OLD MAN	Eric Allan,
MENELAUS	Tim Woodward,
FIRST MESSENGER	Tyler Butterworth,
CLYTEMNESTRA	Fiona Shaw,
IPHIGENIA	Imogen Boorman,
ACHILLES	Graham Sinclair,
SECOND MESSENGER	Greg Hicks,
NURSE	Judith Blakstad
CHORUS	Hetta Charnley, Susan Curnow, Morag Hood, Deborah Makepeace, Janet Maw, Ruth Mitchell, Joanna Myers, Tessa Peake-Jones, Emma Piper, Celestine Randall, Sheila Ruskin, Kate Spiro,
GREEK SOLDIERS	Dominic Arnold, Charles Bates, Timothy Chipping, Neil Conrich, Julian Cope, Charles Dale, David Dandridge, Duncan Duff, Jason Durr, Antony Evans, Nicholas Frost, Oliver Haden, Robert Hands, Jeremy Harrison, Miles Harvey, Michael Hewson, James Hicks, Jeremy Hutton, Jonathan Jaynes, Christopher Kent, Frank Kovacs, Thomas Lockyer, Colin Mace, Danny McGrath, Ritchie Madden, David Monteath, John Moorhead, Roderick O'Grady, Robin Pirongs, Julian Protheroe, Ashley Russel, Richard Ryan, Gary Sharkey, Jon Sotherton, Eric Stovell, Robert Sturt, Lee Warner, Colin Wells, Paul Wimsett

PRIESTS AND PRIESTESSES	Ingrid Baier, Isobel Bradshaw, Eileen Davies, Andrea Duncan, Alison Fielding, Richard Hazell, Teresa McElroy, Nella Marin, Anne Osborne, John Parry, Eryl Royle, Ninka Scott

Director	Don Taylor
Producer	Louis Marks
Designer	Graham Lough
Music	Derek Bourgeois
Costumes	June Hudson

*The scene is set in the Greek camp on the shores of the
Bay of Aulis.* AGAMEMNON's *headquarters hut is the principal
feature, but we are conscious of the presence of a large
army in camp, and a fleet of ships drawn up on the shore.*
*There is a road leading to Argos, and another exit in the
direction of the grove sacred to Artemis.*

It is just before dawn, and a light is burning in
AGAMEMNON's hut.

AGAMEMNON *comes out of the hut, carrying a letter in his hand, and
walks up and down for a few minutes. He stops and looks up at the
sky, then calls quietly to the* OLD MAN *inside the hut.*

AGAMEMNON. Old man. Come out, in front of the hut.
  Stand here.

The OLD MAN *enters from inside the hut.*

OLD MAN.   I'm coming. Another bright idea,
  King Agamemnon, eh?
AGAMEMNON.   Hurry.
OLD MAN.   I'm hurrying.
  I don't sleep much. Too old for that.
  Old age keeps your eyes sharp as a sentry.
AGAMEMNON. What star's that? Like a ship crossing the
                                                  night sky.
OLD MAN. That's Sirius. Next to the seven Pleiades:
  Still rising there, in the mid heaven.
AGAMEMNON. No birdsong. Even the sound of the sea
  Is muffled. But the lack of wind: that silence
  Holds back more than the waves in the straits of Euripus.
OLD MAN. But why come out of your hut, King Agamemnon,
  Just to pace up and down the same
  Few steps? All quiet at Aulis tonight.
  Not a sound from the guard towers on the walls.
  Let's go back in.
AGEMEMNON.   Old friend, I envy you.

7

I envy anyone who can get through life
Unnoticed, avoiding danger, and without fame.
Famous men, great leaders. I don't envy them at all.

OLD MAN. But they get all the glory sir. They win life's
                                                    prizes.

AGAMEMNON. Yes, you say so. But glory is dangerous.
And honour slippery;
You have it, and it's gone. Ambition for leadership
Is an addiction, thrilling, but painful in the end.
If the gods' wishes and a man's will conflict
His life will be smashed.
And men's conflicting demands shred you like a grater.

OLD MAN. I don't like to hear this sort of talk
From a great King, Lord Agamemnon.
Atreus fathered you
Not just for the pleasures of Kingship
And a life of unbroken good luck. Pain
As well as celebration you must expect.
You're a man, born mortal. And the gods
Regardless of whether you like it or not
Will have their way.
You light your lamp, it flares up, and spreads
Enough light for you to write a letter.
You're still holding it in your hand. You write
A bit, then cross it out, then write again,
And cross it out again,
Seal it up, and immediately unseal it,
Even throw it on the ground: all the time
Weeping real tears.
You looked so desperate, you seemed half mad
With some trouble or other. Is it bad news
That causes so much grief? You can tell me, my Lord.
I'm loyal and trustworthy. I came with your wife,
Sent with her from Tyndareus I was,
Part of the dowry!

AGAMEMNON. Thestius' daughter, Leda, bore three daughters:
Phoebe, Clytemnestra – who became my wife –
And Helen. All the leading young men of Greece

8

Were mad for Helen, and came as suitors,
Each one threatening his rivals with murder
And mayhem, if he didn't get the girl.
Tyndareus, their father, was baffled, how, either
In giving or refusing her, to make the best of a bad job.
But then an idea struck him: a pact,
That all the suitors should consent to, shaking hands,
And confirmed with the usual religious ceremonies –
Burned offerings, the pouring of wine, etcetera –
Which would bind every one of them, by oath,
To defend and support whichever man
Won the daughter of Tyndareus as his wife,
In the event that anyone should abduct her
From her husband's bed. Whoever he was,
Greek or barbarian, they would mount a fully armed
Expeditionary force against him, and destroy
His city. When they'd committed themselves,
And old Tyndareus, being a crafty fellow,
Had sewn them up neatly with his logic,
He smartly allowed his daughter to let
The breath of the goddess of love blow her
Towards whichever one of the suitors she chose.
And she chose . . . God help us, *him*, of all people . . .
Menelaus. Not long after that, from Troy,
The principal city of Phrygia, a young fellow
By the name of Paris – the very same man,
According to the story rife among the Greeks,
Who judged between three goddesses, and chose beauty
Before wisdom and power – turned up in Sparta.
The splendour of his dress was barbaric,
A vulgar ostentation of gold and jewels,
Cloth of gold, flowered silk, and gems
In the shape of flowers, glittering, shining . . .
Helen was dazed with lust for him
And he for her. He picked his moment –
Menelaus was out of the country – and dragged her
Off to his byres and bartons and pigsties.
On Mount Ida. Menelaus raved like a madman

9

Through all the cities of Greece, invoking
Tyndareus' old treaty they had all set their hands to,
Claiming, indeed demanding they must all
Stand by their guarantees and launch
A punitive expedition, to sack Troy!
So all the Greeks sprang out of their chariots,
Took down spears, and shields, and body armour from their
walls,
And came here, to this natural harbour of Aulis,
Opposite the narrows, with their ships,
Their heavy armour, thousands of Horse,
And their decorated battle chariots. They gave
Supreme command to me, for Menelaus' sake,
Because I am his brother. And I swear to God,
I wish any other man had been given that honour
Rather than me. And now we are all here,
Mustered at Aulis, this vast army,
There's not a breath of wind, we all wait,
Unable to get even one ship under way.
We have waited, and waited, and we began to despair;
Till the Priest Calchas spoke: and he said . . .
That we must offer my daughter, my child, Iphigenia,
As a sacrifice to the goddess of this place, Artemis,
Who has her sanctuary here. And then, only then
The wind would change, we could put to sea,
Sail across to Phrygia, and sack Troy.
When I heard this, I immediately told Talthybius,
Our communications and propaganda Officer,
To announce the disbandment of the whole army,
Because I couldn't – not conceivably,
Ever be so brutal as to kill my own child . . .
When he heard this, my brother begged me,
He wheedled and exerted every argument
And persuasion he could think of, till finally
He forced me to agree to the damnable business.
I wrote a letter, folded it, and folded it again,
And sent it to my wife. It told her to send
Our daughter here, to be married to Achilles.

I made a great fuss of him, told her how heroic
He was, praised him to the skies, and said
He absolutely refused to sail with us
Unless a bride should be sent from our family
To return with him to his house at Pthia.
I was sure this pack of lies about our daughter's marriage
Would be convincing enough to persuade my wife.
Of all the Greeks, only the Priest Calchas,
Odysseus, and Menelaus, and myself
Know about this . . . I did that . . . And I was wrong!
So in this new letter I have changed my decision,
Back to what I decided in the first place.
That's what I was doing, writing and rewriting,
Sealing and unsealing in my hut in the dark.
Now take it, go on, now, get to Argos
Fast. No, wait, I'd better let you
Into the secret sealed up in there
Word for word. You're a good old fellow,
You've been loyal to my wife and to me for years.

OLD MAN. Yes, you should tell me, so that what I say
    Won't conflict with what's written in the letter.

AGAMEMNON. 'Further to my last letter, Daughter of

                                                    Leda,

    These new instructions: do *not* send,
    Repeat, *not* send, your daughter here
    To this peaceful harbour of Aulis
    On the Gulf of Euboea.
    It seems we must celebrate our daughter's marriage
    At some other, future time.'

OLD MAN. But if Achilles is cheated of his bride,
    He'll explode with anger, surely?
    His fury towards you and your wife will be terrifying.
    You surely don't intend that to happen?

AGAMEMNON. No, no, I'm merely using his name,
    He's not required to do anything. In fact
    He knows nothing at all of the matter, he's party
    To none of our plans, least of all the scheme
    Of his own pretended marriage to my daughter.

OLD MAN. It's clever, Lord Agamemnon, but dangerous,
                                                    to pretend
    You're bringing her to marry the son of an immortal,
    When really, she'll be given to the Greeks, to be
                                            butchered . . .
AGAMEMNON. Don't say that . . . ! It drives me mad to
                                                hear it.
    I feel as if my head's breaking in pieces . . .
    Get moving, superannuated fool. Forget your legs are
                                            old,
    Run like a boy!
OLD MAN.   As fast as I can, my Lord.
AGAMEMNON. Make sure you don't sit down by that spring
                                            in the forest
    And fall asleep.
OLD MAN.   As if I would sir, really!
AGAMEMNON. When you come to the place where the road
                                            forks,
    Look sharply in both directions, and make sure
    No carriage slips past you while you are looking
    The other way, and brings her here,
    To where the whole Greek fleet is anchored.
OLD MAN. I'll take care of that sir.
AGAMEMNON.   Even if you meet her
    At the very gates, with her guards and outriders,
    Stop them, grab the reins yourself, and drive her
    Straight back inside the city walls –
    They're so massive, the one-eyed giants built them,
    So the legend says, when Argos was founded.
OLD MAN. Just a minute though sir . . . why should your
                                                wife
    And daughter believe me, when I tell them all this?
AGAMEMNON. This is my seal . . . see here, on the letter.
    Make sure it's unbroken. Get moving! The sky
    Is greying already. The four-horsed chariot
    Of the sun is galloping towards the eastern
    Horizon, flooding the sea and sky with light.
    It's up to you to save me!

The OLD MAN *runs off in the direction of Argos.*

AGAMEMNON. No man lives happy to the end of his life
  Or avoids his share of bad luck.
  We inherit grief merely by being born.

AGAMEMNON *looks round at the brightening sky, and goes back into his hut.*

The CHORUS *enters, a group of women from Chalcis, across the channel, thrilled by the opportunity to see the Greek army in camp.*

CHORUS. I have sailed across the narrow seas
  Of Euripus, through the fast running tide,
  And landed here on the sandy beach
  Of Aulis. My home is on the other side
  Of the straits, Chalcis, where Arethusa sprays
  Her fountain of fresh spring water within reach
  Of the salt sea itself. I have come to gaze
  In wonder upon the Achaean force,
  And the forest of seagoing oars that will pull
  The slender pine ships, a thousand strong,
  By the strength of brave men's arms, the long
  Journey to Troy led by the powerful
  Red-headed Menelaus,
  And noble Agamemnon, the King!
  They'll drag her back here, our husbands say,
  Helen, whom Aphrodite gave as a prize
  To Paris, the Prince who lived as a shepherd.
  He found her, where the sighing reed beds whispered
  By the river Eurotas – as was promised when the goddess
                                    arose
  Glistening from her bath in a fountain of spray,
  When Hera and Pallas and She
  Competed so bitterly
  For his voice on that Judgement day.

13

I ran through the sacred grove of trees,
By Artemis' shrine, where they offer fresh blood
From the victims' throats – my cheeks are crimson
With embarrassment, that in such a crowd
We should come to gawp at the Greek armies,
Their huge interlinked shields, like a brazen
Wall, the weapons in their armories
Or stacked by their tents, the heavy cavalry,
But most of all, the men! Ajax I saw,
Oileus' son, just sitting there, talking
To the other Ajax, son of Telamon. He was looking
Every inch the part of the superstar
Of Salamis! And nearby,
Protesilaus was playing draughts, and enjoying
The interplay of chance and strategy
With Palamedes, the sea god's grandson! Diomedes too
Was working out with the discus, and revelling
In showing off his strength; and strolling
Close by, Meriones, in battle worth two
Normal men, who claims the war god as his paternity.
And Laertes' son is here
From mountainous Ithaca;
And Nireus, isn't he a beauty!

And Achilles I saw, who runs fast as the wind,
Whom Thetis the sea-nymph bore,
And was tutored by Chiron, in body and mind:
He was sprinting along the sea shore
With a full armour on his back,
Keeping pace for pace with one of the crack
Charioteers, for battle and track,
Eumelos, with a racing four!
And the son of Pheretias spurred on his team
Around the lap marker to win,
And he tickled their flanks with his whip, and the scream
Of the driver himself urged them on.
Their bits and harness were all gold,
The yoke horses grey, with manes piebald,

Red-maned the trace horses, but patterned with bold
Black and white, to the fetlock down.
But the son of Peleus, in full pack,
Ran with them, and matched each stride,
While the whirling wheels
And the screaming axle
And the bouncing chariot rail
Raced inches from his side!

And I saw an Armada of ships in the bay,
Too many to count, awesome beyond measure.
I couldn't speak, I was dumb with the joy,
A sight for my eyes to feed on and treasure
As a bee feeds on nectar and stores honey.
Massing on the right, their oars keeping time,
The Myrmidons' battle galleys hove to,
Fast movers from Phthia, like a full rhyme
Closing the line. And high above the waters,
Carved on the sterns in gold, I saw in full view
Achilles' coat of arms, Poseidon's sea-born daughters!

Keel by keel with them, equal in number,
The fifty ships of Argos stood,
Sthenelus, tough Capaneus' son,
Captained a squadron, and the pride of Talaos' blood,
Mecistes' heir, was supreme commander.
On station beside them rode sixty ships
From Attica, their Admiral
The son of Theseus. For his emblem he keeps
Pallas herself, carved as she flew
In her winged four-handed chariot, a symbol
Sure to bring good luck to any Athenian crew.

With my own eyes I saw
Boeotia's naval power,
A fleet of fifty ships, and each one crowned
With a carven figurehead,
While at each stern post stood

Cadmus, with a golden dragon curled around.
Leitus – born of a giant, the ancient earth
Herself – commanded,
And Ajax, Oileus' son, led fifty, worth
His fame, assembled
From Phocis and from Locris, sailing on
From their port of embarkation, famous Thronion.

From Argos' Cyclops walls
The son of Atreus calls
Men by the thousand to crew his hundred ships.
With him his friend and brother
Sails as co-commander
So that Greece may take full payment for the lips
Sold in marriage to a barbarian, and the hearth
And home destroyed.
And Nestor from Gerenon, loth
To be unemployed
Sails in, ignoring his great age,
With bull-foot Alpheus the river god as his badge.

The King Gouneus captained a line
Of twelve Aeneanian ships, a fine
Flotilla, and alongside them
The tribesmen of Elis, whom everyone
In the army calls Epeians: beside them the squadron –
Whose oars, from stem
To stern were painted gleaming white –
Of the Taphians, mirroring the sun's light.
Eurytus led them: and Phyleus' son was there,
Meges, from the Echinean islands, whose rocks all sailors
fear.

Ajax from Salamis held the centre
Joining right wing and left together
Manoeuvring his line
Of light fast moving craft to meet
And link his wings with the rest of the fleet

16

Like closing a chain.
The task force was ready, as if on parade,
Both army and navy. No commando raid
Or foreign battle fleet would dare to face
So vast a navy, and hope for safe return to base.

Like a city on the sea, I watched the Greek fleet
Assembling in the bay.
Others may speak of it, but my eyes have seen it.
I will never forget this day!

MENELAUS *enters with the* OLD MAN. MENELAUS *has*
AGAMEMNON'S *letter in his hand.*

OLD MAN. Menelaus, you dare not, have you no conscience . . . ?
MENELAUS. Get off! Unquestioning loyalty is as bad.
OLD MAN. Do you mean that as an insult? I call it praise.
MENELAUS. Look, if you overstep the mark, you'll be sorry!
OLD MAN. You had no right to open the letter I was carrying.
MENELAUS. The letter you were carrying betrays every one of us!
OLD MAN. You carry on shouting, but give me that letter!
MENELAUS. I've got it, and I'll keep it!
OLD MAN.   I won't let it go!
MENELAUS. I'll bloody your head for you with this stick if you
                                                            don't.
OLD MAN. I'll die for my master then, and be famous!
MENELAUS. Let go! For a batman, you talk too much.
OLD MAN. My Lord! This is an outrage! Come out sir!
  This man has torn your letter from my hand
  Agamemnon, by force, quite without conscience.

AGAMEMNON *comes out of the hut.*

AGAMEMNON (ENTERING). Hey there . . . !
  What's all this racket, this abuse, at my door?
MENELAUS. Listen to me first, this man's a servant!
AGAMEMNON. Menelaus, what's this brawling! Let go of that
                                                            man!

MENELAUS. Pay attention to me then, I'll tell you from the
start.

AGAMEMNON. Atreus was my father. I'll look any man in the eye.

MENELAUS. This letter is treasonable, a complete betrayal!

AGAMEMNON. I can see it . . . So first of all, give it to me.

MENELAUS. Oh no! Not till I've shown it to the army!

AGAMEMNON. So. You've broken the seal. It's none of your
business.

MENELAUS. Unfortunately for you. I know your filthy plan.

AGAMEMNON. How did you get hold of it? Have you no shame?

MENELAUS. Waiting on the road from Argos – for your daughter.

AGAMEMNON. How dare you spy on me! The impudence . . . !

MENELAUS. When you have an itch you have to scratch. I'm not
your slave!

AGAMEMNON. It's outrageous, to interfere in my family affairs!

MENELAUS. You're devious and unreliable, you always have
been.

AGAMEMNON. Smart talk, excuses for shabby behaviour!

MENELAUS. You've no character or resolution,
   You're quite capable of wickedness, and impossible
   To trust, even for your friends! I'm going
   To show you up for what you are – don't
   Turn away like that, it'll be the truth,
   Without any exaggeration – so don't dismiss it
   With a show of anger! You remember, I'm sure,
   When you were so keen to get the supreme command
   Of the Greek Task Force against Troy,
   And how you wanted it! – There was no pretence
   About that! How very self deprecating
   You were, eager to press the flesh
   With any uniform or suit, doors always open,
   A universal welcome; you always granted
   The pleasure of your company
   To anyone, even if they didn't want it,
   As if by sweet talk and glad-handing
   The whole country, you could buy the command
   In the open market. But then,
   When your appointment had been confirmed,

Suddenly, you were a changed man!
Friends were no longer friends, overnight.
No one could get near you, you were always
Unobtainable, your headquarters' doors
More often locked than open. A great man,
A man of genuine nobility
Who achieves a position of power, does not
Celebrate his good fortune by cutting
All his friends dead, at the very time
When he's able to do them some good! I saw
The contemptible side of your character
Straight away. But then, when you came here,
To Aulis, with the whole Panhellenic
Army trembling at your command,
You became a nonentity, you panicked,
You were struck dumb, or cursed your bad luck
Because there was no wind, and without wind
None of us could get across to Troy!
And the word went round the army, all the Greek
Commanders began to mutter they were wasting
Their time, that we might as well disband
The army, decommission the ships,
Instead of spending time and money at Aulis
For no purpose. You were being called –
Of all damning descriptions – an unlucky General.
You began to see your great dream of leading
A thousand ships to Troy, of darkening
The plain before Priam's city
With division upon division of infantry, disappearing
Before your eyes! You asked my advice
Then, quickly enough. 'What shall I do,
How can we get across, or get out of this trap
Without me losing what I value most,
The glory of command! And then, when Calchas
Came up with a solution, that you should offer
Your child to Artemis, as a sacred blood sacrifice,
In return for fair winds and an easy passage,
You were delighted, you jumped at the suggestion,

You willingly offered to murder your daughter;
In fact, of your own volition – none of us
Forced you, you can't say we did – you hurried
Word to your wife to send your child here,
With a rigmarole about her marrying Achilles.
And now, with yet another U-turn,
You've been caught out secretly changing your story
Once again, with another letter. You will never
Be your own daughter's murderer! But you will!
You know what you said. The very air,
The sky above our heads, heard you say it.
Well, it's not surprising I suppose.
Thousands of men have done the same,
Struggled inch by inch up the slippery slope
To power, and then, when they got there,
Slid ignominiously back down to the bottom.
Sometimes it's because the voters are too dim
To understand what they're doing. Other times
They're simply not up to the job. It's Greece
I feel sorry for. She intended to act
Honourably. Now she's humiliated,
Made a laughing stock, by a bunch of effeminate
Barbarians, and all because of you
And your little girl. It's always a mistake,
In politics, and in military matters
To appoint a leader simply because
He's brave, and bull-headed. Any man
With a modicum of sense can rule a city.
An army commander needs intelligence, brains!

CHORUS. It's a terrible thing when angry words, and the threat
   Of blows, causes such division between brothers.

AGAMEMNON. Now I shall have my say. I shall be
   Critical, but brief, and stay within
   The bounds of decency, without being
   Contemptuous to the point of demeaning myself.
   You are, after all, my brother. A gentleman
   Recognises certain norms of behaviour,
   He treats other people with courtesy and respect.

What is the point of all this blustering
And eyes bloodshot with fury? Has someone
Wronged you? And if so, what do you expect
Me to do about it? If a faithful wife
Is what you want, I'm afraid I can't help you
There. You let the one you had
Run riot. So am I to pay
For your mistakes, when I am myself
Quite blameless? What gnaws at your
Self esteem isn't my rank,
Or the honours that have been heaped upon me.
To hell with reason, forethought, or any
Kind of decent behaviour, all you want
Is to get that lascivious woman back
In your arms, and into bed. The pleasures
Of a degraded mind are like itself,
Degraded. If I, on the other hand,
Initially made a bad decision
And after coming to my senses
Changed my mind, does that make me mad?
No! You're the mad one. You had the good luck
To lose a wife who was worthless, the gods
Granted you that good fortune. Now
You're mad enough to want the bitch back!
All the suitors were half crazed with lust
For her, and like fools, consented to swear
Tyndareus' oath – that most deceiving of goddesses,
Hope, no doubt, leading them on.
It certainly wasn't out of any sense of loyalty
To you! Well then, go and get them
To be your army and do your fighting!
They're ready enough for any madness.
The gods are not lacking in intelligence,
They can tell the difference between genuine vows
And oaths sworn foolishly, or under duress.
I will not kill my children.
You won't get revenge on your worthless wife
At the expense of my sense of justice, leaving me

Years of misery and a guilty conscience
For an unforgiveable crime committed
On a child of my own flesh. So there you are.
A few words, brief, and to the point.
You may choose to act like a madman.
My business, particularly with my own family,
Will be conducted with decency, and common sense.

CHORUS. These words completely contradict what you said
Before. But it must be right to spare your child.

MENELAUS. That leaves me naked, with no friends at all.

AGAMEMNON. You have friends, if you don't try to destroy them.

MENELAUS. No one would believe that you are my brother.

AGAMEMNON. I'm your brother in common sense, not lunacy.

MENELAUS. A brother should share his brother's agony!

AGAMEMNON. If you're just, I'll help you. This way you'll
destroy me!

MENELAUS. Greece needs you. Won't you share her agony?

AGAMEMNON. Greece has gone mad. The gods have touched
you all!

MENELAUS. You glory in the power your Field Marshall's baton
Gives you: and you choose to betray me. Very well.
There are other methods; other friends.

A MESSENGER *enters.*

MESSENGER.   Agamemnon!
King of the Greek army! I am one of the escort
Travelling with your daughter to Aulis, the girl
You called Iphigenia when you were at home.
Her mother is with her, your Clytemnestra
In person, and your baby boy,
Orestes. It'll give you particular pleasure
To see him, having been away from home
For so long. We had a tough journey,
And I left the women relaxing by a fresh
Spring, and cooling their feet in the pond –
We'd unharnessed the horses and turned them loose
To graze in a nearby field – while I ran

Ahead to tell you what's happened. The army
Knows all about it. You know how fast
Rumour travels. Everyone seems to know
About your daughter's arrival. A big crowd
Has already come out from the camp, trying
To get a look at her. Everyone likes to see
Famous people with the good luck to be born rich
And gossip about them. They're all saying,
'What's going on, some marriage, or what?
Or has Agamemnon brought his daughter here
Simply because he's missing her?' I've heard
Some others, though, who say it's a consecration
To Artemis, the Virgin Queen of Aulis,
By way of preparation for marriage.
So who's to be the lucky bridegroom?
If it's true, come on then, we'd better prepare
Baskets of flowers, and floral crowns,
And Lord Menelaus, you must organise the music,
Send for the flutes, and make sure there's plenty
Of dancing, for a day like this, from first dawn
Onwards, should be all happiness for the girl.

AGAMEMNON. Thank you for your news. Go inside for a
                                                    moment.
If the gods are with us, things will turn out well . . .

The MESSENGER, *rather crestfallen, goes into the hut.*

AGAMEMNON. God help me, what can I say
Or do, in a situation like this?
I'm like a slave under the yoke,
Chained and shackled! Bad luck has second-guessed me,
Every move I make is countered, every tactic
Outwitted by a better one! It's better to be born
Nobody, nonentities can cry their eyes out
And blurt out everything to anyone.
For our sort, born in the ruling class,
We must keep our mouths shut, suffer in silence
To protect our position, and our dignity!

The masses are our masters, we their slaves –
And that's my situation exactly.
I'm ashamed to cry about it. But I'd be
Ashamed not to cry too. Nothing could be worse
Than being caught in a trap as appalling as this.
And what, in heaven's name, shall I say
To my wife? How can I face her?
How can I look her in the eyes?
What possible expression can my face wear
As it receives her, and welcomes her to Aulis?
I have troubles enough, she has made them
Far worse by coming here uninvited.
And yet it's reasonable enough, natural even,
That she should want to come with her daughter
To see her married, and to give her a mother's
Kisses and endearments on her wedding day.
And then she'll find out soon enough,
If I know her, what mischief I've planned . . .
But the poor maid herself . . . why do I call her
That? The god of the dead will take
Her virginity soon enough. It's unendurable
To imagine it . . . She's certain to plead
With me . . . 'Will *you* kill me, Daddy,
You? Then let Death marry you too,
Let him marry everyone you love, the same
As me!' And Orestes will be there,
My little boy. He can't speak yet,
But he'll understand, his unintelligible cries
Will speak far too clearly to my heart . . . Paris,
Priam's son, you are the instigator of all
This pain. Your love for Helen has destroyed me!
CHORUS. What a moving speech! He's a King, and I'm a
                                                                        woman
  From a foreign city, but I sympathise with his grief.
MENELAUS. Brother, let me shake you by the hand.
AGAMEMNON. Yes. Why not. You're the winner. I've lost.
MENELAUS. Brother, by Pelops, our famous grandfather,
  And by Atreus, who fathered both of us,

I swear, I'm speaking the plain truth now,
Direct from the heart, with no hidden motives
Or any self-interest, but an honest analysis
Of the facts of the case, and whatever wisdom
I have learned in my life. When I saw the tears
In your eyes, I couldn't help pitying you.
In fact, the tears welled up in my eyes too.
I retract, unconditionally, all the words and arguments
I have used against you. I am not your enemy,
Nor implacable nor destructive in any way
Towards you. I stand in your shoes.
And I beg you not to kill your child
On my account, or put my interests
In any way before your own.
It's not right that you should suffer
For my pleasure, nor that your child
Should die, while my children live and enjoy
The light of day. What is it, after all,
I want to achieve? A good marriage?
I could take my pick anywhere in the world,
If I wanted to. Shall I destroy
The last person in the world I should injure,
My own brother, for the sake of the likes
Of Helen, prefer the wicked woman
To the good man? I've been thinking
Stupidly and selfishly, like an adolescent,
Till watching you, I suddenly had a vision
Of what it means to kill a child.
I was anguished with pity for her, and I realised too
That we are related, that it's my own niece
That is to be killed, to preserve my marriage.
And what has your daughter to do with Helen?
Nothing in the world. So, disband the army,
Send them all home, away from Aulis.
Anything, Brother, to wipe away these tears
From your cheeks, and mine too, weeping
In sympathy. And . . . even if
You have any secret information

About this sacrifice, which makes it particularly
Acceptable to the gods, let me be quite clear
I want no part of it. My share, the guilt
And all the advantages, I willingly hand over
To you. So you see, I've changed my mind.
All my hostility towards you has gone,
Or changed, rather, into something like love.
So it should. You are my brother.
Don't think it cowardice or weakness
That makes me change my mind. Or policy
Masquerading as love. I'm simply determined
To discover the right direction, the best course
For all of us, and follow it through to the end.

CHORUS. Inspiring words, and worthy Tantalus,
    The son of Zeus. Your ancestors would be proud of you.

AGAMEMNON. What can I say, Menelaus, to thank you
    And praise your integrity? Beyond all expectation
    You have spoken with an honesty and justice
    Worthy of the man I know you to be.
    Brothers will always fight, over women
    And money, the most lucrative marriage
    Or the lion's share of the property,
    Or simply because they are brothers, and blood
    Relationships so often turn sour. I hate
    All that, that sibling rivalry
    And family feuding, I reject it as unworthy.
    But. The fact is. Your generosity doesn't help.
    We are boxed in by circumstances, or like an animal in a net.
    There is no alternative. I must murder my child.

MENELAUS. No! Why? Your own child? What compels you
                                    to do it?

AGAMEMNON. This whole Greek army, in camp all round us.

MENELAUS. No, it doesn't. Not if you send her back home.

AGAMEMNON. She might escape in secret. I can't.

MENELAUS. Ignore the rabble! They don't matter.

AGAMEMNON. Calchas will go public. The whole army will
                                    know.

MENELAUS. Not if we kill him first. It's possible.

AGAMEMNON. God damn all ambitious political priests!

MENELAUS. They're useless to man or beast . . . while they live.

AGAMEMNON. The possibilities are terrifying. Don't they
                                                    frighten you?

MENELAUS. I don't know, till you tell me what they are.

AGAMEMNON. Odysseus, of Sisyphus' clan, he knows everything.

MENELAUS. So what? Odysseus can't hurt us two.

AGAMEMNON. He's crafty. And very popular with the troops.

MENELAUS. He's consumed with ambition. That can be
                                                    dangerous.

AGAMEMNON. Don't you think he'll make the most
    Of his opportunity? He'll stand up in front
    Of the whole army, and explain every detail
    Of Calchas' prophecy, line by line!
    He'll tell them I promised to go along with it
    And make the sacrifice, and then retracted
    My promise. With that sort of speech
    In our situation, he could stage a coup,
    Take command of the army, and have us both killed,
    As well as the girl. And if we escaped,
    What could stop him bringing the whole army
    To Argos, Cyclops-built walls and all,
    Taking the place by storm, killing me and mine
    And occupying the whole country?
    With an army this size, it's possible, I have
    To take it into account. So you see
    What an appalling situation I'm in,
    How utterly I'm trapped. I despair
    Of any solution, save a stoical acceptance
    Of the will of the gods, whatever that costs me.
    But one thing, Menelaus, you can do for me.
    Speak to everybody important in the army,
    Make sure that Clytemnestra doesn't hear
    A single word about this – or not before
    I've taken the child away from her
    And seen the whole business through . . . when she's dead
    I mean. That way at least, I'll be able
    To do this evil thing I have to do

27

With the minimum of tears. And you, foreign women
From Chalcis, keep silent! If you value your lives.

AGAMEMNON *goes back into his headquarters, as* MENELAUS
moves away into the camp. The women of the CHORUS *come
forward, disturbed by what they have seen.*

CHORUS. Those people are happy who relish love's pleasure,
    Enjoying Aphrodite's sensual embrace
    As a ship riding easy on a calm sea,
    Avoiding the obsession that leads to disgrace.
    For sex, like a horsefly, can madden with its sting,
    And Eros has two arrows to his string,
    Beneath that deceptive golden hair.
    A mere scratch from the first brings lifelong joy,
    But the second wounds to death, and breeds despair.
    Goddess born in Cyprus, keep my bedroom safe
    From that mortal arrow, make love in my life
    A steady continuing delight,
    Not obsessional or destructive. Let me serve
    The Great Queen with ecstasy, as is her right,
    But commit no crimes for her, nor become her slave.

    The deepest secret of human nature
    Is variety. There are as many ways
    Of living as there are men and women to live them;
    But the morality of the good life obeys
    The simplest of principles: it is clear,
    Straightforward and comprehensible. The wise never fear
    Life's disasters, if virtue has been their discipline
    From childhood. To judge from a moral standpoint,
    Even in details, brings stability to strangers and kin,
    And there is no satisfaction like doing what is to be done
    Properly and well. Reputation is won,
    Even fame, that way, and such fame endures.
    For women, a loving and chaste fidelity
    Is Aphrodite's most secret joy. A man secures,

Through all the variety of his gifts, fame through integrity.

Paris, you returned to the place of your birth
As a shepherd upon Mount Ida's slopes
Where the white heifers graze.
You played the folk melodies of your native earth
On the Phrygian flute, whose simple stops
Olympus invented in legendary days.

Full of milk the cattle grazed
When the goddesses chose you: and that choice
Drove you like a man possessed to Greece,
To a Palace of inlaid ivory, where you stood amazed
At the beauty of Helen's eyes,
Fed deep upon them, and saw desire
Burn there, like the uncontrollable fire
Consuming your own heart: ecstasies
That caused these men to march and ships deploy,
For two goddesses' injured pride, to shatter with chariot
                                         and spear
The citadels and towers of Troy.

CLYTEMNESTRA *and* IPHIGENIA *are seen entering, in a*
horse-drawn chariot, with attendants, and a NURSE, *who*
carries the baby ORESTES. *A group of Greek soldiers excitedly*
follows the chariot, and others gather around as the chariot
enters AGAMEMNON's *compound, excited to see such great*
people.

SOLDIERS. Look now, they're coming, the fortunate
  Ones, the aristocrats, the masters of the earth,
  Princess Iphigenia, the King's daughter, and the great
  Queen Clytemnestra, whose illustrious birth
  Blessed Tyndareus' family. Their happy fate
  Sets them at the summit of good fortune and wealth.
  Power is theirs, and glory, like gods to create
  Pleasure or pain, plenty or dearth.

The women of the CHORUS *gather round the chariot to help the
ladies down.*

CHORUS. Women of Chalcis, stand
    Close by the chariot, offer
    To the Queen a helping hand.
    She must not stumble. Give her
    Gentle support with your arm
    Till she's safe on the ground. And Iphigenia,
    Agamemnon's famous daughter, have no fear.
    We are strangers too. There's no cause for alarm.
    Strangers from Argos will be welcome here.

The SOLDIERS *look on in awe and cheer with delight.*
CLYTEMNESTRA *is used to public relations and knows how to
handle crowds.* IPHIGENIA, *being not much more than a child, is
unused to public appearances, and shy.*

CLYTEMNESTRA. This warm greeting and courteous speech
    Of welcome, promises good luck,
    As much as any fortunate pattern
    Of birds in flight. And I have certainly
    Come here with the best of expectations, to bring
    This bride to a most suitable and happy marriage!

Cheers and applause from the SOLDIERS *and* CHORUS.

    I have brought wedding-gifts as a dowry,
    Unload them from the cart with the greatest care
    And take them into this building!

Recognising the imperious tone, some of the SOLDIERS *begin the task
of unloading.*

    And now, my dear girl, so like a child still,
    So tender and fragile: step down carefully,
    And you women, take her hand, help her from the carriage
    Safely . . . don't fall! And then, one of you

Hold out an arm to support me, so that I
Can get down from my seat with reasonable grace.
For heaven's sake, some of you stand
By the horses' heads, and take their attention!
You know how they panic if something takes their eye
In strange surroundings! Talk to them,
Calm them down!

The rest of the SOLDIERS *hold the horses and steady the chariot.*

                   And now, the child,
The son of Agamemnon, hold out your arms
For him! His name is Orestes. He's not talking
Yet, a tiny baby still, you see?
There. My dear little boy, you're asleep
Aren't you, the rocking of the carriage
Made you nod off . . . Wake up, little fellow,
To wish your sister good luck. The son
Of a fine man, himself a tremendous fellow,
Whose mother was a sea-nymph, one of the Nereids,
Is going to marry her.

She gives ORESTES *to the* NURSE, *as the* SOLDIERS *wheel the
chariot away, and the women of the* CHORUS *retreat to a respectful
position.*

                   Come here, my child,
Take your place close by your mother,
Sit there, Iphigenia, as a daughter should,
To show these people what a lucky woman I am
In my children, and what a family group
We make together.

AGAMEMNON *enters from the hut.*

                  But look, here's your father.
Stand up child, show how pleased you are to see him.

IPHIGENIA. Don't be angry with me if I beat you to it
  Mother, and cuddle him tight before you do . . .
CLYTEMNESTRA. Not yet child!

CLYTEMNESTRA *speaks with great formality, conscious of the
onlookers.*

                              My Lord and Master, Godlike
  Agamemnon, we are here, as you commanded us to be.

IPHIGENIA *can't contain herself, and runs to embrace*
AGAMEMNON.

IPHIGENIA. But I must be first, Father, to hold you
  In my arms after so long, just to look at you.
  I've missed you so much! Mother, don't be angry!
CLYTEMNESTRA. No. This is just as it should be. Of all
  My children, you've always loved your father most.
IPHIGENIA. I'm so happy Father, it's been such a long time . . .
AGAMEMNON. And for me, I feel just the same as you do . . .
IPHIGENIA. You did the right thing, Daddy, bringing me here.
AGAMEMNON. Perhaps so . . . I don't know what to say.
                                                Perhaps not.
IPHIGENIA. What . . . ?
  Why look at me like that, if you're so glad to see me?
AGAMEMNON. A King . . . a General . . . has many things on
                                              his mind.
IPHIGENIA. Forget all that now. This moment is all mine!
AGAMEMNON. All yours then, for one moment . . . No
                                          responsibilities.
IPHIGENIA. Smooth away those frowns then, fill your eyes with
                                                    love!
AGAMEMNON. I am as happy to see you child, as I can
                                            possibly be.
IPHIGENIA. Don't cry then! There's no need to cry now.
AGAMEMNON. We'll be parted too soon. For a long time.
IPHIGENIA. How can you say so! What do you mean?

AGAMEMNON. You speak . . . so honestly. I can't hold back
my tears.

IPHIGENIA. I'll talk nonsense then, if that makes you feel better!

AGAMEMNON. Dear God, how can I not tell her . . . ? Thank
you my dear.

IPHIGENIA. Don't go Father. Stay at home with your children.

AGAMEMNON. I would love to. But I can't. And it's agony
for me.

IPHIGENIA. To hell with all wars, and Menelaus and his
troubles!

AGAMEMNON. Many men will go to Hell for him. Me too, in
the end.

IPHIGENIA. You've been here in the bay of Aulis too long . . .

AGAMEMNON. We should sail at once. But . . . something
prevents us.

IPHIGENIA. Where do they say they live, Father, these Trojans?

AGAMEMNON. Where Paris lives, Priam's son. I wish to God he
didn't . . . .

IPHIGENIA. It's a long journey then; and you're leaving me
behind!

AGAMEMNON. Yours is a long journey too, like mine.

IPHIGENIA. We could travel together then. You could arrange it.

AGAMEMNON. No, your journey is different. You must
remember me.

IPHIGENIA. Will my mother sail with me? Or must I travel
alone?

AGAMEMNON. You'll sail alone . . . without father or mother.

IPHIGENIA. Have you found me a new home, Father? Where is
it?

AGAMEMNON. That's enough . . . There are some things young
girls shouldn't know.

IPHIGENIA. Sort the Phrygians out quickly, Daddy, and come
back to me.

AGAMEMNON. I must perform a sacrifice, before I go.

IPHIGENIA. Of course you must! The right sacred rituals.

AGAMEMNON. You'll be there too. By the holy water.

IPHIGENIA. Shall I be part of the ceremonies at the altar?

AGAMEMNON. What wouldn't I give to be as blessedly innocent

As you are . . . ? Go inside now, child.
You shouldn't be seen in public, only by your women.
But . . . give me a kiss first, hold my hand tight!
You'll soon be gone away from me, a long way,
And for too long a time . . . Your bosom is so soft,
Your cheeks so fresh and childlike, your golden hair . . .
That city of the Phrygians, and Helen,
Why should they lay such a savage weight
Of responsibility on you. . . ! I must stop,
Stop talking like this . . . Even to touch you
Suddenly makes me cry, in spite of myself . . .
Go into my headquarters . . . .

IPHIGENIA *goes in.* AGAMEMNON *turns to* CLYTEMNESTRA,
who has been watching.

                       My apologies to you,
Daughter of Leda, the thought of losing
My daughter . . . to Achilles . . . breaks my heart.
Partings of this kind are happy ones, of course,
But for the parents, and the father particularly,
To give his daughter to another man
After bringing her up with so much love
And care for so long, can't help being painful.
CLYTEMNESTRA. Of course, I understand. You may be sure
I shall feel equally heartbroken
When I hear the wedding hymns sung for my daughter:
So I can hardly blame you for feeling now
What I shall feel then. But time and custom
Will ease the pain. I know the name
Of the man you have engaged to be married
To my child. But is he of good family?
Where is he from? I should like to know.
AGAMEMNON. Aesopus had a daughter, named Aegina.
CLYTEMNESTRA. And who married her? A man, or a god?
AGAMEMNON. It was Zeus. He fathered Aeacus, the ruler of
                                        Oenone.
CLYTEMNESTRA. And which of his sons inherited the property?

AGAMEMNON. Peleus, who married a sea-nymph, Nereus'
daughter.
CLYTEMNESTRA. With the gods' agreement, or in spite of them?
AGAMEMNON. Zeus himself made the match. He gave her away.
CLYTEMNESTRA. And where did he marry this sea-nymph?
Underwater?
AGAMEMNON. On the sacred slopes of Mount Pelion: Chiron's
home.
CLYTEMNESTRA. Where the Centaurs live, half-man half-horse –
so they say.
AGAMEMNON. The gods held a banquet there, in Peleus'
honour.
CLYTEMNESTRA. And who brought up Achilles? Thetis, or his
father?
AGAMEMNON. Chiron taught him . . . to avoid the wickedness
of men.
CLYTEMNESTRA. Oh wise teacher . . . and even wiser father.
AGAMEMNON. This is the man who will marry your daughter.
CLYTEMNESTRA. He could hardly be bettered. Is his home town
in Greece?
AGAMEMNON. In the mountains of Phthia, on the river Apidanos.
CLYTEMNESTRA. And that's where you'll take your daughter –
and mine –
AGAMEMNON. That'll be his business, when he's married to her.
CLYTEMNESTRA. My best wishes to them both. When's the
wedding day?
AGAMEMNON. The next full moon. For good luck.
CLYTEMNESTRA. Have you made the blood sacrifice to Artemis,
for her sake?
AGAMEMNON. I am about to. The matter is well in hand.
CLYTEMNESTRA. The wedding feast itself, will that be held
later?
AGAMEMNON. Yes. The sacrifice to the gods must come first.
CLYTEMNESTRA. And where shall I hold the womenfolk's
party?
AGAMEMNON. Here. In the shadow of the Greek ships.
CLYTEMNESTRA. A case of take it or leave it. Well, we must
hope for the best.

AGAMEMNON. You know what is required of you. Please do
as I say!

CLYTEMNESTRA. Yes, perfectly! I ought to, by now.

AGAMEMNON. Meanwhile, we . . . the men . . . in the
bridegroom's presence.

CLYTEMNESTRA. Will do what? Without me? It's a mother's
business.

AGAMEMNON. Before the Greek army . . . I shall give away my
daughter.

CLYTEMNESTRA. And where, pray, shall I be, while all this is
going on?

AGAMEMNON. Back in Argos. Looking after your other girls.

CLYTEMNESTRA. Leaving my daughter? I must light her
wedding torches . . .

AGAMEMNON. I shall light the flames myself . . . for the
marriage, I mean . . .

CLYTEMNESTRA. That's unheard of, an outrage to all decency!

AGAMEMNON. It's an outrage to see women in an army
encampment.

CLYTEMNESTRA. It's a mother's duty to see her children
married!

AGAMEMNON. It's her duty to look after her daughters at home.

CLYTEMNESTRA. They're quite safe, well guarded, in the
women's wing.

AGAMEMNON. Listen . . .

CLYTEMNESTRA.   No, by the greatest goddess of the
Greeks!
You give your orders out here. Domestic affairs,
Including my daughter's marriage, are my business!

She sweeps angrily into the headquarters building.

AGAMEMNON. Well. God help me, that little plan
Blew up in my face! To get my wife
Out of the way was the first necessity,
And I failed to do even that! Even a conspiracy
Against my nearest and dearest proves
More than I can handle. I must talk to Calchas,

Find out exactly what the goddess demands,
And if this personal disaster, and shameful calamity
For the whole Greek nation, is in any way
Avoidable . . . A sensible man
Keeps a quiet, reliable, domestic wife
Who stays at home – or no wife at all.

AGAMEMNON *goes into his headquarters.*

CHORUS. Now, to the silvery waters and swirling
  Currents of the river Simois, the Greeks
  Will come, with their massive fleet,
  Landing cavalry divisions and uncounted ranks
  Of heavy infantry, assembling
  A terrible war machine on the plains of Troy,
  The city sacred to Apollo.
  And already I can hear the god-driven shout
  Of Cassandra, as she lashes her yellow
  Laurel-crowned hair like a whip, and the voice of prophesy
  Weeps at the horrors it sees in its visionary frenzy.

  On the battle towers of Troy, and along the walls
  Encircling the city, the whole nation
  Of Trojans will stand watching,
  Awestruck, as if the war god himself led the invasion
  Of bronze shields like mirrored fire from the sea, the
                                                rhythmic falls
  Of rank upon rank of disciplined oars, powering
  The high prowed troopships to the many-channelled mouth
  Of Simois, one burning desire driving
  All this machinery of war: that Helen, by birth
  Sister of the Heavenly Twins, should be dragged, protesting
  Or not, by force of Greek swords and shields, to a grim
                                                homecoming.

  Then the vengeful Greek army will draw
  A circle of blood round the stone towers
  Of Pergamon, the rich Phrygian city

The world knows as Troy. Both the wretch who cowers
In the shadows, and Paris himself, will be hauled out by the
                                  hair
And their naked throats severed, or slashed to the ear,
As the columns totter, and the rafters crash
And the whole great city is flattened. The screaming
Of womenfolk, young girls' sobbing, gasps for pity
Even from Priam's Queen, will be drowned in a flood of
                                weeping,
And Helen herself, Zeus' daughter, in the ash
Of her burned out dreams, will understand that rash
Actions have fearful consequences, and the fatal dowry
To be paid for leaving a husband. My most passionate prayer
Is that neither my children nor grandchildren should ever
                                wash
Their eyes with such tears as the gold robed Lydians will
                        weep, or know the fear
Of the millionaire wives of Troy, as they stand by their looms
                              and cry,

'Who is the man who will drag me by the hair
Till the tears start from my eyes
  And tear me by the roots from my native earth
  As a hooligan tears up a flower, while my homeland dies
  All round me? The author of our despair
  Is you, daughter of the long-necked swan.
  For Zeus, the story says, assumed the shape
  Of a white-winged bird to bring your beauty to birth,
  If the legend's true of the immortal rape
  Of Leda. Unless poets weave their fantasies in vain,
  Hoping with childish dreams to soothe our pain.'

ACHILLES *enters. He is between twenty-five and thirty,*
magnificently built, extremely good-looking, and knows it. He has
all the arrogance of the habitual winner, and some of the foolishness
that usually goes with it.

ACHILLES. Where is the Supreme Commander of the Greek

Expeditionary Force? Is this his headquarters?
You there, aide, staff officer,
Or whatever you are, tell him Achilles,
The son of Peleus is here, and must see him.
This hanging about by the straits of Euripus
Inconveniences some men more than others.
Some of us are not yet married, have left
Our fathers at home, undefended, and sit here
Idly sunbathing on the beach. While married men
Have wives and families to consider. It's strange,
This obsession to join the expedition
Against Troy, how it possesses everyone.
It's the gods' business we do here, for sure,
They guide our hands. But I speak for myself –
Any other man can say what he likes –
And my complaint is that I've left Pharsalus
And my old guv'nor Peleus, and now I'm stuck
Here, waiting for the merest breeze
To ripple the straits of Euripus, with my crack
Regiment, the Myrmidons, sitting on their hands!
Day after day they grouse at me.
'Achilles,' they say, 'what are we waiting for,
How much longer must we wait for out little trip to Troy?
Do something, if you can, or else
Let's all go home, instead of wasting time
Here, while the two sons of Atreus try
To make up their minds, and, as usual, fail!'

CLYTEMNESTRA *hurries out from the building.*

CLYTEMNESTRA. Even from inside, Son of the sea goddess,
  I heard what you were saying, and I came out at once.
ACHILLES. Spare my blushes, goddess of good manners,
  At the approach of such a handsome woman!
CLYTEMNESTRA. You don't know me . . . that's not surprising,
  We've never met. But thank you for your courtesy.
ACHILLES. Who are you? And what are you doing here,
  In the Greek camp, surrounded by armed men?

CLYTEMNESTRA. I am Leda's daughter. Clytemnestra is my
name.
The King Agamemnon is my husband.
ACHILLES. Well, that's brief and to the point, just as it should
be.
Can't talk here with a woman. Much too embarrassing.
CLYTEMNESTRA. Wait . . . don't run away! Take my right hand
In yours, and pray for a happy marriage!
ACHILLES. I beg your pardon? You want me to hold hands
With Agamemnon's wife? That's really not done!
CLYTEMNESTRA. Of course it is, it's perfectly right and proper
Since you're marrying my daughter! Son of the sea-nymph!
ACHILLES. I'm marrying . . . I'm speechless . . . What are you
talking about?
Are you making it up? Or are you mad?
CLYTEMNESTRA. Naturally, you're embarrassed. Everyone is
When marriage is on the cards, and they meet their new
relations.
ACHILLES. Madam, I'm not marrying anybody! I've never
Even met your daughter, and the Atreus brothers have said
nothing.
CLYTEMNESTRA. What does this mean? I can see that my words
Come as a surprise to you. Yours leave me staggered.
ACHILLES. Just a moment now . . . Let's think. Put both heads
together.
Maybe neither of us is talking nonsense?
CLYTEMNESTRA. It seems I have been made a fool of. Travelling
To celebrate a non-existent marriage. How insulting!
ACHILLES. Someone has made a fool of both of us. So . . .
(*Icily.*) That's a mere bagatelle. Don't take it to heart.
CLYTEMNESTRA. No sir, goodbye. I've been humiliated,
And made to seem a liar. I can't look you in the face . . .
ACHILLES. Goodbye to you too Madam. I'm going inside
That headquarters building, to find your husband!

They both move away, angry and humiliated, ACHILLES *towards
the headquarters hut. The* OLD MAN *appears, half hidden in the hut
doorway.*

40

OLD MAN. Sir . . . just a minute . . . Aeacus' grandson, aren't
you,
Son of a goddess . . . And you too, Daughter of Leda!
ACHILLES. Who's that in the doorway, too scared to speak
out loud?
OLD MAN. A slave sir, with no pretensions. I know my place.
ACHILLES. Whose slave? None of my people work for
Agamemnon.
OLD MAN. Her's sir, over there. I came with her, from
Tyndareus.
ACHILLES. Well, I'm waiting. If you've anything to say, say it.
OLD MAN. Are you two alone out there, in front of the
doors?
ACHILLES. Yes we are. You can speak. Come away from the
hut.
OLD MAN. With good luck, and good thinking, I shall save
someone's life!

ACHILLES *beckons* CLYTEMNESTRA *across.*

ACHILLES. This old man knows something. Something
important.
CLYTEMNESTRA. If you've something to tell me . . . don't
bother with hand kissing.
OLD MAN. You know me, my Lady, loyal to you and your
daughter.
CLYTEMNESTRA. Yes, one of the house serfs in my father's
palace.
OLD MAN. And I came to Lord Agamemnon as part of your
dowry.
CLYTEMNESTRA. Yes, you travelled to Argos with me, you've
always been mine.
OLD MAN. And my loyalty's to you, ma'am, more than your
husband.
CLYTEMNESTRA. Speak out then. If you've some secret
information . . .
OLD MAN. Your daughter . . . her own father . . . The
murderer. . .he plans to kill her!

41

CLYTEMNESTRA. What! I'll choke you with those words,
                                    old man! Are you mad?
OLD MAN. With a knife he'll do it. Cut her poor white throat!
CLYTEMNESTRA. God help me! My husband! Is the man insane?
OLD MAN. He's sane enough, except about you and your
                                    daughter.
CLYTEMNESTRA. For what reason? What possesses him to do
                                    such a thing?
OLD MAN. The gods demand it, Calchas says, before the fleet
                                    can sail.
CLYTEMNESTRA. Sail where? I'm his wife! How can he? She's
                                    his daughter!
OLD MAN. To Troy, so that Menelaus can drag Helen back
                                    home.
CLYTEMNESTRA. So must my Iphigenia die to ransome Helen?
OLD MAN. That's the gist. Her father will sacrifice your child to
                                    Artemis.
CLYTEMNESTRA. So the marriage was a pretext, to persuade me
                                    to bring her here.
OLD MAN. So you'd be happy to bring her, to marry her to
                                    Achilles.
CLYTEMNESTRA. My daughter! I've brought you to your
                                    destruction. And mine!
OLD MAN. It's terrible for both of you. But that Agamemnon
                                    should dare . . .
CLYTEMNESTRA. This is agony . . . I can't stay here . . . I'm
                                    going to cry . . .
OLD MAN. Who can hold back their tears, when a child dies?
CLYTEMNESTRA. Old man . . . where . . .? I mean . . . listen
                                    . . . how did you find out . . .?
OLD MAN. I was on the way to you, with a second letter.
CLYTEMNESTRA. Confirming or cancelling the order to bring her
                                    to her death?
OLD MAN. Telling you not to bring her. He was thinking
                                    straight then.
CLYTEMNESTRA. Then why . . . with such a message, didn't
                                    you deliver it?
OLD MAN. Menelaus intercepted it. He caused this disaster!

CLYTEMNESTRA. Do you hear, Thetis' child, son of Peleus,
                        these infamies?
ACHILLES. For you, unendurable. And for me, an insult!
CLYTEMNESTRA. They use marriage to Achilles to lure my
                      daughter to her death!
ACHILLES. Your husband has angered me. That is not a small
                          matter . . .

CLYTEMNESTRA *falls on her knees before him.*

CLYTEMNESTRA. I'm not ashamed to fall on my knees
  Before you, Son of a sea goddess as you are.
  I am a mortal woman, and this is not time
  To stand on ceremony or the protocol of rank.
  I'll do anything, humiliate myself at your feet
  If necessary, for my daughter's sake.
  Stand up for me, Son of Thetis,
  Defend me from this unmerited disaster,
  And stand up for your wife, wife in name only
  Admittedly, but none the less yours for all that.
  I brought her here with flowers in her hair,
  As I thought, to a marriage: and in truth I've led her
  Like a sacrificial victim to the slaughter.
  Some of the blame will fall on you
  For certain, if you do nothing to save her.
  You may not be married, but it was common knowledge
  That you were to be the poor girl's husband.
  By everything that makes you a man, your strong right arm,
  Your manly beard, your mother's good name,
  Your own good reputation – because it was the glory
  Of your name that brought us to this danger –
  Save your own honour by saving us.
  No god can help me, I can only abase myself
  Here, at your knees, as though they were an altar,
  And clasp them with my prayers. I have no friends,
  And the unscrupulous savagery of Agamemnon's plan
  You know now as well as I do. I have come here,
  A woman, in a military base

Full of soldiers and marines, whose lawlessness
Is a byword, and whose casual violence
Makes every kind of evil-doing commonplace.
And yet that anarchic energy too can be harnessed
In a good cause, if you can convince them.
If you have the courage to lift up your right arm
In our defence, we'll be saved, for sure!
If not, that's our last hope of salvation gone.

CHORUS. Giving birth is the deepest of life's mysteries:
No animal fights fiercer than a mother for her child.

ACHILLES. All my most noble qualities are inflamed
To immediate action: but I am mature enough
To understand the virtues of moderation, both
In the anguish of grief and the exhilaration of triumph.
Such men as I am are universally acknowledged
To act coolly, with good judgement, and according to reason.
There are certain times when one should act by instinct,
Without too much thought. But there are also times
When one must think sensibly, and exercise one's
intelligence.
I was schooled by Chiron, a godfearing man
Who brought me up to be straightforward,
A direct, decent, uncomplicated fellow.
If the sons of Atreus command the army sensibly,
I shall obey them. If they don't, I won't.
Both here and at Troy, I shall be my own man,
And bring some honour to the god of war
With my sword too, you may be sure.
As for you, my dear madam, who have suffered so cruelly
At the hands of your nearest and dearest, everything
A young man can do, I shall do
To remove the cause of your suffering.
My generosity of spirit will protect you like a shield,
And your daughter will certainly not be killed by her father
Now she is engaged to me! I shall never allow him
To use me as a mere instrument
In the manufacturing of his conspiracies!
If I did, my name would have murdered your daughter

As surely as any sword. But the guilt
Is your husband's, not mine. The very blood
In my veins would be infected, polluted
With murder, if this girl should suffer
Such an intolerable injustice,
And on my account, because of marriage to me,
Be herself destroyed. What would I be worth then?
Nothing at all, the most despicable worm
In the whole Greek camp. Even Menelaus
Would seem a man beside me!
If my name were to become your husband's mercenary
And do his killing for him, some demon
Of destruction must have been my ancestor,
Not Peleus! No, by that son of the Ocean,
Nereus, the father of my mother Thetis,
King Agamemnon, I swear, will not lay a finger
Even on the hem of your daughter's dress,
Much less touch her! Otherwise, call the wilderness
Of Mount Sipylus, where the barbarians live,
And where his family came from, a great city,
And may my own home of Phthia be forever forgotten
In the mouths of men! Calchas, no doubt,
Will bring all his little jugs and basins
To mystify us. But what does a priest matter?
At best he speaks a few fragments of truth
In a whole rubbish dump of lies.
And when his prophecies prove total nonsense
He keeps himself well out of sight!
It's not for the marriage I'm making all this fuss.
Thousands of girls are desperate for the chance
To get into bed with me. It's because
King Agamemnon has insulted me!
If he wanted to use my name as a snare
To trap his own child, he should have asked my permission!
It was my reputation that attracted Clytemnestra
To bring her daughter here, not her husband's command.
If the Greeks had asked for the use of my name
To make the trip to Troy possible,

I wouldn't have refused them, not my fellow soldiers,
My colleagues in this great venture. But as it is
These generals treat me as a nonentity,
As though whether they honour or shame me
Were a matter of not the slightest concern
To either of them! But anyone who tries
To take your daughter away from me
Will be practice meat for my iron sword,
To see how bloodstains suit the blade
Before I go to Troy! Don't be frightened.
I know I must seem like a god, and a very great one
At that! In fact, I'm a man, not a god,
Though by my actions I shall certainly become one!

CHORUS. That speech was worthy of you, Son of Peleus!
And of your mother, whose cradle was the sea!

CLYTEMNESTRA. How can I find the right words
To express my gratitude, or to eulogise you
As you deserve, without embarrassing you
With flattery, or offending you
By undervaluing your virtues?
The best men hate those who overpraise them,
And I feel ashamed to be burdening you
With my private anguish. The pain is all mine,
It's my heart that's breaking, not yours.
And yet, there is something admirable
When a good man stoops from his own good fortune
To help someone less fortunate.
Take pity on me, because my case is pitiable!
I thought you were going to be my son-in-law.
A pathetic illusion that turned out to be!
But think what bad luck it would be for you
In your future marriage to remember
The circumstances of my daughter's death
And your part in it! You should do everything
Possible to avoid that. What you said first
Was to the point, and what you said last.
If you choose to save her, my child will be saved.
Shall I bring her out here, shall she kneel

At your feet and beg for her life? It's not right
To make an unmarried girl do such a thing,
But she'll do it, if that's what you want.
With her eyes decently lowered too,
Not brazenly, staring, like a whore,
But with a modest nobility, as becomes a princess.
If I can persuade you, without seeing her,
Let her preserve her modesty indoors.
But if she must come out, she'll come.

ACHILLES. No, don't bring her out just for me to get a look at
her!

Nor, dear lady, should we give stupid people
The opportunity to laugh at us.
The soldiers have nothing to do, the whole army
Is unemployed, and unrestrained too
By being away from home. They love nothing better
Than malicious gossip. It's irrelevant to me
Whether you implore me on your knees or not.
I've made up my mind that I shall save you
At whatever cost, from this disaster!
Listen to me, take good note of what I say.
I never lie. If I prove a liar,
Or my promises worthless, let me die on the spot.
You have my word that I will save your child!

CLYTEMNESTRA. The heavens bless you for helping people in
trouble.

ACHILLES. Now listen, this is what I want you to do.

CLYTEMNESTRA. What do you suggest? I have no choice but
to listen.

ACHILLES. We'll persuade her father to have second thoughts.

CLYTEMNESTRA. But that's hopeless! He's a coward. He's
scared of the army!

ACHILLES. But good arguments, like good wrestlers, overcome
the bad!

CLYTEMNESTRA. There's cold comfort in that. But tell me what
I must do.

ACHILLES. First, go down on your knees and beg him
Not to kill your child. If he won't listen

47

Come straight back to me. If he does listen,
And agrees with what you say, I need not do anything,
Since by that very action the problem will be solved.
In that case too, my relations with your husband
Wouldn't be compromised, would indeed become closer,
And the army at large could hardly criticise me
If I achieved all this by diplomacy, not force.
That would be a satisfactory outcome
For all of us, for you, and for our friends,
And I need not be involved at all.

CLYTEMNESTRA. You give sensible advice, I'm sure,
Counselling restraint, and I shall act upon it.
But supposing he ignores me, or gives me nothing
In return for my pleading, what then?
Where shall I see you? My situation
Will be desperate. You're the only man
Who can possibly help me. Where shall I find you?

ACHILLES. When you need me I shall be there,
Never fear! But make sure no one sees you
Making a fuss through the whole Greek camp
Looking for me. That would be a disgrace . . .
To your father Tyndareus, who's a good fellow
With a very high reputation among the Greeks.
Don't let him down, or slander his good name.

CLYTEMNESTRA. Of course, you're right. You take command,
I'll do what you say. If the gods
Exist at all, they must surely reward
Such a principled stand as yours. And if not . . .
Then everything is meaningless, and nothing worth doing.

CLYTEMNESTRA *and* ACHILLES *exit, she into the headquarters
building, he back into the camp.*

CHORUS. What a joyful wedding song they sang,
How wildly the music of instruments rang,
The sighing African flute
And the soft voice of the lute,
While the dancers' beating feet

48

Kept time with the song,
And the oboes sang shrill and sweet;
When to Peleus' wedding feast
The nine muses came
On Pelion's high pasture, a host
Whose fair hair swung to the beat
Of their golden sandalled feet,
Singing in praise of Thetis' name
A song so melodious it carried her fame
And her husband, Aeacus' son, beyond Pelion's hills
Where the Centaurs gallop, and the green forest sleeps.
Phrygian Prince Ganymede heard it, and fills
Zeus' cup from the wine bowl's golden deeps,
Dardanus' son, Zeus' favourite, and never spills
The nectar: and in honour of marriage, circling hand in
                hand,
The fifty daughters of Nereus danced on the white sea-sand.

Half horses, half men, to where the gods lay feasting,
Their heads crowned with leaves, the Centaurs came riding,
Each with a lance of pine,
To drink the immortal wine
In Bacchus' golden bowl
At the sea-nymph's wedding.
With one voice they call,
'Good luck to Nereus' daughter!
Chiron, who can see
The mind of Apollo, has brought her
News of a son she will bear
Whose name will be known everywhere,
A great light, shining from Thessaly.
He will lead his Myrmidons over the sea
To Troy, to blast with spear and shield and fire
Priam's great city, in helmet and breastplate of gold,
Hephaestos' masterpiece, such as the gods wear,
His mother's parting gift to her bold
Son.' Was such feasting seen ever before?
The gods sat at table, in immortal company,

When Peleus married the Nereid, first-born child of the sea.

But you, Iphigenia,
On your flowing hair, on your golden hair,
Greek soldiers will set a crown of flowers
As they garland a heifer for the knife and fire,
Pure from the mountain, dappled red and white.
Warm blood from the trembling throat
They will draw, and that blood will be yours,
Not from a beast bred where the herdsman whistles and
                                                    sings,
But a girl her mother nurtured to be bride and mother
                                                of Kings.

Crimson the face of shame.
Can goodness prevail, can virtue prevail?
A godless generation is in power.
Where is decency, who speaks her name?
Lost in the crowd, trampled to death,
Stifled, choked by the stinking breath
Of self interest, in this darkest hour
When the fear of God is dead, brotherhood gone rotten,
And the vengeance the jealous gods exact from men
                                                forgotten.

CLYTEMNESTRA *enters from the headquarters building.*

CLYTEMNESTRA. I've come out here to look for my husband.
    He left the headquarters some time ago,
    And hasn't been seen since. My poor child
    Is in tears, if you can call it that,
    Such moaning and screams of despair and anguish.
    She knows the truth now: that her father plans to kill her.
    But . . . talk of the devil . . . here he comes,
    Agamemnon, that father who will now be exposed
    As guilty of planning the most unnatural crime
    Of all, the murder of his own child.

Enter AGAMEMNON.

AGAMEMNON. Ah, Daughter of Leda, I'm glad to catch you
here
   Outside the building. I have things to tell you
   While Iphigenia is inside, things not suitable
   For a young girl to hear just before her wedding . . .
CLYTEMNESTRA. What things, only suitable to be said outside?
AGAMEMNON. Send the girl out here. Tell her her father
   Is waiting . . . and everything is prepared.
   The chalices are ready, and the barley meal
   We sprinkle to purify the altar fire.
   The victim is ready too. Her red blood
   Must spurt from a pure white neck in honour
   Of Artemis, to celebrate the marriage.
CLYTEMNESTRA. Yes, fine words, it all sounds most admirable;
   But what words will describe your admirable actions,
   How fine will they be? My daughter! Come out here!
   You know it all now. All your father's plans.
   And your baby brother Orestes, bring him too,
   Wrap him snugly in the folds of your dress . . .

IPHIGENIA *enters, carrying the baby* ORESTES.

CLYTEMNESTRA. So. Here she is. Obeying you to the letter.
   Now I shall speak. For her, and for myself.
AGAMEMNON. My child. Why are you crying? No more
   Smiles for me now? All downcast looks,
   Wiping your eyes with the hem of your gown?
CLYTEMNESTRA. Dear gods . . .
   How shall I begin? With pain like this
   There's no beginning, middle or ending.
   Wherever you start, it's the same agony!
AGAMEMNON. What's this all about? You must have rehearsed
   This tearful performance together, I think.
CLYTEMNESTRA. One question, husband. Answer it like a man.
AGAMEMNON. Don't give me orders . . . ! Of course I'll
answer . . .

CLYTEMNESTRA. Your daughter. My daughter. Are you going to
kill her?

AGAMEMNON. Am I *what*?
  What an appalling question, how foul of you to suspect . . .
CLYTEMNESTRA. Be quiet,
  Just answer it. I can't put it more simply.
AGAMEMNON. Ask a reasonable question, you'll get a rational
answer . . .
CLYTEMNESTRA. That question, no other! And I want a straight
answer.
AGAMEMNON. My destiny, my bad luck! I've done nothing to
deserve this!
CLYTEMNESTRA. My bad luck, and hers! All three of us, the
same!
AGAMEMNON. Have I wronged you?
CLYTEMNESTRA.   You ask me that?
  Have you any brains left, or are you quite stupid?
AGAMEMNON. I'm finished . . . no chance . . . they know
everything . . .
CLYTEMNESTRA. Yes, I know it all, the whole filthy plan.
  And this silence of yours, this muttering in your beard
  Is as good as a confession. You don't need to say anything!
AGAMEMNON. Am I trying to speak? There's nothing more to
say.
  Why add to the disaster by telling lies about it?
CLYTEMNESTRA. Then you listen to me, it's my turn now
  And there'll be no obscurity or riddling
  In what I have to say, just plain words,
  That you don't dare deny! In the first place –
  And what a shameful beginning that was –
  You married me against my will,
  Took me by force, killed my first husband,
  Tantalus, dragged my baby from my breast . . .
  And smashed its head open on the ground . . .
  My brothers, the twin sons of Zeus,
  Shining like a vision on their white horses,
  Led an army against you. And you grovelled
  Before my old father, Tyndareus, his diplomacy

Saved your life, and even got you back into my bed
As my second husband. And from that very day
When I reconciled myself to marriage with you
You can appear as my principal witness
When I say that I have been a model wife,
Both personally to you, and in organising your house,
Sexually modest, and utterly chaste,
So that coming home has always been your greatest pleasure
And when you open your front door, the whole world can see
Your good fortune demonstrated. Bad wives are

commonplace,

Never in short supply. But it's a lucky man
That has such a wife as I have been to you.
I have borne you three girls, and finally, this son;
And now, without feeling or conscience
You will tear one of my girls from me,
Like ripping the flesh from my own body.
And if anyone asks you why you will kill her,
For what good reason, what will you say?
Shall I say it for you? So that Menelaus
Can have Helen back! What a glorious action,
To ransom a whore with a child's life,
To buy back, with what is most precious,
The commonest, cheapest thing in the world!
So. You do that, and go off to war,
For years perhaps, leaving me here
At home. How do you think I will feel
Alone in the house, whenever I see
Her empty chair, her empty bedroom
In the children's wing? Shall I sit on my own
With red eyes, always singing the same sad song,
'Your father killed you, little girl,
He gave you your life, and then he took it,
No hired killer, but his own hand
Put an end to your life; what welcome,
What homecoming for him, my little girl?'
We'd need no prompting, would we,
The girls you left behind, and their mother,

To give you the welcome you deserve.
By all the gods, don't force me
To harden my heart towards you, or to think
Thoughts that are evil. And don't force yourself
To think and do what you know to be wrong!
But . . . supposing you do sacrifice your child?
What will you ask for in your prayers, what blessings
Will you pray for, as you cut your daughter's throat?
A homecoming as filthy as your filthy departure?
And what blessings do you suppose
I should call down upon you in my prayers?
Do you imagine the gods to be idiots,
Who will reward murderers, just for the asking?
And when you finally get back to Argos,
Will you open your arms and expect your children
To embrace you? You would have no right
To ask such a thing. Which of them would dare
To look you in the eye, or trust your embraces,
Knowing you killed their sister! Have you followed my
reasoning
So far? Have you thought this through at all?
Or is your only thought how to preserve your position
As General of the army? A real General
Would have stood up proudly among the Greeks
And spoken like a leader, with wisdom and justice,
Saying, 'Soldiers of Greece, do you really want
To sail to Phrygia? Then you must draw lots
To see whose daughter must die. That would have been
The just, the equitable thing to do,
Not picking on your own daughter
As a sacrifice for the whole Greek nation!
If that's to be the case, let Menelaus
Kill his daughter, Hermione, in front of her mother.
It's his business, the whole expedition,
Not yours. But as things stand now,
I, who have been utterly chaste and faithful
To you, must watch my daughter die,
While Helen the whore, whose promiscuity

Was the only cause of this disaster
Can bring her little girl back home
To Sparta, and live in peace and prosperity!
And now, you tell me if anything I've said
Is one whit less than the plain truth.
And even if it is, for God's sake,
I beg you, don't kill our daughter.
For a sane man, there isn't any choice!

CHORUS. To save a child's life is good morality
In anyone's language. Be persuaded, Agamemnon.

IPHIGENIA. Father, if I had Orpheus' voice
And could charm the rocks and stones to dance
To my music, I'd so ravish your ears
With my songs, that everyone would do my bidding
Like slaves. As it is, I have no skill
In singing, no magical powers
Except the power of tears, so they
Must serve for weapons. I have no garlands
To embrace you with, only arms,
This body of mine, which my mother bore you.
Don't end my life before I've lived.
I'm too young to die yet. Life is so precious,
Even the plain daylight is so beautiful,
Don't drive me down into the darkness
Of the grave, not yet! I am the first
Of your children to call you Father, the first
You called your child, the first to clamber
Up onto to your knees to smother you with kisses
And be kissed in return. Do you remember
What you used to say? 'Well my little girl,
Shall I live to see you happily married
In some other man's house, living in a manner
Worthy of Agamemnon's daughter?' And then,
Remember what I said, pulling at your beard
As I stroke it now, 'What shall I do for you?'
I said, 'when you're an old man, I will take you
To *my* house, and look after you there,
Because you looked after me and brought me up

In *your* house, so that makes it fair.'
I remember every word of those childish conversations;
But you must have forgotten them, if you're prepared
To kill me. No, I beg you, by our ancestor
Pelops, by your own father, Atreus,
By my mother, standing here,
Whose agony brought me into the world
And must now endure a more terrible anguish
As I go out of it. That marriage
Between Paris and Helen, what has it got to do
With me? Tell me, Father, one reason
Why that marriage should cause my death!
Look at me now, look me in the eye,
Kiss me again, so that if I die,
If you are quite hardened to persuasion or reason,
I shall have that at least to remember you by.
Baby brother, you're only a little boy,
You can't help those who love you yet,
But you're old enough to cry, as I'm crying,
To beg your father not to kill your sister.
The tiniest child has a sense of evil,
Even before he can speak, he recognises that
With his tears. His silence is the most eloquent persuasion.
Pity me Father. I'm young. Spare my life.
We both beg the same thing, moistening your beard
With our tears, the grown girl and the infant boy
Scarce out of the womb. One word will convince you,
I know. Nothing is sweeter than sunlight
The joy of being alive. To be dead is to be nothing,
Non existent, in the grave. Only madmen want to die.
It's far better to live in misery
Than to die even the most glorious death.
CHORUS. Your wickedness, Helen, that marriage, will bring
                                                                    misery

To the sons of Atreus, and to their children.
AGAMEMNON. You don't have to tell me what's pitiable
And what's not! I love my own children,
Only a madman doesn't! It's terrifying to me,

56

Wife, listen . . . ! To be pushed to such
Desperate extremes, but it's equally terrifying
To refuse! I've got to do it! Look
Around you! Do you see this massive army,
Do you see all these stationary ships
Like a fence shutting us in,
Do you see all this weaponry and armour,
All the kings and leaders of the Greek army,
Who won't get a passage across to Troy,
Nor ever conquer those famous towers
And terraces of the citadel, unless
I sacrifice you. Calchas the prophet
Says so. And there's a terrifying energy
Like the uncontrollable power of lust
In the Greek army, to get across
To those barbarians, and teach them once and for all
That they can't carry off the wives of Greece
Without terrible retribution. And they will kill
My two little girls in Argos, and you two,
And me as well, if I refuse to obey
The commands of the goddess! Do you understand!
Menelaus hasn't forced my hand
My girl, I'm not doing this to please him!
But for Greece. It's for Greece, whether I like it
Or not, you must be sacrificed.
We're all of us under that obligation.
Greece must be free, and as far as it lies in you
To achieve that, so far you must go,
And so must I too! We are all Greeks.
We must not allow the wives of Greece
To be ravished from their beds by barbarians!

AGAMEMNON *marches grimly away into the camp.*

CLYTEMNESTRA. Oh my child – and you strangers from across
the bay,

How can I bear such pain? Your father sells you
As a bride for death, and then runs away!

57

IPHIGENIA. The song of death for us both now, mother and
                                                    daughter,
  A last threnody, and we must sing it together.
  Fate, like a thundercloud, darkens the sky,
  Never bright daylight again for me,
  Never the sun's warm shining, my way
  Is to darkness, and cold eternity.
  Oh you snow-covered valley of Phrygia, and Mount Ida,
  Where Priam took the baby he had dragged from its mother
  And left it alone in your forests to die,
  You sheltered him, nurtured him, so that in Troy
  They called him Prince Paris of Ida, the mountain
                                                    shepherd boy.

  And why so softly did you shelter him there,
  Paris Alexander, in cattle stall
  And sheepfold, like a child of nature, where
  Springs rise in secret, and white streams fall,
  And by the shining mirrored water
  Nymphs comb their golden hair
  In river meadows thick with bluebells, which goddesses
                                                    gather
  For garlands such as immortals wear.

  To that fated place, where Paris lay,
  Came Pallas Athene, one ominous day,
  And dangerous Aphrodite from Cyprus, and Hera,
  And Hermes, Zeus' messenger. All three –
  Aphrodite, voluptuous with sex, Pallas the bearer
  Of the spear of law, and Hera, she
  Who shares the bed of Zeus, determined to play
  The bitter game of beauty, and bear away
  The prize that will breed bloodshed and horror,
  And bring death for me, my death,
  For a promise of immortal fame, and a few feet of earth.

  This sacrifice, my life, Artemis demands,
  My blood must launch the ships for Troy.

Oh Mother, my mother, my father commands
My obedience, betrays me, then runs away,
Leaving me defenceless. My bitterest curse,
All bitterness, on Helen, and the fate that binds
My life to expiate her sin – what could be worse? –
Murdered by a father's sacrilegious hands!

Oh why did the bronze-beaked ships come here
With their oars of slender pine, to be beached on the shore
Of Aulis, on their way to Troy?
And why did Zeus send a contrary wind
Against our fleet, while he smoothes the way
For other sailors? Who knows the mind
Of a god, who makes the sailing fair
For some men and blows others to despair,
Fills some ships' sails till they bulge with joy,
Slack canvas for others, breezes abating
To a dead calm, and the misery of waiting.

So many agonies, so much suffering
Mortal men inherit.
Our term is fixed, terror our ending,
None can escape it.
But never greater agony, never more terrible slaughter
Inflicted on the sons of Greece, than by Helen, Tyndareus'
daughter!

CHORUS. I pity you, child. In your short life, nothing
Could deserve such bad luck, such injustice, such an ending.

A great noise of shouting and riot from inside the Greek camp.

IPHIGENIA. Mother, there's a crowd of men, running this way!
CLYTEMNESTRA. It's him. The man you came for! Thetis' son.
IPHIGENIA. Women, open the doors, let me hide my face . . .
CLYTEMNESTRA. Don't hide.
IPHIGENIA.   I can't look at Achilles without
blushing.

CLYTEMNESTRA. Why not?

IPHIGENIA. That sham marriage! I'm too ashamed!

CLYTEMNESTRA. You're in no position to be fastidious.
    Swallow your pride, girl, it's your last chance.

ACHILLES *comes in, followed by two batmen who carry a*
shield and helmet, and a shower of stones from a large group of
soldiers who stand at a distance. ACHILLES *is out of breath, scuffed*
and dirty, bruises and blood on his face.

ACHILLES. Unhappy child of Leda.

CLYTEMNESTRA.   You call me my true name.

ACHILLES. There's a riot in the army.

CLYTEMNESTRA.   They're shouting. What about?

ACHILLES. It's your daughter, they're saying . . .

CLYTEMNESTRA.   God help us, what?

ACHILLES. That she must be killed.

CLYTEMNESTRA.   And does no one speak for her?

ACHILLES. I got into a fight myself . . .

CLYTEMNESTRA.   My dear friend, what fight?

ACHILLES. The real thing. They stoned me.

CLYTEMNESTRA.   Because you tried to save her?

ACHILLES. That's right.

CLYTEMNESTRA.   And who dared to lay hands on
                                                you?

ACHILLES. The whole bloody army!

CLYTEMNESTRA.   Weren't the Myrmidons there?

ACHILLES. They threw the first stones!

CLYTEMNESTRA.   My darling, it's the end . . .

ACHILLES. I've been bought off by marriage, they said.

CLYTEMNESTRA.   Did you answer?

ACHILLES. Said, don't you lay a finger on my wife!

CLYTEMNESTRA.   That's right!

ACHILLES. Said her father promised her.

CLYTEMNESTRA.   Had her brought here from
                                                Argos.

ACHILLES. But they shouted me down.

CLYTEMNESTRA.   Uncivilised rabble!

ACHILLES. But I'll fight them for you still.

CLYTEMNESTRA.   One man against an army.

ACHILLES. See these chaps with my armour . . . ?

CLYTEMNESTRA.   God bless you for your courage!

ACHILLES. The whole world will bless me!

CLYTEMNESTRA.   Who dares sacrifice her now?

ACHILLES. No one, while I live.

CLYTEMNESTRA.   Will they come for her by force?

ACHILLES. Thousands of them, Odysseus in command.

CLYTEMNESTRA.   Of Sisyphus' family?

ACHILLES. That's the one.

CLYTEMNESTRA.   Was he elected, or did he choose
                            himself?

ACHILLES. Elected, but it was fixed.

CLYTEMNESTRA.   Filthy choice! Child murderer!

ACHILLES. Don't worry, I'll stop him!

CLYTEMNESTRA.   Will he drag her away?

ACHILLES. Right first time. By her golden hair!

CLYTEMNESTRA.   What shall I do?

ACHILLES. Hang on to her tight!

CLYTEMNESTRA.   My bare arms will protect her.

ACHILLES. It may come to that . . .

IPHIGENIA.   Mother, listen to me!
   Don't be angry with your husband, that's pointless now.
   No one can easily bear what's unbearable.
   Achilles deserves our thanks for trying to help us,
   But we musn't let him destroy his position
   In the army, and maybe lose his life
   For our sakes, and to no purpose.
   That will be a disaster for him,
   And won't save us. Listen Mother,
   Let me tell you what I think . . . I must die . . .
   That has suddenly become very clear to me.
   And if I must die, let me do it decently,
   With dignity and courage . . . No, no Mother,
   You can't deny what I'm saying, if you look at it
   My way, you'll know I'm right!

The SOLDIERS *have gradually become aware of what she is saying,
and the stone throwing and shouting has stopped.*

What nation is greater than Greece? And all
The Greeks now look to me for an answer,
Everything depends on me, the safe passage
Of the invasion fleet, the destruction of Troy,
And safety, in the future, for all Greek wives
From abduction by foreigners. No woman again
Will ever be dragged from her home and contentment
By force, when the whole world will have seen
The price Paris will pay for the rape of Helen!
I shall achieve all that at a stroke, simply
By giving my life. I shall become famous
As the woman who set Greece free . . .
So why should I hang on to life so desperately?
When you gave me birth, Mother, it was as a Greek woman,
Part of the Greek nation, not just for yourself.
There are ten thousand men here, armed to the teeth,
Another ten thousand stripped at the oars
Ready to row – and why? Because
Their fatherland, the beloved country,
Has been wronged, and insulted, and for its sake
They will dare anything, however dangerous
Against their enemies, and die for Greece
If need be. How can my single life
Stand against that? How could that be right?
How could it be just? Could I say one word
In my own defence? What arguments could I use?
And there's one thing more. Why should Achilles
Take on the whole Greek army single handed,
And probably be killed, for the sake of a woman?
What use are women in war? One brave man
Is worth ten thousand of us. And if Artemis,
Being a great goddess, demands my body,
Who am I, a mere mortal, to oppose her wishes?
That's out of the question.

She turns and speaks to the assembled SOLDIERS.

                           I dedicate my body
As a gift for Greece. Take me. Sacrifice me.
And then to Troy, plunder the whole city,
When you leave it, leave a ruin! That will be
My memorial. A Greek victory
Will be the marriage I never celebrated,
The children I never bore, a name
Remembered through the generations!
It is Greek destiny, Mother, to rule barbarians:
Barbarians must never rule Greeks.
Why? Because they are born slaves,
And for Greeks, freedom is our birthright!

A huge cheer from the SOLDIERS.

CHORUS. The young girl is a model of nobility. But there's
                                      something
Evil in a goddess that demands such sacrifices.
ACHILLES. Daughter of Agamemnon, what a blessing
It would have been, if the gods had allowed me
To win you for my wife. I envy Greece,
Whose bride you now become, and I envy you too
For giving your body for Greece. Everything
You said was admirable, memorably expressed,
And worthy of your fatherland. You have decided
Not to fight the gods, they are too powerful.
You have faced the inevitable by doing the wise
And the correct thing. Such strength of character
Only increases my passionate desire
To have you for my wife. You're a remarkable woman,
And worthy of your country. Now listen to me.
I want to do everything I can to help you.
For the chance of taking you home with me
I'd dare anything. And – by Thetis, my mother,
I swear it! – I'm angry and disappointed
Not to be able to save you, even if

That means fighting the whole Greek army!
Think for a moment. It's a dreadful thing to die.

IPHIGENIA. No, listen to me. I have no hope now,
And no fear either. They mean nothing anymore.
It's bad enough that Helen's body
Should cause men to fight and kill each other.
You mustn't die, my friend, nor kill anyone
On my account. So, leave me now.
Let me save Greece, if it's in my power to do it.

ACHILLES. What courage, what greatness of spirit!
What can I say to such resolution?
Let me speak the plain truth, and call you
A superior being, an aristocratic soul!
Nevertheless, it is possible you might regret
What you said in the heat of the moment, and want
To change your mind, so listen carefully
To what I'm saying. I shall place my weapons
Right next to the altar! Fully prepared
Not to allow them to kill you. To stop them
By force, if necessary! It may be
That even you, when the knife is at your throat,
Will see things differently, and remember my promise.
You won't lose your life for a momentary impulse
Afterwards regretted. Not in my presence!
I shall go now, taking my weapons with me,
To the sanctuary of the goddess Artemis. I shall stand
Right by the altar; and wait there, till you come.

ACHILLES *goes, as priestesses of Artemis enter ready to prepare*
IPHIGENIA *for sacrifice, and unobtrusively,* AGAMEMNON's *guards.*

IPHIGENIA. No sound, Mother but tears. Why are you crying?
CLYTEMNESTRA. I have some cause to cry. My heart is broken.
IPHIGENIA. I'll be frightened if you cry. Do one thing for

me . . .

CLYTEMNESTRA. What is it? Whatever, I can't refuse.
IPHIGENIA. Don't wear black for me, or cut off your hair.

CLYTEMNESTRA. How can you ask that? When I've lost my
daughter . . .

IPHIGENIA. No Mother, not lost. Remembered for ever.

CLYTEMNESTRA. What do you mean? When I've lost you, I
must grieve . . .

IPHIGENIA. Why should you grieve? There won't be any grave.

CLYTEMNESTRA. It's not the grave, it's the death people greave
for.

IPHIGENIA. My tomb will be the altar of Artemis, Zeus'
daughter.

CLYTEMNESTRA. I'll do what you ask child. I know you must
be right . . .

IPHIGENIA. I'm the lucky one. To give all I have for Greece!

CLYTEMNESTRA. And your sisters, what message shall I give
to them?

IPHIGENIA. That they must never wear black for me either.

CLYTEMNESTRA. But something personal . . . some loving word.

IPHIGENIA. Just say . . . 'Goodbye'. Tell Orestes to be a
man.

CLYTEMNESTRA. Cuddle him close then. You'll never see him
again . . .

IPHIGENIA. My little darling . . . you did all you could, didn't
you.

CLYTEMNESTRA. Can I do anything for you, when I get back
home?

IPHIGENIA. Yes. Don't hate my father. Remember he's your
husband.

CLYTEMNESTRA. He's running his own race now. Against
terror.

IPHIGENIA. He doesn't want to kill me. He's doing it for
Greece.

CLYTEMNESTRA. It's a disgusting sham! His ancestors would
disown him.

IPHIGENIA. Who will escort me. . . ? They'll hold my head
back, by the hair.

CLYTEMNESTRA. I'll come with you . . .

IPHIGENIA. No Mother, that wouldn't be right.

CLYTEMNESTRA. I'll hang on to your clothes. . . !

IPHIGENIA. No Mother, believe me!
  Stay here. It will be better that way
  For both of us. My father's guards, please,
  Let one of them escort me to the garden
  Of Aretemis, where I am to be slaughtered.

AGAMEMNON's *guards come forward to lead* IPHIGENIA.

CLYTEMNESTRA. My child, you're going. . . !
IPHIGENIA. And I shall never return.
CLYTEMNESTRA. Leaving me, I'm your mother . . .
IPHIGENIA. We don't deserve this, do we?
CLYTEMNESTRA. Don't go, wait a moment . . .
IPHIGENIA. Not one tear Mother. Not one!

The Priestesses come forward, and begin to prepare
IPHIGENIA *for the sacrifice, dressing her hair with flowers,*
garlanding her body, washing her hands with holy water, as
music begins.

IPHIGENIA. Women, sing a hymn for me, chant of my fate
  In honour of Artemis, the Daughter of Zeus.
  Let all the sons of Greece throughout the camp
  Be silent. This moment is holy. Let the Priests
  Prepare the instruments of sacrifice.
  Sprinkle the barley to purify the flames,
  And let my father begin to circle the altar,
  Always to the right, according to the ritual.
  My sacrifice brings salvation to the Greeks, and victory!

The procession that is to lead IPHIGENIA *to the sanctuary*
begins to form, more the enactment of a ritual than an exit.

IPHIGENIA. Lead me now, Troy's destroyer,
  The Phrygian people's despair,
  Crown me with flowers, bind me with garlands,
  Set blossoms like jewels in my hair;
  Wash my hands in the ewers of holy water

And dance to Artemis, link hands
In circles round the shrine
To where her altar stands.
All honour to the goddess. This blood of mine
Will cancel the gods' decree
And the ships will put to sea.
Oh Mother, dear Mother, my eyes
Flow like fountains for you here.
They must be dry at the altar. Sing,
Women, from the temple, where
It faces across the straits to where Chalcis lies.
At Aulis, the crowded harbours ring
With the shouts of soldiers, fired
For war, a forest of weapons waving,
By my name alone inspired.
Glory to the fatherland! I shall never
See Mycenae again. Goodbye, for ever!

CHORUS. Do you praise the Cyclops' masterpiece
   The stones their hands laid, Perseus' city?
IPHIGENIA. That city bred me to be a beacon for Greece.
   I give Greece my life now, give it willingly.
CHORUS. Your glory will shine through eternity.
IPHIGENIA. Goodbye, daylight.
   Great torch of the world, goodbye.
   Another life for me now, another time
   All unknown and strange, my eternal home.
   Goodbye, daylight,
   For ever, for ever, goodbye.

*She is led out in a ritual exit, half dance, half solemn
procession, by the priestesses and the guards.*
CLYTEMNESTRA, *unable to bear any more, rushes into the
headquarters building.*

CHORUS. See where she goes now, Troy's destroyer,
   To bring Phrygians to despair.
   Clusters of flowers weaved in garlands
   For death in her golden hair,

Veiled in the purity of holy water,
To where the fearful altar stands
Of the bloodthirsty goddess, to offer
For the blood sacrifice she demands
Her own white throat, and suffer
The gash of the knife, and flood
The altar with sacrificial blood.
Your father waits there, he fills the bowl
With wine and pure water.
The whole Greek army is assembled, burning
To begin the Trojan slaughter.
Grant us luck, Queen Artemis, to achieve that goal.
Great lady, we've satisfied your ancient yearning
For blood. Launch our expedition
Against Phrygia, and Trojan cunning.
And may the greatest soldier of the Greek nation,
Agamemnon, end the story
Crowned with immortal glory.

The MESSENGER, *a young captain of* AGAMEMNON'*s personal guard, rushes in from the direction of the sanctuary, shouting as he comes.*

MESSENGER. Clytemnestra, Tyndareus' daughter! If you're
                                                        inside
  The headquarters, come out! I've something extraordinary to
                                                        tell you!

CLYTEMNESTRA *comes out, distraught, and close to collapse.*

CLYTEMNESTRA. I heard you shouting, and came out at once.
  Something in your voice made me shudder with terror.
  Can there be greater disasters than I already endure?
  There can be nothing worse.
MESSENGER.   It's your daughter.
  Something happened. It was awesome . . . wonderful!
CLYTEMNESTRA. Then tell me, quickly. Don't hold anything
                                                        back!

MESSENGER. My dear mistress, not a word, I'll tell you
                                                    everything
Right from the beginning – though my mind's confused
Still, my tongue might garble it a bit.
When we came to the sacred grove
And the gardens thick with flowers where Artemis' sanctuary
Stands, we found the whole Greek army on parade
There, all pressing forward, and eager to see everything.
And when Agamemnon saw his daughter
Entering the temple precinct, correctly prepared
As a sacrificial victim, he cried out, aloud,
In terrible pain; then tried to turn his head away
From her, and from the army, and wept like a child,
Hiding his face in his cloak. She came
Close enough to touch him, this man who was her father,
And said this, or something like it:
'Here I am, Father, as you commanded me,
Ready to play my part. I give my body
For the sake of my country, and all the nations
Of the Greeks, most willingly. Take me by the hand
To the altar. Sacrifice me there, if that
Is what the goddess requires. I wish
You luck, and insofar as it lies in me
To influence a goddess, all prosperity.
May you win the great prize of victory,
And return in triumph to your fatherland.
But because I come willingly, please
Don't let any of the Greeks touch me.
I won't make a noise, and I'll stretch my neck forward
Without any fear.' Everyone present
Was immensely impressed at this young girl's
Extraordinary courage, and her decorum,
Her sense of what was right. Then Talthybius,
Whose duty it was, stepped forward, and called aloud
To the army that speaking was utterly forbidden,
And that each man should observe a reverent silence.
The Priest Calchas drew the knife from its sheath –
So sharp it almost cut you to look at it,

Placed it on a golden dish, and crowned
The girl's head with flowers. Then Peleus' son,
Achilles, took the golden dish, sprinkled it
With holy water from the vessels, then
Solemnly bearing it around the altar,
Uttered this prayer. 'Daughter of Zeus,
Artemis the hunter, thirsty for the blood
Of wild animals, moon goddess,
Bright light wheeling in the dark heavens,
Receive this sacrifice we offer,
The whole Greek army, and its leader, Agamemnon,
The pure blood from the white neck
Of an innocent virgin. Grant us in return
A fair wind and good passage for our ships
To Troy, and that we may storm the city
And overwhelm the citadel by the force of our arms.'
The two brothers, the sons of Atreus,
Stood there, eyes down, staring at the ground,
And the whole army followed suit.
Then the priest lifted up the knife,
Said a short prayer over the girl
And took level aim at her throat, ready
To cut it. And I can tell you,
As I stood there with my head down,
I was sick to the stomach, I could feel the pain
In my own heart. Then suddenly . . .
Something wonderful happened. I can only call it a miracle.
We all heard the knife strike her throat
Horribly clearly, but . . . there was no girl
Stretched out on the ground where we expected her to be!
Calchas suddenly shouted out, and the whole army
Cried out in amazement, like an echo,
Seeing before their eyes what was clearly
The visible hand of the gods, something
We couldn't believe, even though it was there
Before our eyes. What lay gasping
Its life out on the ground, and flooding the altar
With its blood, was a deer, a large one too,

Worthy of a goddess. Calchas spoke up
At once, with what joy in his voice you can imagine,
'Leaders of the Greek army, feast
Your eyes on this sacrifice, which the goddess
Herself offers on the altar, a deer
Bred to run like the wind on the mountains.
This is a sacrifice she welcomes, prefers
Even, before the girl, not wanting to stain
Her altar with the blood of a virgin
So noble, both in her birth and her actions.
This is an offering she delights in,
And she grants us in return a fair wind
And a fast passage to sweep down upon Troy!
So let every soldier and sailor now
Summon up his courage, and return to his ship
And be ready to embark this very day,
Leaving these safe harbours here at Aulis
To launch into the long swell of the Aegean!'
Then, when the whole sacrifice had burned to ashes
On the altar in the sacrificial flame,
He made the customary prayer for a good
Passage and safe return for the army . . .
And Agamemnon sent me to tell you the news,
And, particularly, to emphasise what a marvellous favour
He has received from the gods, and how it confers
On him imperishable glory among the Greeks.
I was there, and I'm telling you what happened
Exactly as I saw it, with my own eyes!
The girl, quite obviously, has been transported
Up to the heavens, to live among the Gods.
So you can put an end to all your grief
For her, and there is no cause at all
For anger towards your husband. Divine
Intervention into the affairs of men
Is always unexpected, and those whom the gods
Especially love, they'll save, some way or another.
In one day you have seen your daughter's death
And rebirth, darkness transformed into light.

CHORUS. Could any messenger bring happier news?
    Your daughter is alive, living among the gods!
CLYTEMNESTRA. My dear child, which of the gods
    Came like a thief and robbed me of my treasure?
    How shall I think of you, or speak of you now?
    Shall I pray to heaven, or weep to earth?
    And you Captain. Do you expect me to believe this story?
    Isn't it a lie, concocted for my benefit,
    To soothe me and keep me quiet?
    You bring me plasters for a broken heart.
CHORUS. Here comes the Lord Agamemnon. He'll tell you
    The same story, I'm sure, and understand what it means.

AGAMEMNON comes in, his face breaking into a ghastly
smile as he sees his wife. Her face is a mask of stone.

AGAMEMNON. Wife. Everyone will envy how our marriage has
                                        been blessed
    With our eldest daughter. She is one of the company
    Of the gods, of that there is no question.
    Your duty now is to take good care
    Of that little soldier of mine, and go back home.
    The army, as you can see, is ready to embark,
    And it may be some considerable time
    Before I return and pay my respects to you
    In person. I hope things go well with you.

She looks at him with an arctic coldness, turns, and
leaves without a word. The marriage is over, the events
of the Oresteia are already implied. AGAMEMNON *stands*
looking after her, and turns his corpse-like smile on the
CHORUS.

CHORUS. Make your journey, Son of Atreus, with joy
  To the land of Phrygia, and joyfully return
  Loaded with the treasure of plundered Troy!

AGAMEMNON *turns stiffly, and goes into his headquarters,
followed by his officers. The women of Chalcis slowly
begin to leave. Nothing has ended. Many things are beginning.*

THE WOMEN OF TROY

Characters

POSEIDON, god of the sea
ATHENE, goddess of wisdom
HECUBA, widow of Priam, King of Troy
CASSANDRA, their daughter, a prophetess
ANDROMACHE, their daughter-in-law, widow of Hector
TALTHYBIUS, a Greek Officer
MENELAUS, King of Sparta
HELEN, his wife
CHORUS, of Trojan women, captured, and soon to be enslaved
ASTYANAX, a small boy, Hector's son (unspeaking)
GREEK SOLDIERS

*Troy is in ruins, a panorama of shattered smoking
buildings, collapsed roofs, masonry and rubble spilled
across the streets. The general devastation expresses a sense
of anarchy and uncontrollable violence, liberated
from normal restraints.*

Only one figure is visible, HECUBA, *lying quite still outside
a building that is damaged but still standing, and secure
enough to act as a refuge for the captured women of Troy.
The God* POSEIDON *enters, and looks round at the smoking
ruins.*

POSEIDON. I have come here from the bottom of the sea,
   The salt waters of the Aegean, where the daughters
   Of Nereus, fifty sea-nymphs in chorus,
   Circle in their intricate and beautiful dance.
   My name is Poseidon. I am a god.
   I built this city – with Apollo I built it –
   Every stone we laid, every tower,
   Even the walls we dressed and levelled
   With plumb line and mason's square.
   So I've always had a particular love
   For this city of the Phrygians: and look at it now:
   A smoking ruin, devastated by the power
   Of the Greek war machine. A Phocian inventor
   By the name of Epeios, who lived on Parnassus,
   With skills he learned from Athene, and probably
   With her help, designed and built
   A horse, whose capacious belly was pregnant
   With armed commandos, and managed to get it –
   Together with its murderous payload –
   Inside the walls; so that no one
   In the future will ever forget the stratagem
   That goes by the name of the Wooden Horse,
   Nor the ferocious strike force it concealed.
   And now, the temple gardens are deserted,
   And puddles of blood smear the sanctuaries
   Of all the gods. King Priam lies dead

On the steps of the temple of Zeus Protector
Of the city. More gold than can be counted
And anything soldiers can loot finds its way
Down to the Greek ships; and all
They're waiting for now is a following wind,
So that after ten years, and ten sowing seasons,
They can joyfully set eyes on their wives and children,
These Greeks, who brought an army to sack Troy!
As for me, I have been defeated
Too, by Athene, and Hera, goddesses
Who supported the Greeks, and who, between them,
Have utterly devastated this city of the Phrygians.
So now I too shall desert famous Troy,
And all those altars and temples raised
In my name. For when a town
Is destroyed, and becomes a wilderness,
All worship ceases, and there's no longer
Anything left worth a god's consideration.
Now the riverbank of the Scamander echoes
With the screams and moans of captured women,
As various Greek lords draw lots for them
And they become their slaves. Arcadian
Princes draw some, Thessalians others,
And the Princes of Athens, Theseus' descendants,
Get their share. All the women
Of Troy who've not yet been allocated
Are in this building here. They've been reserved
For the leaders of the Greek army. And with them,
A prisoner, like the rest – and quite right too –
Is the Spartan daughter of Tyndareus, Helen.
But to see the true face of misery
You need look no further than the poor creature
Lying here, in front of the gate, Hecuba,
Whose unnumbered tears match the numberless dead
She grieves for. Her daughter, Polyxena,
Has been secretly and brutally murdered
At the tomb of Achilles, in payment for his death.
Priam is dead too, and her sons by him:

And her daughter Cassandra, the frenzied visionary
Whom even the god Apollo left
Untouched as a virgin, Agamemnon
Intends to make his concubine –
A dangerous business, best kept in the dark,
That flouts all religious feeling.
Well then, most prosperous of cities, home
Of the rich and fortunate, time to say goodbye!
Shining towers and citadels, farewell for ever.
If Pallas Athene, daughter of Zeus,
Had not determined to destroy you, your foundations
Would be as firm and solid as ever they were.

ATHENE *enters, and moves across towards* POSEIDON.

ATHENE. May our old antagonism be forgotten?
  I have something to say to you, brother of my father,
  Great god as you are, whom other gods honour.
POSEIDON. Certainly it may. We are blood relations,
  Queen Athene, and that warms my heart.
ATHENE. You are generous to say so. The question at issue
  Is a matter of equal concern to us both.
POSEIDON. What is it? Some new dispensation from the gods?
  From Zeus himself? Or some other divinity?
ATHENE. No, it concerns Troy, on whose ground we now
                                                stand.
  I want to make a pact: join your power to mine.
POSEIDON. Is that so? You pity your ancient enemy now,
  You see her a smoke blackened ruin, do you?
ATHENE. That's not the point. First, give me your answer.
  Will you join me, and help to carry out my plan?
POSEIDON. By all means. Though I'd be glad to know what it
                                                is.
  Are you helping the Greeks now, or the Trojans?
ATHENE. My former enemies, the Trojans, will be comforted.
  I shall make the Greeks' return home a disaster.
POSEIDON. A somewhat cavalier change of mind, surely?
  Are you usually so casual whom you love or hate?

81

ATHENE. Haven't you heard. I've been insulted, my temple
desecrated!

POSEIDON Yes, I know. When Ajax dragged Cassandra from
sanctuary.

ATHENE. The Greeks didn't punish him. Not even a reprimand.

POSEIDON. When your power had enabled them to bring Troy
to its knees!

ATHENE I shall punish them for that. With your help.

POSEIDON. I'm entirely at your service. What can I do?

ATHENE. I want their voyage home to be complete disaster.

POSEIDON. Before they set sail? Or out at sea?

ATHENE. When they've left Troy and are nearing home.
Zeus has promised me a savage hail storm,
Torrential rain and gale force winds
In the middle of the night. And he's given me
The use of his thunderbolts, to strike the Greek ships
With lightning, and burn them at sea.
Your task will be to make the Aegean
Heave with mountainous waves, every third wave even higher
Than the rest, and swirl and eddy the salt waters
With dangerous whirlpools, and fill
The whole bay of Euboea with floating corpses
So thick you could walk on them. So that the Greeks
Will learn their lesson, and in future, respect
My temples, and fear the power of the gods.

POSEIDON. Athene, you need not waste more words,
I shall do that with pleasure. The whole Aegean
From the shores of Mykonos and the rocks of Delos
To Skyros and Lemnos and the headlands of Capheria
And the open salt sea, I shall whip up to a foam,
So that the number of the drowned will be beyond counting.
You get off to Olympus now, get hold
Of the thunderbolts, and watch your opportunity
When the Greek fleet casts off for home.
When a man sacks a town and destroys everything,
Even sacred temples and the tombs of the dead,
He's asking for trouble. The same destruction
Sooner or later, will fall on his own head.

The two immortals depart in opposite directions. HECUBA *slowly raises herself up on one arm.*

HECUBA. Lift up your head from the dust,
  Heave up from the earth
  The weight of your misery, you whom the gods have cursed.
  Troy has ceased to exist: and we, by birth
  Troy's Kings and Queens, rule nothing now.
  The old life is gone, old gods, old hearth
  And home, destroyed. We must endure it, flow
  With the stream, let the new wind fill our sail,
  Not breast a running tide with our fragile prow.
  Oh, weep, weep, for my burning home, howl
  For my children dead, for my husband dead, the boast
  Of my noble family, empty as a sail when the winds fall.

Some agonies are beyond telling,
  And some must be told.
  Let my stretched limbs shake with it then, this keening,
  On my rack of pain, my bed of cold
  Stone. My temples are throbbing, my head
  Will burst, my heart shatters the walled
  Prison of my breast. Oh to sway, flow, lifted
  By the gentle rocking of a boat, to keep time
  With the dirge I must sing now, the song of the dead,
  My threnody of tears. This is the only theme
  For the black clad Muse of the destroyed, no dancing
  Can express it, dissonant music, harsh rhyme.

Oh you ships, whose sharp prows
  Cut the purple sea
  As your oars pulled in a cloud of spray
  From the sanctuary
  Of the harbours of Greece, till your bows
  Grounded in the bay of Troy, sad Troy,
  Ominous your flutes' bleak song,
  Your pipes' deathlike cry
  As on taut Egyptian cables you swung

At your moorings at Troy, sad Troy,
Like hunters on the scent
Of Menelaus' Helen, born to dismay
Her brother Castor, and bring
Shame to the banks of Eurotas, you brought
Death to Priam whose seed bred fifty sons, a headlong
Fall to suffering Hecuba, and a broken heart.

Look at me now, throned in the dust
By Agamemnon's tentflap,
An old woman, dragged as a slave
From my home, all hope
Plundered from my god-cursed
Ravaged grey head, with no reprieve
From my punishment of everlasting sorrow.
Weep, wives of the bronze armoured Trojans, grieve
For your heroes dead, daughters, harrow
The clouds with your tears for husbands lost!
Troy is burning.
Like the mother bird at her plundered nest,
My song has become a scream, no music can I borrow
From the stately dance or the solemn psalming
To the gods of Troy I sang among the women, nor the slow
Rhythm I began, Priam's sceptre in my hand, when I led the
dancing.

The FIRST SEMICHORUS *enters from the ruined building, the captive
Women of Troy, all ages, from young girls to grandmothers, all
dirty, cut, bruised, raped, with torn clothes, or half covered in rags,
the trembling survivors of a city that has just been sacked by a large
and violent army.*

SEMICHORUS ONE. Hecuba, did you shout aloud,
Or was it a howl of agony?
How far did it carry? Through the walls we heard
A sound that made us shiver in our misery
As we hid in the ruins, wretched Women of Troy,
Facing a life of slavery.

HECUBA. My women, my girls, already the Greeks deploy
  Their ships, their hands reach for the oars!
SEMICHORUS ONE. No, No! Will they really drag us away
  From our homes, and ship us overseas to theirs?
HECUBA. I know nothing: but sense that the worst will come.
SEMICHORUS ONE. I can't bear it! Soon we will hear them
                                                    shout,

  'Get moving, you Trojan women, hey, slave,
  Kiss your home goodbye, and now, move out
  And get on board. We're sailing for home!'
HECUBA. But not Cassandra, not her, dear heaven, leave
  That child inside, my god-crazed daughter
  In her visionary ecstasy.
  Don't let the Greek soldiers deport her,
  Not a poor mad girl. How can I grieve
  More than I do, is there more pain for me?
  Oh Troy, you are lost.
  We all leave you now. And whose misery
  Is greater, the dead, whose day is passed,
  Or the living, who must live in slavery?

The SECOND SEMICHORUS *enters from* AGAMEMNON's *temporary
tented headquarters nearby. They have already been rounded up
by the commander's guards, and are in as desperate a state as the*
FIRST SEMICHORUS.

SEMICHORUS TWO. I'm so frightened, look, I'm shaking with
                                                    terror!
  I crept from Agamemnon's tents, dear Queen,
  When I heard you cry out. What new horror
  Must I suffer? Surely the Greeks don't mean
  To kill me here? Are they mustering at their ships,
  Getting ready to row, in groups by the stern?
HECUBA. My children, a blasted mind never sleeps.
  I came out here at dawn. But there's no relief.
SEMICHORUS TWO. Is there any decision? No message from
                                                    the Greeks
  About the slave allocation? Who'll be master of my grief?

85

HECUBA. It won't be long now till you hear the worst.
SEMICHORUS TWO. I can't bear it. Who will it be, which lord
 Of the Greeks will carry me over the sea
 To Argos, or Phthia, or some bleak island
 Far, far from Troy, one of the accursed!
HECUBA. Oh you gods, where in my misery
 Shall I go, what corner of the earth
 Shall I burden with my old age,
 Like a drone in the hive, or an image of death
 Still in the flesh: a shadow from the country
 Of forgotten shadows. I'll be a concierge,
 They'll sit me at the outer gate,
 Or in the nursery with the children, in the entourage
 Of some Greek Princeling: I, who in Troy held my state
 As a Queen, half divine, with Kings to pay me homage!

The two SEMICHORUSES *combine to create the full* CHORUS.

CHORUS. Oh the pity of it, the pity! What words,
 What howling, can give tongue to a pain
 No animal could endure! Never again in the shadow
 Of Mount Ida will these hands of mine
 Pass the shuttle back and forth between the threads
 As I sit at my loom. For the last time I harrow
 My heart with the sight of my dead sons,
 The last time, before greater sorrow
 Overwhelms me, and my slavery begins:
 Perhaps forced into the bed of some loathsome Greek,
 – Gods curse such a night, and the evil
 Powers that bring me to it! – Or maybe my slave's back
 Will break drawing holy water from Peirene. O, Athens,
 God-favoured city of Theseus, may I come to you, not grovel
 By the turbulent Eurotas, at Menelaus' mercy, part of

             Helen's

Loathed household, under the Troy-sacker's heel!

I have heard men say that the foothills
Of Peneius, beneath Olympus, are famous for their wealth

And the fertility of their green fields.
There, of all places on earth,
Would be my second choice, after the sacred halls
Of Athens. And the land of Mount Etna, which scalds
Its slopes with Hephaestos' fire, the mountain homeland
Of Sicily, across the strait from Tunis, holds
Pride of place for integrity, and is renowned
For its brave men. And there is a secluded valley
They tell me, watered by a beautiful river
Named Crathis, close to the Ionian sea,
Whose dark streams, like hair, as they flow become reddened
Into the richest gold. Its springs are sacred, and for ever
Blessed with plenty is that valley, breeding heroes hardened
For war. I'd be happy enough to live there.

But look: a staff officer of the Greek army
Has some news for us. I can see him hurrying
At a brisk march in our direction.
What will he tell us? What more worth saying?
The Dorian Greeks have reduced us to slavery.

Enter TALTHYBIUS.

TALTHYBIUS. Hecuba . . . you are not unaware that on many
occasions
As officer in charge of negotiations, or outlining our
proposals,
I have come here from the Greek Camp. So I'm no stranger –
Talthybius, you may remember me – I have some news
for you
HECUBA. This is it my dears, what we've feared for so long . . .
TALTHYBIUS. You've been allocated to your masters . . . if
that's what you're afraid of.
HECUBA. Aieeeee . . . ! Where then? Phthia? Somewhere else in
Thessaly?
Or is it to be Thebes, Cadmus' city?
TALTHYBIUS. You are allocated separately: not all together.
HECUBA. So who goes to whom? Which of the Women of Troy

87

Has been lucky, and will dance for joy?

TALTHYBIUS. The fact is . . . ask one at a time, not all at
once . . .

HECUBA. My poor child, who has won her, Cassandra,
My god-stricken daughter?

TALTHYBIUS. Agamemnon made a special note of her, and took
her for himself.

HECUBA. Ah God! – Must she be slave to his Spartan wife,
Her bondservant for life?

TALTHYBIUS. Not at all, she's for him. In darkness. In his bed.

HECUBA. What! She is a consecrated virgin, Apollo's nun.
Lifelong virginity she was promised, by Zeus' golden-haired
son!

TALTHYBIUS. He wants her *because* she's sacred. He's shot
through with lust.

HECUBA. Throw away the keys of the temple, my child,
Strip off your sacred habit,
Trample the flowers on the ground!

TALTHYBIUS. Now look here, to be a King's mistress is no
bad thing.

HECUBA. And my youngest child, where's she? You tore her
from my arms.

TALTHYBIUS. Polyxena, you mean . . . or is it someone else?

HECUBA. Yes. Who gets her by the luck of the draw?

TALTHYBIUS. She is to serve Achilles, at his tomb.

HECUBA. Dear heavens, must a child I bore
Be a servant at a tomb?
Is this a custom among you Greeks, my friend, or some new
law?

TALTHYBIUS. Consider your child fortunate. All's well with her.

HECUBA. What does that mean? She is alive? Is she?

TALTHYBIUS. Her fate is settled. All her troubles are over.

HECUBA. And the wife of Hector, the incomparable warrior?
What happens to Andromache? What Greek draws her?

TALTHYBIUS. She was chosen specially, by the son of Achilles.

HECUBA. And whose slave am I? Grey-haired Hecuba.
Who needs a stick as a third foot to support her?

TALTHYBIUS. Odysseus, King of Ithaca drew you, as his slave.

HECUBA. Ah . . . pain, and still more pain . . . !
　Let me tear the hair in handfuls from my head,
　Plough my face with my nails, till the wrinkles run red,
　Still agony, and greater agony . . . !
　I've drawn the shortest straw, even worse than I feared –
　To be the slave of a man without morality,
　A liar, a deceiver, to whom laws of gods and men
　Mean nothing, whose animal appetite
　Savages all decency, and whose double tongue
　Twists truth into lies, friendship to enmity!
　Weep for me, Women of Troy, this last lottery of fate
　Will be the end of me. Veil me in shadows, I belong
　In the deepest pit of misery.
CHORUS. We know the worst now for you, dear Queen,
　But which of the Greeks has my future in his power?
TALTHYBIUS. All right you men, guard detachment,
　Go in there and bring Cassandra out.
　And move it! When I've handed her over
　To the Commander in Chief, I can take the rest
　Of you enslaved women to your masters,
　According to the allocation. Hey . . . ! What's that?
　Have they got lighted torches in there?
　Are they setting fire to the place, or what?
　These Trojan Women, just because we're taking them
　From their homes across to Argos . . . dear God,
　Are they trying to commit suicide in there,
　Setting light to themselves? To tell the truth,
　These are a proud people. In circumstances like these
　They don't take kindly to humiliation.
　All right, open up, open up in there!
　It may suit their dignity to insult the Greeks
　Like this, but I shall have to carry the can.
HECUBA. No, no one's setting fire to anything. It's my poor
　Manic daughter, Cassandra, she's running out here . . . !

CASSANDRA *enters, dirty and bruised, her hair wild, her*
clothes torn carrying two flaming torches. She is a young
girl, by a modern diagnosis schizophrenic or manic

*depressive, her mania taking a religious form, obsessed
with virginity. We might conjecture that she has been given
as a priestess to Apollo's temple as a child, as good
a form of shelter and therapy as any other. But the events
of the last twenty-four hours have stoked up the fires
burning in her brain, and she is now in a high manic phase,
acting out a grotesque parody of the rituals
of marriage.*

CASSANDRA. Hold it up, the torch, take it, let it flame
  Higher, oh hold it higher!
  Let it burn everything sacred to Apollo!
  Hymen, god of marriage, hallow
  The bridegroom and his desire,
  And bless me, the bride, and my new home,
  The royal bedroom of Argos! Hymen, bless my wedding,
  As I glorify you with my singing!

  You Mother, you sing
  For my father murdered, our city
  Destroyed, a sad keening song,
  Dirge for our country!
  But I fired these torches, illuminating
  My holy wedding feast, a blazing light
  To celebrate the marriage of virginity,
  And Hymen, god of lust, and the dark night
  Of Hecate, the consecrated virgin's deflowering!

  Begin the dance then, let our feet take wing, float higher
  In ecstasy, ah, ecstasy,
  As if this were a feast in celebration
  Of my father's good luck, the zenith of his fortune!
  This ritual dance is holy,
  God Apollo, lead us to your altar
  Under the laurel tree, where I dedicated my life.
  Now, Hymen, god of marriage, make me a good wife!

Dance, Mother, dance with me!
You should be laughing. Let your flying feet
Keep time with mine, whirling in ecstasy
Faster and faster, and shout,
Shout, Mother, the old songs of matrimony!
Sing, sing, Women of Troy,
Put on your most glittering dresses, celebrate
The virgin's lucky marriage! I shall enjoy
A husband bedded by the hand of destiny!

CHORUS. Dear Queen, your daughter's possessed! Hold on to
                                               her,
  Or she'll dance her way right down to the Greek Camp.

HECUBA. Oh Hephaestos, you gave flaming torches
  To mortal men, to carry in honour of marriage.
  But these torches are a grotesque parody
  Of everything I hoped for for my daughter.
  Oh my dear child, when I dreamed of your marriage
  I never imagined it would be like this, thrust
  At spear-point into some Greek's bed
  As a slave of his lust! Give me the torch,
  Poor child, you're not fit to carry anything burning
  In your half-crazed state. All this suffering
  Hasn't brought you to your senses, has it,
  You're just as much a poor mad thing
  As you ever were. Here, Women of Troy,
  Take these torches back inside,
  And let her dreadful parody of a wedding song
  Be drowned by the sound of your tears.

CASSANDRA. Mother, you must cover my hair with flowers,
  A victory crown to celebrate my triumph,
  Marrying a King. You must lead me to him,
  And if I don't seem overwhelmed at the prospect,
  Take no notice, give me a good shove,
  Force me, by violence, if you have to!
  Because, if the god Apollo exists
  At all, then Agamemnon, the world famous leader
  Of the Greeks, will find me more destructive
  As a wife than ever Helen was!
  Because I'll kill him, and destroy his whole family

In return for my father and brothers destroyed.
But that's enough. No more now. Some things
Are best passed over in silence. Why should I sing
Prophetic songs about the axe that will sever my neck,
And some other necks too? Or the son
Murdering the mother, or the total annihilation
Of the House of Atreus, all the rich fruit
Which the tree of my marriage will bear!
Look! Let me tell you. This city of Troy
Is far happier than the whole nation of the Greeks:
And I'll prove it to you. Yes, I'm possessed,
Inspired, call it what you like. But,
For one moment, let me stand outside
This god-drunken ecstasy, and speak
As though my voice were my own. These Greeks,
For the sake of one woman, and one moment
Of uncontrollable lust, sent a hunting party
To track down Helen, to smoke her out,
And it cost them tens of thousands dead!
And their oh-so-wise Commander, to achieve
What he hated most, lose what he loved most,
Giving up the pleasure of his family and children
For the sake of his brother Menelaus' wife,
Who was not dragged away from her home by force,
But ran away and was unfaithful, because she wanted to!
And when they came here, to the banks of Scamander,
These Greeks, then they began to die,
And they kept on dying. And for what reason?
They weren't being robbed, they weren't being invaded,
They didn't see the towers and battlements
Of their homeland being occupied.
And those who became the war god's victims
Had forgotten what their children looked like.
They weren't washed and shrouded and laid to rest
By their wives' loving hands: and now
Their bodies lie forgotten in a foreign country.
And things were no better at home. Their women
Died in the loneliness of widowhood,

Their fathers became childless old men,
Who had bred up their sons . . . for nothing,
To lie in a distant country, with no relatives
To honour them and make sacrifices at their graves.
Oh yes, the whole Greek nation
Has a great deal to thank their army for!
There were other things too, terrible things,
Things better left unsaid, not fit
To be spoken by the tongue of a consecrated virgin.
But our Trojans! What a contrast there! They won
The greatest of all glories. They died
Fighting for their fatherland! And if an enemy spear
Found its target, and in a moment made a living man
Into a corpse, that man was carried from the field
By his own platoon, the earth that covered him
Was the sacred soil of the land of his fathers.
The hands that wrapped him in his shroud
Were the right hands, according to the customs
Of burial in our country. And those Trojan soldiers
Who didn't die in battle, lived at home,
Spending every day with their wives and children,
The simplest of pleasures, denied to the Greeks.
And when you grieve for Hector, remember this.
Listen to me now, because this is the truth.
He proved, in action, he was the greatest of men.
And now he is gone. Dead. And all this
Has been the direct result of the coming of the Greeks.
Supposing they had stayed at home? We would never
Have seen Hector's glory, all that brightness
Would have remained hidden! And Paris. He married
The Daughter of Zeus. If he hadn't married her
Who would have sung songs in his honour in our palaces?
Any sensible man must hate war,
He does his best to avoid it. But if it should come,
Even if it should end like this, it is no shame
For a city, indeed, it is a crown of honour
To die nobly, with dignity. The really shameful thing
Is to die dishonourably, ignobly, without pride.

So you see Mother, you need not pity our country,
Nor weep for my 'marriage'. Think of those
We hate the most, you and I,
And be sure, that by means of this marriage of mine
I shall destroy them.

CHORUS. You make light of all these horrors, and laugh at your
own pain.

The disasters you prophesy are fantasies. They won't happen.

TALTHYBIUS. If it weren't for the fact that your devotion
To Apollo has left you mentally disturbed,
You would be severely punished for cursing our Generals
Like that, just as they are about to set sail.
It's surprising how often those that seem the wisest
And of the highest regard, do things which show them
To be something a good deal less. The greatest,
The most powerful General in the Greek army,
The son of Atreus himself, has let uncontrollable lust
For this madwoman get the better of him.
I'm a poor man. But there's no way
I'd let her anywhere near my bed!
And as for you. Since you're out of your mind,
We'll let your insults to the Greeks, and ridiculously
Overblown compliments to your own side, float away
On the breeze, with the breath that uttered them.
Come on then, follow me, it's time
You were getting on board. What a lovely bride
For my Commander in Chief! And you, Hecuba,
You can follow us down when Laertes' son
Comes to get you. You'll be his wife's slave,
Penelope. She's a decent, sensible woman.
You won't find a Greek at Troy to say otherwise.

CASSANDRA. What a clever fellow he is,
This underling! Officers of your kind
Are always hated by everyone, lackeys,
Slaves yourselves, doing great men's dirty work.
You say my mother will be taken from here
To Odysseus' palace. But what about the words
Of Apollo, spoken through my mouth?

They say that she will die here,
And other things, about her death,
Too terrible to be spoken. And as for Odysseus,
What can I say about his sufferings,
Except that what I suffer, and what Troy suffers
Will one day seem like a golden age
To him. He will add ten further years
To the ten years he has spent here
Before he reaches his fatherland,
And he'll reach it alone. He will have endured
The terrifying passage through the rocky gorge
Of Charybdis, and the mountain pastures
Of the Cyclops, who eats human flesh.
On the Ligurian coast he will meet the witch
Circe, who turns men into pigs;
He will be shipwrecked more than once
In the open sea, and have to face
The seductive desire for oblivion
In the drugged land of the Lotus eaters,
And the sacred oxen of the sun god,
Whose slaughtered and jointed flesh will moan
Like a human being in pain, a sound
To strike terror into Odysseus' breast.
Finally, to cut short this catalogue of horrors,
He will pass through Hell, while still alive,
And after crossing the marshes of the lake of the dead,
When he reaches Ithaca, he will find his old home
Torn apart by troubles, ten thousand of them!
But why should we waste our breath on the sorrows that
                                            lie in wait
For Odysseus? That arrow has left the string, but not yet
Hit the bull. Take me then, to marry my bridegroom
In the very doorway of Hell! In the dead of night they'll
                                            come
To bury you, vilest, filthiest of men, as though
The daylight were ashamed to see you, the great Greek leader
                                            brought low
Who dreamed of mounting so high! Me too, my naked flesh

Will be thrown into a rocky gulley, where the storm waters
                                                    rush
Close by my bridegroom's grave! Wild animals will eat
Apollo's consecrated priestess. My crown of flowers, my
                                                    white
Robe of the most beautiful of the gods, and all the ritual of
                                                    Dionysus,
Goodbye to all of it, the feasting and celebrations, so precious
To me! Tear them all off, and my skin too in strips, let
                                                    the wind
Carry them back to the god of prophecy, while my flesh is
                                                    still untouched.
Where is the General's flagship? Which way must I go?
                                                    Who
Could wait for the wind that fills her sails more eagerly
                                                    than I do?
One of the avenging furies, dragged from the ruins of Troy!
Goodbye Mother. No tears. Oh land of my fathers, dead
                                                    brothers who lie
Under this earth, Father who sired me, soon, soon we'll
                                                    meet,
Short, oh short my journey, in the house of the dead, and
                                                    you'll greet
Me with joy for the victory I bring: the family at whose
                                                    hands Troy died
And all her people perished, the House of Atreus, destroyed!

TALTHYBIUS *motions to his guards, who roughly take*
CASSANDRA *away with them, her voice rising in a weird ululation
or scream.* HECUBA *collapses in a dead faint, and
the* CHORUS *gathers round her, calling to her women.*

CHORUS. Where are Hecuba's women? Your venerable queen
    Has fainted, she's collapsed, and lies speechless on the ground.
    Don't let her just lie there, you bitches, an old woman
    Fallen flat on her face. Get her up on her feet!

The frightened servant women run to HECUBA *and try to
raise her.*

HECUBA. No, leave me alone. Your kindness, my girls,
　　Is no kindness to me. Let me lie here
　　Just as I fell. What I am suffering,
　　And have suffered, what I will suffer yet,
　　Is more than enough to make anyone fall
　　And never get up again. Oh you gods,
　　What good were you to us? Betrayers!
　　And yet people still call upon gods
　　When bad luck, or history, has flattened them
　　And the whole of their world has collapsed.
　　So let me tell you how fortunate I was,
　　Born lucky, to heighten the tragedy
　　Of what has happened to me now. I was royal
　　By birth, and I married a King. My sons
　　Excelled, not merely because I bore so many,
　　But because they were the best among the Phrygians.
　　What's more, they were Trojans, and such Trojans
　　As no Greek woman or barbarian
　　Could ever boast of bearing. And I saw
　　Every one of them slaughtered by the swords
　　And spears of the Greeks! By their open graves
　　I have stood, and cut my hair in mourning
　　To cast upon their bodies; and so many bitter tears
　　I have wept for their father, Priam. No one
　　Told me of his death, no one
　　Brought me the news. With my own eyes
　　I saw him hacked down on the altar steps
　　Of our holiest temple, and the whole city sacked
　　As the Greeks ran riot; all the daughters I brought up
　　With such care, to make them fit brides for Princes,
　　I saw them snatched from my arms, their good breeding
　　Wasted on brutal soldiery and foreigners.
　　There's no hope they'll ever see me again
　　Or that I will ever see them. And now,
　　Like the keystone to my arch of misery,

In my old age I must go to Greece
To finish my life as a slave. And what work
They will give me, a woman of my years,
To be a gatekeeper, looking after the keys,
Me, the mother of Hector, or a kitchen skivvy
Kneading the bread dough. I won't sleep
On a royal mattress any more, the floor
Will be good enough for my bony back
And wasted flesh; worn out, second hand
Dresses will do for me, rags even,
The sort that well bred women never see
Let alone wear, they will have to make do
For my worn out, second hand body.
Dear gods, what a terrible retribution,
All that has happened to me, and will happen,
Because of that one woman and her love affair!
Cassandra, my child, what violation will end
Your consecrated virginity, that mystic ecstasy
You shared with Dionysus, and all the gods?
And you, my poor girl, Polyxena,
Where are you now? None of my children
Neither sons nor daughter – and there were so many of
them –
Can give me so much as a helping hand
In my misery. They are all gone.
So why try to help me up? What for?
What have I to look forward to ? Well. Take my hand
And lead me step by step – these feet of mine –
So used to deep carpets, all the luxury of Troy,
They belong to a slave now. Bring me to my bed,
My straw paliasse and stone pillow,
Throw me down there on my face
And let these tears, my torturers, whip me senseless.
Wealth, good fortune, it's all worth nothing.
There is no happiness. The lucky ones are the dead.
CHORUS. Teach me, gods of song, some harsh lament
    Dissonant with tears and howls,
    Help me to sing Troy's sorrows, invent

New sounds for my grief: the Greek Horse on wheels
Has ruined me, brought me to the edge of the grave
Made me a slave.
Unguarded they left it, by the main gate,
Its gold cheek pieces gleaming,
And from its belly the clash of armour plate
Rumbled like thunder, muffled and threatening.
So we ran to the rock of the citadel
The whole population, shouting,
'Come out everybody, all
our troubles are over, wheel
This wooden offering for Zeus' daughter,
Athene of Troy, inside the wall!'
And who ran from their houses the faster,
The young men or the old? All high
On the singing and the joy, as they laid hands on the monster
That was more than it seemed, and would doom them all to
                                                        die.

Then it seemed the whole nation of the Phrygians ran
To the gates, eager to bring
That smooth planed icon of mountain pine
And the Greek ambush within it, as an offering
To the virgin who drives the immortal horses of heaven –
For the Trojans, destruction.
Roped with cables of twisted flax
They heaved it, like a black ship,
To the stone shrine at the heart of the temple complex
Of Pallas Athene – altars soon to drip
And smooth floors run slippery with Trojan blood.
Then the melodius African pipe
Honeyed the air, as the dark hood
Of night enfolded Troy. In celebration
After the day's exhaustion, the whole city was singing,
Dancing feet stamping in exhilaration
To the rhythm of young girls' voices, flickering
Torches casting puddles of light
In the darkened palaces, and on the faces sleeping,

And in eyes wide awake and glittering in

At that time in our great hall
With the others, I was singing
All our favourite songs to Artemis, Zeus'
Virgin of the mountains, and joining in t
When suddenly I heard a terrible howl,
The unmistakable sound of murder,
A terrified scream rising from the streets of the whole
City. Children grabbed hold of their mothers'
Skirts, their pale hands plucked at her gown,
Fluttering with fear. The god of war
Had sprung his trap, the ambush strategy
Worked perfectly, thanks to Pallas Athene, whose power
Secretly inspired it. The Trojans were cut down
In their own homes, in sanctuary, beheaded where they
lay
Sleeping, a whole generation of women raped in their own
Bedrooms, breeding bastards for the Greeks, desolation for
Troy.

Look, Hecuba, they're bringing Andromache
In a Greek baggage waggon. Her bosom is heaving
With sobs, as she grasps Hector's son, Astyanax, clinging
To her breasts, as they rise and fall like a bank of oars in
the sea.

*Enter a baggage waggon, loaded with all kinds of plunder,
including* HECTOR's *weapons and armour, dragged by a group
of female slaves.* ANDROMACHE *stands on it, amid the spoils
of her city, desperately clutching the three or four-year-old*
ASTYANAX *to her bosom, as if fearful to let go of him.*

CHORUS. Where are they taking you, woman of grief,
In an enemy cart, with the bronze armour
Of Hector stacked beside you, all the loot
Ransacked from Troy at sword point?

The son of Achilles will hang up Troy's plundered splendour
As a trophy under some Phthian temple roof!
ANDROMACHE. My Greek masters are only taking what's theirs.
HECUBA. Aiee, Aiee!
ANDROMACHE.   Don't sing *my* victory song!
HECUBA. Agony!
ANDROMACHE.   The agonies are all mine.
HECUBA. Oh Zeus!
ANDROMACHE.   Hard learned, to be suffered long.
HECUBA. My children!
ANDROMACHE.   No longer. Grown old in tears.

HECUBA. All our happiness. Troy, our city. Gone.
ANDROMACHE. Into misery.
HECUBA.   My children, my heroic sons!
ANDROMACHE. All gone, gone.
HECUBA.   What grief is like mine?
ANDROMACHE. My suffering.
HECUBA.   The sobbing, the moans.
ANDROMACHE. Of our city.
HECUBA.   Ruined. Smoke blackened stone.

ANDROMACHE. My husband! Where are you? I need you now.
                                                    Save me!
HECUBA. You're calling for a dead man. My firstborn son
Is in Hades, and I am in misery.
ANDROMACHE. Protect me now, as you've always done.

HECUBA. Oh my Priam, whom the Greeks barbarously killed!
ANDROMACHE. Old man, great King, princely father,
Your sons were famous throughout the world.
HECUBA. Let me sleep in the arms of death for ever.

ANDROMACHE. So bitter, these longings,
HECUBA.   Sharp pains now, and sorrows unceasing.
ANDROMACHE. For the city we have lost,
HECUBA.   And miseries ever increasing.

ANDROMACHE. The gods always hated us. Their malice spared
your son.

So that his contemptible marriage should bring ruin
To the citadel of Troy! Now in bloody pieces he's lying
For the vultures, in Pallas' temple. Our slavery is his doing!

HECUBA. Troy, mother of us all!
ANDROMACHE.   Tears blind me. Deserted. A ruin.
HECUBA. This pitiful end.
ANDROMACHE.   The house my children were born in.
HECUBA. I've lost my home. I've lost my children. Everything.
No grief can encompass what I feel. No funeral song.
Flow, tears, for a city, and family, shattered past hoping.
Only the dead shed no tears. They are beyond weeping.
CHORUS. Suffering people find some comfort in tears.
To give voice to grief is a kind of pleasure.
ANDROMACHE. Oh Hecuba, mother of the son who speared
So many of these Greeks, do you see what they are doing?
HECUBA. I see what the gods are doing, making monuments
Of worthless men, and demolishing the good.
ANDROMACHE. We are loot, my son and I, soldiers' plunder,
Born royal, and made slaves! The whole world's overturned.
HECUBA. Necessity is logical, and merciless. Cassandra
Has just been torn from my arms by force.
ANDROMACHE. No, no more. I can't bear it . . .
So some second Ajax flatters his masculinity
By dragging off your daughter. But . . . there's worse pain
to come.
HECUBA. Of course there is. There's no end to pain.
The next horror will always be worse than the last.
ANDROMACHE. She's dead. Your daughter, Polyxena. Murdered
At Achilles' tomb, as a sacrifice to the dead.
HECUBA. And it is . . . So that's what Talthybius meant,
The truth his diplomatic evasion concealed.
ANDROMACHE. I saw it with my own eyes. I got down from
the cart,
Cut down the body, covered it with her dress.
HECUBA. My poor child . . . ritually murdered, filthy,

Sacrilege . . . oh my poor girl, butchered like an
animal . . . !

ANDROMACHE. Anyway she's dead, however it happened,
And she's happier dead than I am living.

HECUBA. No, no one is happier dead. The living
At least have hope. To be dead is to be nothing.

ANDROMACHE. Dear Mother, listen. You are my mother too,
Even though you didn't give me birth; listen
And draw some comfort from what I'm saying.
To be dead is the same as never to have been born.
But to die is better than a life of agony,
Because the dead feel nothing, and no pain
Can touch them any more. Whereas someone whose life
Has been prosperous and lucky, and is then overwhelmed
By disasters, knows what it's like to have been happy,
And is heartbroken to be excluded from that paradise . . .
For your child, it's as though she had never seen
The light of day, she's dead, and knows nothing
Of her suffering now. It's different for me.
Being Hector's wife, I aimed at the highest
A woman could wish for, and I hit the mark.
And now I have lost everything. Living with Hector
I made it my business to be the perfect wife,
Never wanted even to leave his house,
Because that's the certain way to compromise
A woman's reputation, gave up all desire
To go anywhere and was joyfully fulfilled at home.
And even at home, I admitted no fashionable
Gossip or women's chatter, but used my intelligence
To improve my own mind, and was content with that.
I lived quietly with my husband, my happiness was obvious
Whenever our eyes met. I knew what things
Were my prerogative, and how to give in gracefully
To his authority in matters that were his.
But my reputation as the ideal wife
Reached the Greek Camp, and that ruined me.
As soon as I was captured, Achilles' son
Asked for me as his wife, meaning his whore,

To be a slave in the very house
Of the man who murdered my husband . . .
If I drive the memory of my beloved Hector
Out of my mind, and open the doors
Of my heart to the man who owns me now,
I shall betray the love of the dead man,
And mine to him. And if I refuse
To allow this Prince to touch me, I'll provoke
The hatred of the man whose power is total
Over me and mine. They say one night
In bed with a man will convince any woman
And pleasure away her hatred. I spit in the face
Of any woman who forgets her dead husband
To jump into bed with the next one. Dear God,
Not even a mare, uncoupled from her old yokefellow
And stablemate will pull in harness willingly!
And animals are supposed to be inferior to men,
With no power to reason or speak their thoughts!
But you, Hector, my love, you had everything
I dreamed of in a husband, in intelligence, good family,
Wealth and courage the greatest of men!
You took me as a virgin from my father's house,
And I gave my body for the first time to you
In our marriage bed. Now you are dead,
And I am to be transported across the sea
To Greece as a prisoner, to be yoked as a slave.
And Polyxena, whom you groan and weep for,
Isn't her suffering far less than mine?
You say everyone living has hope. What hope
Have I? I'm not stupid enough to delude
Myself with false expectations, pleasant
Though such comforting daydreams might be . . .

CHORUS. Your suffering is like mine. Your anguished words
    Give voice to my deepest agonies and fears.

HECUBA. I've never been on board ship in my life,
    But I've seen pictures of them, and heard men talking,
    So I know that if the storm is not too violent,
    And there's some chance of survival, the sailors

Will do everything they can to come through it, hanging on
To the tiller, scrambling aloft to the sails,
And bailing out the water for dear life.
But if the waves run higher, and towering rollers
Overwhelm them, they accept the inevitable
And give themselves to the sea. And so do I too.
The gods have drowned me in an ocean of misery.
After so many sorrows, and in such despair,
Words mean nothing. There's nothing left to say.
But you, dear daughter, dry your eyes.
No more grieving for Hector now.
You must forget him. Even your tears
Can't help him now. My advice to you
Is to make much of your new master.
Be pleasant, make yourself attractive to him.
That way you will make everyone's captivity
Easier to bear, and your own life more pleasant.
With luck, you may bring up this grandson of mine
To be the saviour of Troy. Sons of yours
May return to the ruins of Ilium one day
And build a new city from the ashes . . .
But look . . . the next chapter is already beginning.
The Greek minion is coming back,
To tell us, no doubt, what the Greek Council
Has finally decided to do with us all.

TALTHYBIUS *returns, with an armed guard detachment. He
looks round at the women very uneasily, then walks across
to* ANDROMACHE.

TALTHYBIUS. Hector's wife, widow of the greatest of the
                                          Trojans . . .
    I ask you not to hate me. With the greatest reluctance
    I must tell you the news, the joint decision
    Of the Council of the Greeks and the two sons of Pelops.
ANDROMACHE. What is it? That sounds like a prelude to
                                          disaster.

105

TALTHYBIUS. This child. They have decided . . . I don't know
how to say it.

ANDROMACHE. No, don't take him away . . . ! We have
different masters . . . ?

TALTHYBIUS. No Greek will ever be his master.

ANDROMACHE. How . . . ? Is he to be the last of the Trojans?
Left here?

TALTHYBIUS. There's no decent way to say an indecent thing.

ANDROMACHE. Thank you for your decency . . . but no more
bad news . . .

TALTHYBIUS. They mean to kill him. That's the worst. Now
you know.

ANDROMACHE. Oh my God . . . ! That sentence is worse than
my marriage . . .

TALTHYBIUS. Odysseus' speech carried the whole Council . . .

ANDROMACHE. Aieee, Aieee, I can't bear it, I can't . . . !

TALTHYBIUS. That the son of such a father must not be allowed
to grow up . . .

ANDROMACHE. May those arguments condemn his own son!

TALTHYBIUS. And that he should be thrown from the battlements
of Troy.

This has to be. So please be sensible.
Don't hang on to him like that, but bear this pain
Like the Queen you are. There's nothing you can do.
You are quite without any power to prevent it
So don't imagine otherwise. No one can help you.
The city is in ruins, your husband dead.
You are quite alone, and believe me
We are capable of dealing with a single woman
If we have to. So don't make a fight of it,
Or kick or struggle, or curse the Greeks.
If you say anything to anger the army
Your child may not be properly buried
And no tears be shed at his grave. But if
You keep quiet, and resign yourself to what must happen,
They might allow you to bury your child
Decently, and treat you with more consideration.

ANDROMACHE. My darling, my precious, too dangerous to live,

Your enemies will kill you, and leave your mother in misery,
Your father's courage, that saved so many,
Is a death sentence for you. Everything
That made him great for you proves fatal.
Ah, God, when I came into Hector's palace
On that unlucky wedding day,
And that unluckier wedding night,
I thought I would conceive a son to rule
Over the whole of Asia, not a victim
To be callously murdered, butchered by the Greeks!
My dear little boy, are you crying too?
Do you understand what's happening? Why else
Do you hang on to my hand like that, and bury
Your timid face in the folds of my dress
Like a bird creeping under his mother's wing?
There is no Hector rising from the grave
With his spear in his hand, coming to save you,
Nor any of your father's brothers, no army
Of Trojans. You must jump from that terrifying height,
Fall, and break your neck, smash the breath in your mouth
Without pity from anyone! My sweet baby,
So tender in my arms, dearer than all the world
To your mother, the softness of your breath,
The baby smell of your skin . . . ! All for nothing,
My labour pains when you were born, all for nothing
When I gave you my breast, and dressed you so tenderly
In your baby clothes, all nothing, all for nothing.
Hold me tight now, hang on to me, for the last time,
I gave you birth, put your arms round my shoulders
And hang on to me, hard, and kiss me, my boy . . .
You Greeks! You have dreamed up such cruelties
Even the barbarians would flinch at! Why
Are you killing this child! What has he done
In his innocence? He's guilty of nothing!
Helen! You Daughter of Tyndareus! You
Are not Zeus' daughter! More fathers than one
You had, and I know their names too!
Destruction, first of all, and Envy and Murder

And Death, and every evil thing
That crawls on the face of the earth! Zeus could never
Have fathered you to bring ruin and slaughter
On Greeks and barbarians alike, by thousands!
Die in agony, and be damned for ever,
You and your beautiful eyes, whose inviting looks
Have brought this famous country of Phrygia
To complete destruction! Come on then! Take him!
Carry him away. Throw him down from the walls
If that's what your generals have decided, and then
Make a banquet of his dead body! The gods
Are destroying us all. I can't save
My own child from death! Parcel up
My disgraced body, and throw it on board ship.
It's a fine wedding I'm sailing to
With my poor son left dead at my back!

CHORUS. Poor Troy. Ten thousand men are dead
For one woman, and her hated marriage bed.

TALTHYBIUS. Come on boy. You must break that embrace
Now, in spite of your mother's agony,
And climb the walls to the highest bluff
That crowns ancestral Troy. At that place,
According to the vote of the Army Committee,
You must give up your life. Take him then.

*At this point the soldiers drag the screaming boy from his
distraught mother by force.*

TALTHYBIUS.   Someone tough
And unthinking they need for this job, without pity
And no scruples. I'm not half hard enough.

HECUBA. Poor child, son of my dead son,
To tear you like that from your mother and from me
Is wicked. How can I suffer
This, and learn to bear it? What can be done
To help you now, enduring this? We can only
Beat our breasts in anguish, tear our hair,
And that's all we can do. Our city is gone,

108

And soon you will be gone too. There is no agony
We don't already feel, no abyss of pain to discover.

ANDRÓMACHE *is dragged out by the guards one way as*
ASTYANAX *is taken the other.* HECUBA *sinks down in despair.*

CHORUS. From the sea-fringed shore of Salamis, the island of
                                                                    beehives
That faces the sacred slopes where the first bough
Of the blue-grey olive was unveiled by Pallas, ancestor of
                                                                    the groves
That sit like a wreath of honour on the shining brow
Of Athens, came Telamon, Salamis' founder, across the
                                                                    waves
Of the Aegean to destroy
The ancient city of Troy,
With the archer Heracles, in the distant past
When Greece first came to Ilium, to bring it to the dust.

The flower of Hellas he led in his rage for the
                                                          immortal horses
Of Zeus, first promised, then denied. In the calm
Shallows of Simois they rested their sea-going oars, cast
                                                                    hawsers
To make fast the sterns, while Heracles' mighty arm
Took the bow from his ship and killed Laomedon, and
                                                              with flashes
Of fire like a whirlwind
Shattered and burned
The very stones of Apollo's city. Once in the past
And now again, Greek arms have brought Dardanus' city to
                                                                    the dust.

Oh Ganymede, son of Laomedon,
As you step so delicately among the golden
Wine cups, pouring the vintage
For Zeus, enjoying a favourite's privileges,
What use are you to your city, as it rages

109

In flames, and the Greeks bring carnage
To the land of your birth? Is that the cry
Of seagulls screaming for their young
On the sea shore? No. Women of Troy,
Wives for their husbands screaming,
For their dead sons, daughters weeping desperately
For mothers too old to live slaves for long.
Your pools for freshwater swimming, that trackway
Where you always loved to go running,
All obliterated now. While you were reclining
Serene in your youthful beauty
By the throne of Zeus, the Greeks were destroying
Troy's people and Priam's city.

Love, consuming love, once came
To the palace of Dardanus, Laomedon's home.
The gods themselves were trembling
With the excitement of it, and Troy
Seemed promised an immortal destiny
At the Olympian wedding
Of Tithonus with Aurora, goddess of the dawn.
No further reproach will pass my lips
Against Zeus or his doings. What's done is done.
But the pure light of morning
That cheers everyone, saw destruction
Dawn on our city, saw our citadels collapse;
And yet, Aurora herself had a Trojan
Husband in her bed, was breeding
Children by him, after abducting
Him in her four-horsed chariot, to enjoy
Her love among the stars. For us, vain dreaming,
False hopes. The gods hate Troy.

Enter MENELAUS, *with his guards.*

MENELAUS. Even the sun shines brighter today,
This most glorious of days when I shall finally
Get my hands on that wife of mine, Helen.
Yes, I am the man, Menelaus,

Who for ten years have endured this terrible war –
Together with the Greek army. But it wasn't only
For my wife's sake that I came to Troy.
People say that, I know. My real motive
Was to get my hands on the man who stole
My wife, violated the sanctity
Of my much loved home, treacherously
Deceived me, his host, and thumbed his nose
At every known principle of hospitality!
Well. I've certainly made him pay for that –
With the gods' help of course – him,
And all his people – the Greeks have butchered
The lot, and turned his great city
Into a wilderness. But certainly, too,
I have come to fetch the Spartan woman –
It gives me no pleasure to speak her name –
The woman who was my wife. She's been counted
Into this temporary prison with the rest
Of the Trojan women. The Greek soldiers,
Whose blood and guts have been tested and spent
In so many battles to get her back
Have handed her over to me, to kill her
Here on the spot – unless I decide
To take her back to our Argive homeland.
That's up to me. In fact, I've decided
To pass up the opportunity of killing Helen
Here in Troy, and to row her home
To Greece, where she will be handed over
To the relatives of all those who died at Troy
To be executed in payment for their blood.
Get in there, you guards, into that building,
And bring her out here, drag her out
By the hair, sticky with dead men's blood,
The murderess! And as soon as the wind's
In the right quarter, we'll ship her off to Greece.
HECUBA. Oh Zeus, you who at the same time
  Support the earth like a great pillar
  And sit throned upon it, unknown, unknowable,

111

Whether we call you a force of nature
Or an image in the mind of man, hear
The prayer I offer, as mysteriously, unheard,
You lead men's footsteps in the paths of Justice!

MENELAUS. That's a new way to pray to the gods!

HECUBA. If you mean to kill your wife, Menelaus,
You'll have my support. But don't see her,
Don't risk becoming a slave
Of your lust again. With one look
She makes men's eyes her prisoners, she sacks
Whole cities, burns houses to the ground
With that bewitching smile! I know her,
And so do you, everyone who's met her
And suffered for it knows her well enough!

HELEN – *terrified, bruised, frightened, but still managing
to make herself look more than presentable, in far better
clothes than any of the others have managed to salvage,
and still awesomely beautiful – is dragged in by the
guards.*

HELEN. Menelaus . . . if this is just the start
I'm terrified of what may come next . . . ! Your guards
Have dragged me out here in front of the building
With such violence and contempt . . . You hate me, I know.
I'm almost sure you do. But this one question
I must ask you nevertheless. What have the Greeks
Decided – what have you decided –
To do with me. Am I to live or die?

MENELAUS. Nothing definite was decided. But the army
unanimously
Gave you to me, your wronged husband, to kill you.

HELEN. Can I speak in my own defence, and show
How unjust it would be to kill me – if you do?

MENELAUS. I've come for an execution, not an argument.

HECUBA. Hear her Menelaus, let her speak,
Don't let her die without a word
In her own defence! And then let me

Make the case against her! What do you know
Of the havoc she has caused in Troy? Nothing.
When I've had my say, read the whole indictment,
There'll be no room for any doubt that she's guilty.
MENELAUS. You're asking a favour, and that will take time.
But if she wants to speak, that can be allowed.
It's for your sake, be quite clear, that I allow it, not hers.
HELEN. It probably doesn't matter if I speak well
Or badly, if you've already decided
Against me. You won't even bother to answer.
But if your accusations against me
Are what I think they will be, I shall answer
Your arguments with arguments of my own.
First of all, this woman, Hecuba,
She gave birth to all the trouble by giving birth
To Paris. Secondly, *he* destroyed Troy,
Priam did, the old king, and he destroyed me too,
When he failed to strangle his brat at birth,
Paris Alexander, seeing in him, as he did,
An image of that firebrand that would burn Troy.
And then what happened? Listen, and I'll tell you.
Paris had three goddesses in one harness,
And sat in judgement on their beauty. Pallas
Offered him the leadership
Of a Trojan expeditionary force
That would take out the whole of Greece! Hera
Promised that if he gave her the prize
He would become the master of Europe
And the whole of Asia. But Aphrodite
Simply and rapturously described how beautiful
I was, promised him he should have me
If he chose her as the most beautiful
Of the three goddesses. Think carefully
About what happened next. Aphrodite won the prize,
And think what a blessing my marriage to Paris
Was to Greece! You are not under the heel
Of a barbarian conqueror, not defeated in battle,
No totalitarian dictator has you at his mercy.

113

But Hellas' good fortune was my ruin,
Exported, I was, sold off abroad,
My exceptional beauty was a saleable asset
For Greece! And now all I get is vulgar abuse
Instead of the respect and honour I deserve!
You will say, no doubt, that I have ignored
The main point, the reason why
I ran away from your home in secret.
He came, call him Paris, or Alexander,
Whichever of his names you like, that genius
Of destruction Hecuba gave birth to, and with him
Came a goddess, well, not exactly a weakling
As goddesses go . . . And you, spineless idiot,
You chose that moment of all moments
To leave your home and take ship for Crete!
Are you beginning to understand? The next question
Is the crucial one, and I ask it of myself,
Not you. What, if anything at all,
Was I thinking of when I tamely followed
This foreigner, whom I hardly knew,
Betraying my country, and my home, and my family
In the process? Ask the goddess, not me,
Punish her, punish the destructive power
Of love; and in doing so, proclaim yourself
Superior to Zeus, who is the master
Of all the gods, but the slave of that one,
Aphrodite! That being the case,
What can you honestly do but forgive me?
There is, I suppose, one further accusation
You might make against me. Once Paris was dead
And in his grave, since my marriage was no longer
The direct responsibility of the goddess, I should
Have left his house and made my escape
To the Greek ships. God knows, I wanted to,
And God knows how I tried! Ask the guard commanders
At the great tower posterns, ask the sentries
On the walls, ask them how many times
They caught me lowering my clumsy body

In secret from the battlements of Troy,
Or shinning down ropes to reach the ground!
But my new husband Deiphobus – he's dead too –
Took me by force, made me be his wife!
All the Trojans were against it. Well then.
Husband. Can you still think it right to kill me?
Could you do such a thing with any justice?
I had no choice. I was raped, not married.
My life in Troy was the most abject slavery,
Nothing glorious about it. And I have destroyed them.
The gods have acted. Will you oppose them?
Only a fool would dare to do that.

CHORUS. Speak up for your children now, Dear Queen,
Speak for your country! Show her arguments for what they
are,
Fluent, but wicked. She's a dangerous woman!

HECUBA. First I shall speak for the goddesses, and expose
This woman's slanders for the rubbish they are!
The gods are not fools. Hera and the Virgin
Pallas would never have perpetrated
Such acts of brainless stupidity. Would Hera
Ever sell her own city of Argos
To the barbarians? Or could Pallas conceivably
Allow Athens to come under foreign domination
Simply for the sake of a game? If they went
To Mount Ida at all, for mere childish amusement,
And the vanity of beautiful women!
Why should Hera so suddenly fall victim
To an insatiable craving to be thought beautiful?
To get a more aristocratic husband
For herself than Zeus? And is Athene
Now on the lookout for a husband among the gods?
Her hatred of marriage is well known, she pleaded
With her father for eternal virginity,
And he granted it. Don't attempt to disguise
Your own wickedness by accusing the Immortals
Of such stupidity. No sensible person
Will be taken in. And Aphrodite herself,

115

You say – this is ludicrous, laughable –
Came with my son to Menelaus' house!
Is it likely? She could have stayed at home
On Olympus, and taken you, the Royal Palace
At Amyclae, the whole lot, to Ilium,
With the merest gesture, if she'd wanted to.
But that wasn't it! My son had the sort
Of good looks women run mad for,
You were wet with lust the moment you saw him!
That was your Aphrodite! And doesn't everyone
Dignify their appetite and stupidity
By invoking the goddess's name, blaming her?
Sensuality and senselessness have more in common
Than a first syllable. The moment you saw him
In his exotic oriental dress
And dripping with gold, you lost your head
Completely. Life in Sparta was austere
By comparison; but once Sparta was behind you
You saw yourself drowning in an ever flowing river
Of Phrygian gold, submerging the whole city
Under a tidal wave of riotous expense!
They were too bleak a stage for you, the bare
Rooms of Menelaus' palace, to overplay
Your fantasies of luxury and indulgence!
And then, my son, you say, dragged you off
By force, that's your version of the story!
Which one of the Spartans saw this happen?
Were there no witnesses? How loudly did you scream?
Your brother Castor was a young man, still alive,
Still living there with his twin, neither of them
Had yet been transformed into heavenly bodies
And taken their places among the stars.
And when you arrived in Troy, with the Greek army
Hot on your heels, and the battles began,
If news reached you that this man's divisions
Had fought a successful engagement, Oh Menelaus,
No praise was too good for him, so that my son
Ran mad with jealousy and despair

That his rival in love had the upper hand.
But if the Trojans won the day, Menelaus,
Pooh, what was he, he was nothing!
Yes, you always kept a very beady eye
On the main chance, you would make sure
You were on the winning side! Loyalty, duty,
Love? Not worth that much to you, any of it!
And as for this story of yours, how desperate
You were to escape, how you lowered yourself
By rope from the city walls, as if we
Kept you here against your will –
Well, how many times, may I ask, were you caught
In the act of hanging yourself, or sharpening
A knife to cut your own throat, things
Any woman of breeding or nobility
Would be expected at least to attempt, if she were truly
Grieving for her former husband? Not you.
I've lost count of the times I said to you,
'Listen, Daughter, you should get out of here.
My sons can find other women
Easily enough. I'll help you to escape
In secret, I'll arrange an escort for you
To the Greek ships, and so we'll make an end
Of this pointless slaughter of Greeks and Trojans.'
But that was not at all the kind of thing
You had in mind. In Alexander's palace
Your most arrogant whim could be indulged,
You loved nothing better than seeing Asiatics
Prostrating themselves at your feet! And how
That mattered to you, how important it made you feel!
And even now, you dare to parade yourself
Like this, wearing make up, your hair brushed,
With your best dress on, brazenly confronting
Your husband in the open air
Under the eye of heaven! You're worthless.
Respectable women spit at you in contempt.
If you had any decency in you at all
You would have come here on your knees in rags,

117

Shaven headed, and shivering with fear,
Prepared to humiliate yourself
With every kind of self abasement and shame
For the wicked things you have done. Menelaus,
You can see what I'm getting at. My arguments
All point the same way. Consummate
The Greek victory by killing your wife!
Death is what she deserves. And other women
Will learn from her example that wives who betray
Their husbands must expect to die for it.

CHORUS. Menelaus, punish your wife in a way
Worthy of the traditions of your family. Rescue
The reputation of Greek womanhood by the nobility of your
revenge!

MENELAUS. Your conclusions are exactly the same as my own,
That this woman left my house of her own free will
To go to bed with a foreigner.
To drag in Aphrodite is a mere smokescreen
Of pretentious self importance! Take her away.
Let her face death in the stoning pit.
You can atone for the ten year suffering of the Greeks
With an hour of dying: or however long it takes.
That'll teach you what it costs to humiliate me.

HELEN. I beg you on my knees, I implore you,
Don't kill because the gods are diseased!

HECUBA. Remember all your friends who are dead, murdered
By this woman! On my knees, I beg you, remember!

MENELAUS. All right old woman, that'll do! I'm not listening
To her. I'm speaking to my staff . . . Take her
To where the ships are moored. We're sending her back
home.

HECUBA. Don't travel in the same ship with her!

MENELAUS. Why? Has she put on weight? Will she sink it?

Sycophantic laughter from MENELAUS' *officers and guards.*

HECUBA. Once a lover, always besotted.

118

MENELAUS. No. A sensible man loves someone worthy of his
love.

    However, I shall do as you say. We won't
Go on board the same ship. A reasonable precaution.
When we arrive in Argos she will be punished
As she deserves. She's a wicked woman,
And she will endure a terrible death
That will be a warning to all women in the future
To be chaste and moral in their behaviour.
That's by no means an easy lesson to teach,
But the manner of her death will terrify
The most frivolous of females, or others who might be
tempted

To be even more degraded than she is.

MENELAUS *gestures sternly to the soldiers, who take* HELEN
*away. Before she leaves she catches his eyes and smiles in
a way that suggests a secretive mockery, even triumph.
Even at a distance she can see the sweat on his temples.
She knows she is safe.*

CHORUS. Oh Zeus, our eyes are open now!
    You have betrayed us to the Greeks – the great
Temple of Ilium, the flames that glow
Eternally on the altar of offerings, the sweet
Pillars of myrhh smoke that rise to heaven,
The incense thick in the air, even
The sanctuary of Pergamon, the sacred mountain
Of Ida, where the melted snow leaps
In torrents down the ivy covered slopes,
And first light flushes the eastern crest of dawn's
handmaiden.

The beauty of ritual is destroyed, all the sacrifices
Are over, no more hushed singing
Of sacred psalms, watch night services,
Vigils from first dark till dawn, no carrying
Of images cast in gold to the festivals

Of the twelve full moons of Troy. A shadow falls
Like ice in my heart. Do you care, on your radiant throne
In the heavens, do you even remember, King of gods,
That we exist, while the very air explodes
Around us, and fire reduces our city to ashes and stone?

Oh my love, my husband, you are dead!
You are out there somewhere – unwashed, unburied
Your poor ghost wanders aimlessly in the dark.
And ships will carry me over the sea,
Their fast oars beating like wings, to the city
Of the horse breeders, Argos, whose great stone walls are
                         the work
Of the Cyclops, and seem to touch the sky.
But our children, a great crowd of them, weep and moan
Down by the gates, clinging desperately to their mothers, all
                         their pain,
Screaming and tears to no avail.
'Mother,' they sob, 'the Greeks will haul
Me away to their black ships, I shall be all
Alone, and the sea-going oars
Will sweep me across to sacred Salamis,
Or to where between two seas the Acropolis
Of Corinth guards Pelops' doors!'

I have one wish: that when Menelaus' ship
Is in the open sea, with a terrifying thunderclap
From the hand of Zeus it will be struck by lightning
Amidships, right between the oars,
And far out in the Aegean! I shall be in tears
Then, exiled from Troy, dehumanised, reduced to a thing
That slaves for the Greeks: while Helen peers
Like a self-regarding schoolgirl in her mirrors of gold
Admiring her good looks. My wish for her's soon told.
Dear gods, let her never come safe home
To Sparta, never repossess that bedroom
In her own house and hearth, never come
Again to the village of Pitana, as once she could,

Nor re-enter Athene's temple with the great bronze door,
This woman whose promiscuity shamed Greece, and stained
                              the pure
Waters of Simois with blood.

The CHORUS *catches sight of the Greek execution party*
bringing back the body of ASTYANAX.

CHORUS. No, no, no more agony!
  Our land is under the whip, the next
  Stroke falls while we still bleed from the last.
  Yes, yes, you may weep, Women of Troy! But the worst
  Is still to come. They are bringing Astyanax' body, cast
  Like a stone by the Greeks from the towers of Troy.

TALTHYBIUS *leads in the execution squad, with* ASTYANAX' *body,*
carried in HECTOR's *battle shield, which is big enough*
to protect a six foot man from shoulder to knee, and
therefore easily carries the little boy. The child is naked,
but for a cloak, which half covers him, put there by one of
the soldiers for decency's sake. The golden-haired boy has
been washed, so that there is no dirt and blood upon him,
and at first sight he seems angelic as he lies there: but
all the hair has been torn from one side of his head by
the impact, and his skull is smashed. TALTHYBIUS *has done*
his best to make him look presentable.

TALTHYBIUS. Hecuba . . . there's only one ship
  Of Neoptolemus' squadron still here. The crew
  Are currently loading his share of the booty
  Before sailing for Phthia. Neoptolemus himself
  Has already set sail, having heard bad news
  From home – his grandfather Peleus, apparently,
  Has been the victim of a military coup,
  Organised by Acastus, the son of Pelias,
  And has had to flee the country. Time
  Is of the essence, so he left at once,
  Taking Andromache with him, whose heartbroken

Tears as she left her native land,
And grief-stricken outbursts over the tomb
Of Hector, brought tears to my eyes too.
She begged the Prince that you should be allowed
To bury the body, the son of your son Hector,
Who gave up his life, as ordered, thrown down
From the walls of Troy. She begged too, that this shield
With its bronze back, which has terrified
The Greeks so many times in the hands
Of the boy's father, when he advanced protecting
The whole of his body behind it, should not
Be sent across the sea to Peleus' house,
Nor stand as a mute reminder in the same chamber
Where the boy's mother, Andromache, to her grief,
Must give herself a second time as a bride,
But be used instead of a coffin and cairn
Of stones, and that the boy should be buried
Lying beneath it. She asked me to make sure
That the body came into your hands, so that you
Could shroud it with some of your own clothes
And garland it with flowers – insofar as you can
In your present difficult circumstances.
She, because of her master's great haste,
Is robbed of the opportunity of burying her child
Herself, and is already gone. We, let me emphasise,
As soon as you have laid out the body,
Buried him, and heaped up the earth on his grave,
Must step the mast, make sail, and away.
So you must do what you have to do
As quickly as possible. One thing
I have done for you. As we came back
Across the Scamander, I took the opportunity
To wash the body, and wipe away
The dirt and blood from his wounds. Well then . . .
I shall now make it my business to dig
A grave for the boy, so that my work will end
As quickly as yours must; and then, with the greatest
Possible expedition, we can all go home.

At a gesture from TALTHYBIUS, *the soldiers bear the shield*
containing ASTYANAX *forward to* HECUBA. TALTHYBIUS, *not*
knowing where to look, and near to tears, looks down at the ground.

HECUBA. Oh, the great arc of Hector's shield! Here,
   Put it on the ground . . . My eyes
   Are stabbed to the brain. I never dreamed
   They would see such a sight. Oh you Greeks,
   You are so proud of yourselves as fighting men
   And thinkers! Are you proud of this too?
   Why him? Were you so frightened of a child
   You had to invent this unheard of savagery?
   Did you think he would rebuild fallen Troy
   From this rubble on his own? You're nothing,
   You're worth nothing, we could all see that
   When Hector was riding his good fortune,
   With ten thousand men fighting at his side,
   Destroying you beneath his spear. But now,
   When the city is taken, and every Trojan
   Fighting man lies dead, you have become terrified
   Of a little child. What cowards you are,
   How I despise blind panic,
   Unreasoning terror in rational men!

TALTHYBIUS *gives a curt order, and the Greek soldiers*
march away.

HECUBA My little darling . . . what a wretched, meaningless
                                   death
   Has been meted out to you! If you had died
   On your feet, defending your city,
   In the full glory of your young manhood,
   Having tasted the pleasures of marriage,
   One of the god-Kings of Troy, everyone
   Would have called you a happy man – if
   Any of these things is worth the name
   Of happiness. But though your child's soul
   May have glimpsed or sensed the glories

You were born to, they have slipped from your grasp.
Before you were old enough to enjoy them.
My poor little boy, how dreadfully your head
Has been shaved by the walls of your own city,
Built by the prophetic god Apollo
For your ancestors. These beautiful curls
Your mother so much loved to stroke and kiss
And bury her face in, torn out, shorn to stubble.
The blood's still oozing from the broken bones
Laughing at us in its mockery of life . . .
No . . . no more of that. It degrades the decency
Of speech to put such things into words . . .
Sweet little hands, the image of your father's,
So limp and lifeless now, mere appendages
Flopping at the end of your arms. And your lips,
So delicious in all their childish chattering,
And now so cold and dead! What lies you told me
When you snuggled down among my bedclothes.
'Grandmother,' you used to say, 'I shall cut
The biggest curl you ever saw from my head
For you when you are dead, and I'll bring
All my friends to your tomb, to make speeches
And sing songs of farewell.' But now,
That promise will never be kept. And I
An old woman, with her city destroyed
And all her own children dead, must bury you,
So much younger than I am, such a tender corpse.
My dear little sweetheart, what use were all
Those cuddles I gave you, the times I nursed you,
Fed you, and got you off to sleep,
All my love wasted when it comes to this,
With you dead in my arms. What memorial verses
Would a poet write to be carved on your tombstone?
'This child was murdered by the Greeks
Because they were afraid of him!' May all Hellas
Forever be ashamed of such an epitaph!
Well, little grandson, everything
You should have inherited from your father you have lost,

Except this shield with its curved bronze back,
And that, my dear, you will keep forever
As it covers you in the earth. Women,
Do you see? This is the shield that protected
Hector's magnificent arm! He for sure
Was this shield's best protector, and now he is dead.
Look, you can clearly see the imprint
Of his powerful hand on the grip, and here
On the brass facing and the smooth rim
You can see how his beard has burnished it
As he held it up to his chin, and where
The sweat, pouring down from his forehead and temples
In so many hot fought afternoons of battle
Has left its dark stain. Come now, my women,
See what you can find, some robe, if you can,
Or some flowers somewhere, to dress his poor body
For burial.

Some of HECUBA's *women go off stage.*

                   It's little enough, child,
We can give you, in this time of disaster.
But what we can find, you shall have. Anyone
Born mortal and living in this world, who thinks
Himself prosperous and secure, is a fool.
Historical necessity, or whatever else you call
The force that governs our lives, what else is it
But a madman dancing, leaping one way then the next
Without pattern or meaning. What's certain
Is that luck always runs out, and that no happy man
Ever stays happy or lucky for long.

HECUBA's *women re-enter, with torn and dusty robes, some
of them of great finery, stripped from the bodies of the
dead, or pulled out from under collapsed rubble. There
are even a few dented chalices and vases, and some broken
jewellery, not worth stealing, and, by a miracle, some
bunches of yesterday morning's flowers, only partly*

smashed by falling ceilings and beams.

CHORUS. Look Hecuba, we found these things among the ruins.
　　They'll do to prepare the body for burial.
HECUBA. Dear child, it's not after some victory
　　At horse racing with fellows your own age,
　　Or archery, that I, your father's mother,
　　Award you these meagre prizes. We Trojans
　　Esteem such achievements, and honour them as they deserve.
　　These poor things are the only remnants
　　Of the legendary wealth of Troy, your inheritance,
　　Of which Helen, whom all the gods hate,
　　Has robbed you. And more than that, she has taken
　　Your life, and utterly destroyed your family.
CHORUS. Let your tears flow!
　　My heart is breaking, weep and sing
　　For the dead child who was born to be King!
HECUBA. This magnificent robe, the height of Trojan fashion!
　　You should have worn it at your wedding
　　To the most aristocratic Princess of Asia.
　　Now I can only use it as a shroud
　　Or winding sheet to wrap round your body.
　　And for you, great shield, who protected Hector
　　Like a mother, and gave birth to victories
　　Beyond number, a garland of flowers.
　　You are not dead, nor will ever be,
　　Though you lie with the dead in the earth: an honour
　　Greater than the Greeks can pay to the armour
　　Of that black-hearted politician, Odysseus!
CHORUS. Howl then, howl!
　　Now, if ever, tear the tears from your breast
　　As the earth receives this child to rest.
　　Mother, you must share our pain.
HECUBA. 　　　　　　　　　　Howl . . .
CHORUS. Lead our song for the dead.
HECUBA 　　　　　　　　For grief!

CHORUS. Who can forget these sufferings? Time will bring no
relief.

HECUBA. With these strips of linen, as if I could heal them
Let me bind up your wounds. The mere shadow of a doctor
Without the substance. My fingers are skilful
But have no art to cure. Your father's hand
Must care for you now, among the dead.

CHORUS. Beat your temples, tear out your hair
Let your nails rake your face like a bank of oars.

HECUBA. My daughters, listen, Women of Troy . . .

CHORUS. We're still here. Say what you want to say.

HECUBA Everything I have done in my life has meant nothing
To the vindictive gods – and Troy, of all cities,
They have persecuted with a particular hatred.
All our sacrifices, all our offerings
Have been quite worthless, a waste of time.
And yet . . . if the god had not decided
To make the greatest suffer most
And trample us all in the mud, what nonentities
We would all have been! No one would ever
Have heard of us, no songs would have been written
In memory of our suffering, nor would the poets
A hundred generations hence have taken us
As their great theme. So take up the body,
And let us bring it to its dishonoured grave.
We have given it all we can of the flowers
And offerings customary for the dead –
And what difference does it make to them
If they are buried in luxury, loaded with gifts.
None at all, I think. Funerals are for the living,
An empty show to impress their friends.

Some of the women slowly take the body of ASTYANAX *on its
decorated shield away for burial.*

CHORUS. Weep and sing
For your suffering mother, who teased out the cloth
Of your life with such care, all torn and rumpled in death.

127

And for the child, a hero's son, no family could be greater
Than his, born to be King.
His terrible death men will remember with horror.
But look. What are they doing?
There are men with torches, will they destroy
Even these ruins? On Ilium's surviving towers
In many hands the bud of flame flowers.
What more can they do to Troy?

TALTHYBIUS *enters with several officers, who carry lighted
torches with them.*

TALTHYBIUS. All company commanders with orders
    To fire the city, there's no need to wait
    Any longer, till your torches burn out
    In your hands. Burn everything down!
    When we have reduced the whole lot to ashes
    Then we can celebrate, leave Troy, and go home!
    My other orders concern you women.
    As soon as you hear the sound of the trumpet
    Follow these officers along that path.
    They will lead you to the Greek ships.
    You, old woman, you're the unluckiest
    Of the lot. You must go too, with these
    Officers of Odysseus' regiment. You must leave
    Your old home. You're designated one of his slaves.
HECUBA. So this is how it ends. My crown of pain,
    All my sufferings, each new loss
    Worse than the last, till it comes to this:
    To leave my homeland, to leave my city,
    To watch them burning it to the ground.
    Come on then, old worn out feet,
    Make one last effort, so that I can say
    My last goodbyes to my poor city
    In its death agony . . .

*She climbs up to a higher part of the ruin, overlooking
the fire.*

HECUBA. Troy! While you lived, you were the greatest
　And most glorious of all the cities of Asia.
　Now they are destroying even your name.
　They are burning you to the ground, and taking us
　Into exile to be slaves. Oh, you gods!
　But why bother to call on them? We called before,
　And they didn't hear us. They ignored our prayers.
　Well then. Why not run into the flames?
　What could be better for me, the Queen
　Of this burning city, than to die in its embrace
　And make its funeral pyre my own!

*She begins to stagger towards the fire, but with a sudden
burst of shouting,* TALTHYBIUS' *officers seize her and stop
her, and* TALTHYBIUS *himself runs across.*

TALTHYBIUS. Poor woman. You've suffered so much
　It's unbalanced you, like an ecstasy of pain.

Almost foaming at the mouth she tries to break away.

TALTHYBIUS. Hang on to her! You need not treat her with
　　　　　　　　　　　　　　　　　　　　　　　kid gloves!
　She belongs to Odysseus now, and your orders
　Are to deliver her personally into his hands.

*She howls like an animal. Awestruck, the soldiers let go of
her and watch her final agony with the* CHORUS.

HECUBA. Howl! Howl! Howl!
　Son of Cronos, god of Troy,
　Father of our fatherland, do you see?
　Dardanus' children don't deserve such a fall!
CHORUS. He sees, and does nothing. Troy, our beautiful city,
　No longer exists. They are burning, burning it all.

HECUBA. Howl! Howl! Howl!
　Troy is burning, every house is in flames

Even the citadel, walls and domes,
The hungry flames are consuming it all!

CHORUS. The black wing of heaven shadows the dying houses
Of the murdered Trojans. Smoke is their funeral pall.

HECUBA. My beloved city, my children's nurse.
CHORUS. Weep louder, weep long.
HECUBA. My children, do you hear your mother's voice?
CHORUS. Cry to the dead. Can they hear your song?
HECUBA. Let me kneel, lay my old legs on the ground,
And my old woman's hands, let them beat the earth!
CHORUS. Let me kneel beside you, let my voice sound
In the dark halls of Hades, the Kingdom of Death!
Husband, can you hear me underground?
HECUBA. Like loot they are stealing us.
CHORUS.   Let the dead hear our pain.
HECUBA. To live in their slave huts, to be a slave.
CHORUS. Home gone, country gone.
HECUBA. Priam, you are dead, but you have no grave,
No friend to weep or keen,
Can you hear my anguished moan?
CHORUS. He hears nothing. The black veil of death
Has darkened his sacred eyes with the desecration of earth.

HECUBA. My beloved country, temples of the gods . . .
CHORUS. Weep louder, weep long.
HECUBA. The fire consumes, and the spear invades.
CHORUS. Soon anonymous earth, like a forgotten song.
HECUBA. A cloud of dust darkens the sky
Like a shadowy wing, blots out my old home.
CHORUS. Soon no one will remember this city,
Everything is dying, even the name;
There is no place on earth called Troy.

*A tremendous sound, part earthquake, part explosion, part
the collapse of a vast building.*

HECUBA. Do you hear that sound?

CHORUS.   Troy has fallen!
HECUBA It's like an earthquake. Everything's shaking!
CHORUS. The city sinks, we all drown!
HECUBA. Into the abyss. My legs are trembling,
    But I won't fall. Old limbs, strengthen
    Yourselves. Your slavery is beginning.

The trumpet call is heard, HECUBA *begins to trudge away
along the path down to the harbour.*

CHORUS. Troy is finished. We must turn our weary feet
    To the harbour. The oars are waiting. March down to the
                                            Achaean fleet!

The CHORUS *follows her out, followed by the Greek guards.
Troy burns.*

HELEN

Characters

HELEN, daughter of Zeus and Leda, wife of Menelaus
TEUCER, a Greek officer, brother of Ajax Telamon
MENELAUS, King of Sparta
CONCIERGE, an old woman keeping the gate at
  Theoclymenus' Palace
A SHIPWRECKED SAILOR, one of Menelaus' crew
THEONOE, sister of Theoclymenus, a prophetess
THEOCLYMENUS, King of Egypt
MESSENGER, one of Theoclymenus' sailors
THE HEAVENLY TWINS, sons of Zeus and Leda, now
  deified
CHORUS, of captured and enslaved Greek women
HUNTSMEN, GUARDS, ATTENDANTS,
  THEOCLYMENUS' RETINUE

We are close to the Royal Palace of THEOCLYMENUS, *King of Egypt, which stands near to the sea shore. The sea is visible in the distance beyond a ridge of sand.*

Near the palace is an ornamental tomb or mausoleum, dedicated to THEOCLYMENUS' father, PROTEUS, the former King. Up some steps, on a platform, and technically in sanctuary, is a rather comfortable mattress, and one or two knick knacks, suggesting someone is camping out.

HELEN, a radiantly beautiful woman in her late thirties, speaks confidingly to the audience.

HELEN. That's the Virgin river, the most beautiful Nile
    Over there: so called because pure melted snow
    Not rain, feeds the stream. It irrigates
    The whole country. It never rains here.
    This is Egypt. Proteus was King –
    While he was still alive, of course –
    And from his palace on the island of Pharos,
    He ruled the whole of the land of Egypt.
    He married Psamathe, who was one of the daughters –
    Of Nereus, the Old Man of the Sea,
    And her upbringing was utterly nautical,
    A life, as you might say, on the Ocean wave.
    She had been married before to Aeacus,
    But he, of course, was dead by then.
    In this very palace she gave birth
    To two children, a son, Theoclymenus –
    His name means 'Honoured by the Gods',
    Though you wouldn't think so from his behaviour –
    And a very noble daughter, doted on by her mother,
    And called, at first, Eido, 'the one who knows'.
    Only when she was grown up they changed her name
    To Theonoe, 'the one who knows
    All about the gods, and the past and the future,
    And pretty well everything there is to know' –
    A talent which she inherited from her grandfather,
    Nereus, I suppose. As for me,

Well, my homeland, Sparta, you will have heard of,
And my father, Tyndareus, too, I'm pretty sure.
There is, in fact, this story about Zeus –
That he had changed himself into a white feathered swan,
And was being chased by an eagle, so flew
Into my mother, as it were, and seized the opportunity,
While she wasn't looking, of taking his pleasure:
Though whether that story makes any sense at all
I don't honestly know. My name is Helen,
And I've had a quite dreadful life
Really, so sad: I must tell you about it.
Three goddesses came to a delightful rustic valley
On Mount Ida, where Alexander was living at the time –
Alexander, you know, was Paris's other name –
And asked him to judge which was the most beautiful,
And so settle the matter once and for all.
These three were Hera, Queen of the gods,
Aphrodite of Cyprus, and Athene the Virgin
Daughter of Zeus, no less! My beauty –
If anything so unlucky could be called beautiful –
Was dangled by Aphrodite as a bait, so that Paris,
If she won, would marry me. Which she did,
Naturally. Paris soon kissed goodbye
To his cattle sheds on Mount Ida, I can tell you,
And came to Sparta, to get into bed
With me, at the earliest possible opportunity.
Hera, of course, was furious that she hadn't won
And put the other goddesses in their place,
So she turned Alexander's relish at having me
In his bed, into thin air – literally.
Because it wasn't in fact me that she gave him at all,
But a walking talking living doll,
A non-existent image made in my likeness
Conjured up out of clouds and mist and things
To deceive King Priam's son. He thought
He was having me, which was the purest fantasy
On his part, because he certainly wasn't!
Zeus was behind the whole thing, of course,

And besides, he had his own plan which slotted neatly
Into all this confusion, and multiplied the mischief,
Which was to create a catastrophic war
Between all the Greek peoples and the unfortunate

                        inhabitants

Of Phrygia. Why? Merely to dispense with
So much superfluous humanity, I suppose,
To rid mother earth of the weight of so many
Useless human beings, and to make the most powerful
Man in Greece – Achilles – world famous.
I was made the sole cause of the war,
Stood up like a prize between the two armies
For the Trojans to defend, and the Greeks to strive for,
Or rather, not me at all, merely
My name, because I simply wasn't there!
But Zeus hadn't forgotten me. I was wrapped up
In a cloud of mist, whipped up to heaven
By Hermes who always does this sort of job
For the gods, and plonked down here, at the palace
Of Proteus, the idea being that he was the purest
And most moral chap of the whole human race,
So he would look after me, and I would be able
To keep Menelaus' bed entirely chaste!
Which is exactly what happened. And here I am,
While my poor dear husband has recruited
A vast army, and sailed all the way
To the topless towers of Troy, in pursuit
Of his supposedly ravished wife! And men
By the thousands, poor things, have died for my sake
On the banks of Scamander; and I, what's more,
Who have had to put up with all this ghastliness
And inconvenience, have become an object
Of universal hatred, who cheated on her husband,
And who personally caused the Great War
Which has overwhelmed all the peoples of Greece!
So why am I still here? Why stay alive?
Well, Hermes told me that I would eventually
Get back to the famous land of Sparta,

And with my husband – when he had realised
That I hadn't been to Troy at all –
So that I need not even consider, as they say,
Opening up the bedclothes to any other man.
Now, while Proteus was still living and breathing
This was no problem, my chastity was in no danger
At all from him! But he, as they say,
Now wears the veil of darkness, and is dressed up
In an overcoat of earth: and his son,
Theoclymenus, is most importunate
In his pursuit of me. I, of course,
Am utterly loyal to my dear husband,
So I have come here, to the tomb of Proteus,
To claim sanctuary, hoping, by this means,
To keep myself safe and pure
For my dear Menelaus: so that even if my name
Is synonymous with everything ghastly and evil
And hated throughout the Greek world,
My body, at least here in Egypt,
Will be pure, and my reputation above suspicion.

TEUCER *enters across the sand dunes. He is an ex-soldier,*
wearing the worn remnants of clothing much patched and
improvised as a result of years spent at sea, and carrying a hunting
bow slung across his shoulders. He sees the palace before
noticing HELEN, *who has withdrawn a little into the*
shadows.

TEUCER. What an impressive building! I wonder who owns it?
  Only a millionaire, or some kind of plutocrat
  Could afford such imposing towers and battlements.

HELEN *emerges into the light, interested.*

TEUCER. Good God!
  I can't believe my eyes! The spitting image
  Of that dreadful woman who ruined me
  And the whole Greek nation, single handed!

May the Gods spit you out like a roll of phlegm,
You must be Helen's double! If it wasn't for the fact
That I'm a stranger here, in a foreign country,
I'd put an arrow in you and finish you off,
You're so exactly like the daughter of Zeus!

He begins to go.

HELEN. My dear fellow . . . whoever you are, don't run

away . . .

And please don't hate *me* because *she* caused trouble.
TEUCER. Well . . . er . . . sorry. Made a mistake. Got angry
Rather more than I should. But the whole of Greece
Hates that woman's guts! Sorry if I was rude.
HELEN. Who are you, where from? What are you doing here?
TEUCER. One of those Greeks I am ma'am, worse luck.
HELEN. Then no wonder you can't stand Helen. Who are you,
Where do you come from, and who's your father?
TEUCER. My name is Teucer. Telamon's my father,
And I was born and bred on the island of Salamis.
HELEN. What are you doing here then, in the valley of the

Nile?

TEUCER. I'm an exile. My fatherland kicked me out.
HELEN. Oh, isn't that sad! Who kicked you out?
TEUCER. My father, Telamon, who should love me the most.
HELEN. Why? You must have done something dreadful.
TEUCER. Ajax, my brother, died at Troy. That's why.
HELEN. How? You didn't kill him did you? With your own

sword?

TEUCER. No, his sword did the job. He fell upon it.
HELEN. Was he mad? No one sane would do such a thing.
TEUCER. Have you ever heard of Achilles, the son of Peleus?
HELEN. I believe he was one of Helen's suitors, wasn't he?
TEUCER. When he died, there was terrific competition for his

armour.

HELEN. So? Why should that cause Ajax any harm?
TEUCER. Someone else won it. So he killed himself.
HELEN. And his suicide has caused your exile?

TEUCER. That's it, in a nutshell. Because I didn't die with him.
TEUCER. So you were on the expedition to the famous town
of Troy!
TEUCER. I was there when she was sacked. Now I've been
sacked too.
HELEN. Has the city been burned down, completely destroyed?
TEUCER. Flattened. You can't even trace the line of the walls.
HELEN. Poor Helen, poor woman! All the Trojans died for you!
TEUCER. Plenty of Greeks too. All that suffering. All her fault.
HELEN. How long ago was Troy destroyed?
TEUCER. There have been seven harvests, since the harvest of
blood.
HELEN. And how long was the siege? How long were you
at Troy?
TEUCER. A long time. Many months. Ten years it dragged
on.
HELEN. And the Spartan woman? Did you really get hold
of her?
TEUCER. Menelaus did. By the hair: last I saw.
HELEN. Did you see the wretched woman? Or are you speaking
secondhand?
TEUCER. I saw her, as clearly as I can see you.
HELEN. But supposing . . . it was all unreal . . . you
imagined it?
TEUCER. Let's talk of something else, not her, do you mind?
HELEN. But you believed what you saw? It wasn't an illusion?
TEUCER. I saw her with my own eyes. I can just see her
now . . .
HELEN. And has Menelaus got back home with his wife?
TEUCER. He has not. Not to Argos, let alone Sparta.
HELEN. Oh how dreadful. That's sad news, for both of them.
TEUCER. Completely disappeared, and her with him, so they
say.
HELEN. But didn't all the Greeks sail home together?
TEUCER. We set sail together. Then a storm scattered
us.
HELEN. Whereabouts? In what part of the sea?
TEUCER. We were just half way across the Aegean.

HELEN. And there's no news of Menelaus arriving anywhere
                                     since then?

TEUCER. No. Everyone in Greece says he's dead.

HELEN. Oh no, don't say that! Is Leda still alive?

TEUCER. Leda? No, Leda's dead. Dead and buried.

HELEN. Not because of Helen's disgrace? Don't say that.

TEUCER. So they say. She hanged herself. With a rope.

HELEN. And Tyndareus' twin sons? Are they alive or dead?

TEUCER. Well, they're dead, and then they're not. There's two
                                 versions of the story.

HELEN. Which is the true one? I could hardly suffer more!

TEUCER. Some say they're gods, now: that they've become twin
                                      stars.

HELEN. That would be splendid! What do the others say?

TEUCER. That their sister's shame drove them to suicide.
  Look, I've had quite enough of this story, I've lived through
                                      it

  Once, and I don't want to sob my heart out again!
  The point of my coming here is to see Theonoe,
  The famous spiritualist and clairvoyante,
  To find out my chances of getting to the island
  Of Cyprus with a fair wind in my sails.
  Perhaps you can help me get an interview with her?
  Apollo told me through his oracle that I
  Would eventually settle there, and name the place
  Salamis, after the island where I was born.

HELEN. You can't possibly miss Cyprus from here.
  But you must cast off immediately, and get away from the
                                    shore
  Before the son of Proteus sees you.
  He's the King here, and at the moment he's out hunting:
  There's nothing he loves better than watching his dogs
  Tear some animal to pieces – ghastly fellow!
  The point is, he can't stand Greeks,
  If he gets his hands on one, he kills him!
  Don't ask me why, I've no idea –
  And if I had I wouldn't waste precious time
  In telling you, because it won't do any good.

TEUCER. Dear lady, nothing in the circumstances
  Could be more to the point than what you've just said.
  May the gods do you a similar good turn
  One of these days . . . You know, you really are
  Extraordinarily like Helen to look at.
  It's quite amazing . . . and so utterly unlike her
  As a person. I hope she rots in hell
  And never comes within a thousand miles
  Of Sparta! But the very best of luck to you!

*He shakes hands with her, and hurries off across the sand
dunes.* HELEN *looks up at the heavens and assumes a tragic
expression, thinking in the circumstances she really ought
to try some sort of choral ode, if only for the sake of form.*

HELEN. Ah, what foundations shall I lay for the great tomb of
                                                       my grief!
  And what songs of misery shall I sing to win first prize for
                                                       keening!
  What mourning Muse shall I invoke, ah, miserable life!
  Oh Gods, Oh men . . .

She runs out of ideas, but fortunately sees the CHORUS
*approaching. This stimulates her invention into a new
rhapsody. The* CHORUS, *who carry baskets of purple washing
with them, initially stand at a distance listening, but
gradually move into the centre for their own verse.*

HELEN. Legendary Sirens, women with wings
  Born from the womb of earth, come
  To help me sing my mournful songs,
  Bring your African flutes to inspire my dumb
  Sorrows, breathe life with your lyres into my numb
  Griefs, so that my lamentations will echo
  Your own, and my singing will be inspired
  By your voices, whose melodies match my sorrow,
  My threnodies for blood! And may Persephone send
  Her funeral music from hell, and accept the honesty

144

Of my tears, and these inadequate songs of grief, offered
To my dead in the dark city of eternity!

CHORUS. By the blue river water, where luxuriant grass
Grows thick and green, I was hanging out
These purple dresses, spreading them across
The tops of the reeds, where the full golden heat
Of the sun would dry them, when I heard a voice like a
shout
Of pain, or rather a miserable wailing
No instrument could ever accompany, like the howl
Of a pack of hunting dogs, or a nymph, shrieking
In agony, till the echoes of her sobbing roll
Across the mountain tops, and her anguished accusing
Of Pan, who raped her, booms through the valleys like a
waterfall:
And then I realised it was my lady, singing.
HELEN. Weep and sing,
Daughters of Greece, kidnapped and enslaved
By foreign pirates! A wandering
Greek sailor has arrived
Bringing tears to add to my tears, and new griefs for my
grieving.

Troy has been destroyed! A firestorm
Has left nothing but ashes. And I
Because of my name must bear the guilt
Of so many dead, so much blood spilt,
All this murder, suffering and agony!
For my mother, Leda, the shame
Of my disgrace made her take a rope
And hang herself. Now my husband has gone,
His endless sea voyage has ended in death.
And my two twin brothers, the flower and the crown,
Castor and Pollux, of their country's hope,
Have vanished into thin air! No longer on the heath
Where the racehorses gallop shall we see them ride,
Or working out on the track, by the reedy riverside!
CHORUS. Howl, oh howl

For Helen, whose brutal destiny
Would make anyone weep, a cruel
Joke of a life, black comedy,
When Zeus in white feathers disguised as a swan, like a bolt
                       from the blue, fell
From the sky, and impregnated your mother!
In one single life there's scarcely a pain
You haven't endured. Your mother's dead,
And the twin sons of Zeus have disappeared –
All the joy and energy of their youth is gone.
You live in exile, probably you will never
Open your eyes in the land of your birth
Again. And in every village in Greece,
And in every street of every town
Rumour blackens your name with the disgrace
Of sharing a barbarian's bed! And now death
Has taken your husband: the seas he travelled have sucked
                       him down.
You will never bring honour to your ancestors' homes
Or see again Spartan Athene, in her temple of burnished
                       bronze.

HELEN. Ah, who was the Trojan who cut down the pine
That began the process that ended in tears
For Troy, and no less for Greece? For Priam's son
Built a ship from those timbers, and manned the oars
With his oily foreigners, and set sail
On his god-cursed voyage to my hearth and home,
My beauty his prize, the fatal
Marriage, whose dowry was total
Disaster for both sides! And Aphrodite came,
Shadowing his footsteps like a murderess
With her treacherous gift of death for the Greeks. Yet her
                       scheme
Came to nothing in the end. It all blew up in her face.

But haughty Hera, from the golden throne
Where she snuggles up to Zeus, sent Hermes

HELEN

The Son of Maia, who moves faster than thought, down
To where I was gaily gathering rose leaves,
Fresh green sprays for Athene, to grace
Her Temple of Bronze, in my pretty apron.
He whipped me up into space
To this god-forsaken place,
And forced the sons of Priam into open,
No, bloodthirsty and unrelenting war with Greece,
And blamed it all on me – so my name is never spoken
On the banks of the Simois without this undeserved disgrace.
CHORUS. Yes, you've had a ghastly time. But we must
Bear life's little troubles, and make the best of them.
HELEN. Life's little troubles! My dear girls.
Is that what you call this millstone my fate
Has hung around my neck? I think
I was born as a dire warning for the whole
Of Humankind, don't you? For instance,
Have you ever heard, in Greece or anywhere else,
Of a woman giving birth to her children
By laying an egg? Because that's the way
My mother, Leda, gave birth to me,
And to my brothers, in the popular version
At least – and what's more, Zeus was our father!
And if this isn't dire warning enough,
The whole of my life and everything that's happened
Most certainly is! It's Hera's fault,
At least half of it. The other main cause,
Is, I'm afraid, my ravishing beauty.
I sometimes wish I could simply have been
Rubbed out, like a drawing, and sketched again
From scratch, in a much uglier version
Instead of this masterpiece. Then, perhaps, the Greeks
Might have forgotten all the bad luck
I bring to everybody and remember nice things
About me, instead of horrible ones.
When a man focuses all his hopes
Upon a single objective, and the gods decide
To smash it to pieces, that's bad enough.

147

He just has to put up with it. But in my case,
Whichever way I turn, I'm surrounded with disaster.
First of all, I've done nothing wrong,
But I have this appalling reputation.
It's bad enough to be a byword for wickedness
When you've actually been wicked, but it's unendurable
To be castigated as a monster, when you haven't.
And then, the gods have spirited me away
From my own country, and dropped me here
Among these dreadful uncultured foreigners,
Without any of my friends. In effect, I'm a slave,
Though I was born free, and of free parents,
Because in this country, as with all barbarians,
Everyone's a slave except one man,
The one at the top! One anchor I've hung on to,
To keep my ship steady through the dreadful weather
Of my life – that some day, my husband
Would come and take me away from all this!
And now, if he's dead, even that little anchor
Has come adrift. My mother's dead too,
And they say I killed her, quite unjustly,
But nevertheless, that's what people say.
My daughter, the whole family's pride
And joy, and my own little darling,
Will be grey before she loses her virginity
At this rate. And my two twin brothers –
Everyone *will* call them Zeus's two lads! –
Have simply ceased to exist! I'm surrounded
With so many disasters, I'm as good as dead,
And might just as well be, though the plain fact is
I am still alive. The worst of it is
That even if I were to return to my homeland,
The Spartans would probably put me in prison,
Assuming me to be that Helen
For whom Menelaus went chasing off
To Troy! If only he were alive
He would recognise me at once, by certain
Private proofs of identity known

Only to the two of us. But as it is,
That will never happen either, because
He's dead. And I might as well be dead.
What have I got to look forward to?
Marriage to some appalling barbarian
Merely to get myself out of this?
Eating gigantic and disgusting dinners
Alone with him every night, and then
Going to bed with him, how loathsome
That would be, and how loathsome
I would become too! Certainly death
Would be better than that. But if I am to do it,
It ought to be done properly, with some style.
Naturally, I won't hang myself. Even slaves
Think that beneath them, and it would be most
Unbecoming to be seen dangling from a beam.
To use a knife would be rather heroic.
But terribly painful. What a ghastly situation
To find oneself in! It's most unfair.
For other women their beauty is an asset
That gets them everything they could wish for.
It's no blessing for me. It's an utter catastrophe!

CHORUS. Helen, the man who was here, the stranger,
Don't assume every word he said was true.

HELEN. He told me quite plainly that my husband was dead.

CHORUS. Plain words can sometimes be plain lies.

HELEN. But more often they tell the plain truth.

CHORUS. You're assuming the worst. It may never happen!

HELEN. I'm in such a panic now, I'm sure it will.

CHORUS. What's your situation in the palace? Are they friendly?

HELEN. Dear friends. Except the one who pesters me with
marriage.

CHORUS. Then I'll tell you what to do. Leave your sanctuary at
the tomb.

HELEN. What kind of advice do you call that?

CHORUS. And go into the house. The woman who's psychic,
You know, the daughter of the sea-nymph,
What's her name, Theonoe, ask her

149

Whether your husband's still alive
Or has given up daylight for good. Once
You know that for certain, then you can celebrate
Or cry your eyes out accordingly.
But what's the point of making a fuss
Before you know, one way or the other? Just listen,
And trust me for a moment. Come away from the tomb
And go and see the woman at least!
Inside that house you have the means to find out
The whole truth of the matter. Why look any further?
Look, I'll come in with you if you like,
We'll ask her together to use her psychic powers
To reveal what the spirit world says about it.
We women should stick together. Shouldn't we girls!

A great cry of 'yes' from the CHORUS, *as the music begins,
and we move into a parody of a traditional tragic choral
dialogue.*

HELEN. My darlings, you're absolutely right,
  I'll do what you say – go quickly, straight
  Into the house, to learn my fate,
  Whether to laugh or cry!
CHORUS. We're eager to help, every possible way!
HELEN. I warn you, I might die
  If the news is bad! Think what she might say!
  This could be a dreadful, appalling day!
CHORUS. Why anticipate pain before it hurts,
  Or weep buckets before the crying starts?
HELEN. My poor husband! If I knew what they were I'd cry
  For the horrors you have had to face.
  Do you see the light of day,
  The sun's chariot crossing the sky,
  Or the stars in their endless journey through space?
  Or do you sleep with the dead for eternity?
CHORUS. Why not hope for the best? It's certainly the case
  That the future will happen. Accept it with good grace.

HELEN. Oh River Eurotas, oh water, green reeds,
  Be my witness, what I shall do
  If this rumour is true
  Of my husband's death, mark my words, oh weeds!
CHORUS. I don't know what she's talking about, do you?
HELEN. Yes, with such joy I shall swing
  By the neck, choking
  On a rope, or with a heroic thrust
  Of a lethal sword the blood will burst
  From the gash where I've cut my throat, the cold knife
  Plunging deep into my life,
  As a sacrifice to those goddesses, the gang of three,
  And dear Paris on Ida in his cave by the cattle shed,
                            thinking of me!
CHORUS. May you never again pull the shortest straw,
  It's time you had some luck of the draw.
HELEN. Yes, and don't forget Troy!
  Wiped from the face of the earth to pay for crimes
  That were never committed, a tissue of dreams
  And illusions! What horrors you suffered, what savagery!
  What bloodshed, how many tears, has Aphrodite
  Inflicted on you by the glorious gift
  Of my legendary beauty!
  Pains redoubled, tears multiplied, suffering
  Beyond computation, weeping
  Mothers desperately seeking
  For lost children, sisters bereft
  Of reason, kneeling with shaven head
  Dedicating their curls to their brothers dead
  By the banks of the rolling river Scamander!
  And Greece just the same, what a cry of pain, like a
                            communal scream
  Rose up from her, a great national shudder
  Of weeping and beating of heads, fingernails that gleam
  With fresh blood from scratched cheeks, and all that
  Simply because of me! Arcadian Callisto was lucky,
  She went down on all fours as a shaggy
  Bear to pleasure Zeus. How very much nicer

To be long haired and wild eyed and fierce, than what happened
to my poor mother!
And Merops' girl by the Titan was changed to a deer and
kicked out
Of Artemis' dance troupe, that's all! But my beauty brings
despair
To the Towers of Troy, and death to the Greeks. It's
horribly unfair!

Feeling very hard done by, and on the point of tears, HELEN *leads the* CHORUS *into the palace.*

After a few seconds, MENELAUS *peeps nervously over the sand dunes. He is an appalling mess, dressed only in a fragment of sail which he has lashed crudely around his body, and covered in seaweed, etc.*

MENELAUS. Oh Grandfather Pelops, the winner
  Of that famous chariot race against Oneomaus
  At Olympia, when your father brought you
  To the great dinner party he gave for the gods –
  As the main course – it's a pity
  You didn't end your life there and then,
  On the gods' tablecloth before ever begetting
  My father Atreus, who subsequently,
  In Aerope's bed, sired Agamemnon
  And me – Menelaus – international superstars
  Both of us, of course – that goes without saying.
  In fact – I say this without boasting –
  I think I commanded by far the larger
  Part of the Greek Expeditionary Force
  That sailed to Troy: and I, let me say,
  Was no dictator either. The young men from Greece
  Who sailed under my command, sailed willingly.
  It isn't possible to be precise about numbers –
  Some of them, of course, are dead now,
  But some, most fortunately, have survived the sea voyage

And made it back home, bringing with them
The names and effects of their comrades who died.
I, on the other hand, ever since I sacked
The Towers of Troy, have suffered appallingly
In my never ending voyage across the long rollers
Of the grey wastes of the ocean. No one
Could more earnestly desire to get home than I do.
But the gods, apparently, think me unworthy
Of this simple favour! I must have landed
On every single desolate beach
In Africa by now! But every time
I get anywhere near my beloved country,
The damned wind changes, and blows me back again!
I have never once had a following wind
Filling my sails enough to get home,
Never once! And now, to crown it all,
I'm bloody well shipwrecked, some of my friends
Are drowned, and I'm washed up here, wherever
It is. My ship hit the rocks, and is now
Battered into a thousand pieces.
By the greatest good luck I managed to escape –
Just – by hanging onto the keel –
A beautifully crafted bit of shipbuilding, incidentally,
Which broke free from the rest; – and Helen too,
Whom I dragged away with me from the sack of Troy.
I haven't the slightest idea what this country is called,
What sort of place it is, or who lives here.
I was far too embarrassed to find people
And ask them, dressed like this!
When one looks such a mess, one ought to try
To keep decently out of sight. A chap
Like me, of the very best family
And proud of his breeding, feels poverty
Far more than the poor do, I'm quite convinced,
Because they're used to it, and I'm not!
I am, in fact, in somewhat of a state.
There's no sign of any food anywhere,
Nor anything decent to wear. That much

Is perfectly obvious from my present attire,
All I could salvage from the wreckage. Normally
I wear the most resplendent clothes, marvellous cloaks,
All top quality stuff; but the sea,
Unfortunately, has swallowed the lot!
I hid the woman who started all the trouble
In a cleft in the rock deep inside a cave
Before coming here, and ordered my friends,
The ones who survived, to keep a very sharp eye
On her there. I came here alone, scouting
To see if I can somehow find
The necessities all my poor chaps need.
As soon as I saw this house, complete
With battlemented walls and magnificent roof,
And that splendid gate that clearly indicates
A man of some wealth, I decided to come closer.
Shipwrecked sailors might reasonably expect
To get something at least from a rich man.
No point in asking a pauper. People
With nothing, give nothing, however willing.

He hammers on the gate.

Hallo there! Is there a porter? Come out
And tell the people inside I need help!

The CONCIERGE *appears, a terrifying, grey haired, grim-faced
old woman.*

CONCIERGE. Who's that at the door? Be off with you, go on,
   We don't want your sort hanging about at the gate
   Making a nuisance of yourself to the master.
   Are you a Greek? If you are, they'll kill you.
   We don't have nothing to do with no Greeks here!
MENELAUS. Now look here old woman, you don't need to be
                                                    rude.
   I'll do what you say by all means, but abuse . . .
CONCIERGE. You get out then! I'm just doing my job, I am,

Stranger, we don't want no Greeks round here!

MENELAUS. Hey, you don't have to push me, do you! Stop
shoving!

CONCIERGE. It's your fault if you won't go when I tell you.

MENELAUS. Now listen my good woman, tell your master from
me . . .

CONCIERGE. He won't want to know you. Not when I've said
my say. . . !

MENELAUS. I'm a stranger, I've been shipwrecked. You have an
obligation to help me!

CONCIERGE. You can tell them all about it at some other
house . . .

MENELAUS. No, I'm coming in here . . . ! Now, just listen to
me. . . !

CONCIERGE. You're a bloody nuisance! I'll have you thrown out!

MENELAUS. God, my glorious army, if I only had them
here. . . !

CONCIERGE. You may be somebody there, but here you're a
nobody.

MENELAUS. Dear gods, how outrageous to treat *me* like this!

CONCIERGE. No good you making a fuss, it don't impress
me.

MENELAUS. I was powerful and famous! Where's it all gone?

CONCEIRGE. Cry your eyes out to your friends then, tell them
all about it.

MENELAUS. What country is this? Whose is the Royal Palace?

CONCIERGE. It's Proteus' house. And the country is Egypt.

MENELAUS. Egypt! Oh my God. What a place to end up in!

CONCIERGE. What's wrong with Egypt then? Don't you like our
lovely Nile?

MENELAUS. No, no, the Nile is fine. It's my bad luck I'm
complaining about.

CONCIERGE. Lots of people are unlucky. You're not the only
one.

MENELAUS. The fellow you called your master. Is he at home?

CONCIERGE. He's in there. In that tomb. His son is King now.

MENELAUS. And where might he be? Out somewhere? Or at
home?

CONCIERGE. No, he's not at home. And he hates all Greeks.

MENELAUS. Doesn't affect me, not at all! Why does he hate
                                             Greeks?

CONCIERGE. Because of Helen, Zeus' daughter. She lives in
                                         the palace.

MENELAUS. I beg your pardon. . . ? Would you say that again?

CONCIERGE. The Tyndareus girl. Her from Sparta.

MENELAUS. Where did she come from? I don't understand you.

CONCIERGE. From Sparta of course. From there, to here.

MENELAUS. When. . . ? My wife? They can't have grabbed her
                                      from the cave . . .

CONCIERGE. It was before the Greeks went to Troy. Now,
                                          stranger,
You can get lost. We've got troubles at the moment
Inside the palace, and anything could happen.
You've come at the wrong time, and if his lordship
Finds you, the only hospitality
You're likely to get from him will be death.
Now me, personally, I like Greeks,
In spite of that mouthful I give you just now.
But I'm scared of *him*. Have to do what I'm told.

She snaps her door shut and goes in.

MENELAUS. I don't know what to think, or what to say.
It really is too much, if what she says is true.
After everything I've had to put up with,
To have to cope with another disaster –
Like bringing my wife under arrest from Troy,
Shutting her up safe in a cave, and then finding
Some other woman with exactly the same name
Living in this palace! And that old crone said
She was born the daughter of Zeus! Is it possible
That there's some chap by the name of Zeus living here
On the banks of the Nile? No, of course it isn't!
There's only one Zeus, and he lives in Heaven.
And then, she said Sparta! Where on earth can that be
Except on the banks of the river Eurotas

By all those famously beautiful reed beds!
And there's only one Tyndareus, as far as I know.
Is there another land called Lacedaemon,
And another city called Troy? Well,
I don't know what to think about that.
Certainly the world's a big place, there's lots
Of people in it, and a good many of them
Have the same names. Two cities *can* be called
By the same name, and so can two women.
Nothing amazing or out of the ordinary
In that, is there! And I certainly won't
Run away from a slave, just because she's aggressive
And tries to frighten me. There can be no one so provincial
And out of touch as to refuse *me* food
When he hears my name! The great fire of Troy
Is famous everywhere, and so am I,
The fellow who lit it! Menelaus!
Not unknown, that name, everyone in the world
Has heard of me! So I must simply wait
For the master of the house to come back home.
There are two available tactics, both reasonably safe.
If, on the one hand, he's a dreadful brute,
I can keep out of sight, and creep back to the wreck.
But if he looks like he might be a wimp,
I'll ask him, quite openly, to give me what I need
In my present unfortunate situation.
Nothing can be more humiliating
For people who are broke or starving
Than to have to go down on their knees and beg
The bare necessities of life from powerful people,
And especially when you're a King, like I am!
But needs must, as they say. There's no motive
Stronger than necessity. I didn't say that,
I mean, it's not original. But it's profoundly true!

The CHORUS *re-enters quickly from the palace, full of news.*
MENELAUS *dodges down for a moment behind a palm
tree.*

CHORUS. I have heard the psychic virgin speak
   Here in the house, and she clearly revealed
   That Menelaus has not yet entered the dark
   Passages of hell, where black
   Lanterns cast shadows on the dead underground!
   But still, exhausted and sick at heart
   He tramps the salt ocean, and has never returned
   To the harbours of his homeland! In this lonely state
   Without friends, and depressed by his journey
   That never ends, he has landed on every coast
   In the world since leaving Troy,
   And never strayed far from his ship, but raised the mast
   Dipped oars and rowed away!

Re-enter HELEN, *distinctly cheerful.*

HELEN. Well, here I am, back again!
   And now that I've heard such encouraging news
   From Theonoe, who knows the truth
   About absolutely everything, I shall return
   To the safety of my mattress at the tomb!
   She says that my husband's still alive,
   Above the ground in the daylight and enjoying the sun,
   But wandering about here and there and everywhere
   Sailing to the most unlikely places, and by now
   Worn out, and thoroughly fed up with
   The life of a kind of nautical tramp:
   And that when this aimless existence is over
   He will, finally, come back to me.
   What she didn't tell me, however,
   Is if he'll be safe when he gets here. And I
   Was far too nervous actually to ask her
   In so many words. I was relieved enough
   To hear at least that he's not dead yet!
   She also said, intriguingly, that he's not far away
   From here, shipwrecked and cast ashore
   With a few friends! Dear Menelaus,

I do hope you'll come soon. I long for you!
It really has been an awfully long time. . . !

She sees MENELAUS *peeping from behind his tree, not sure if
he can believe his eyes.*

Hallo, who's that? I hope this isn't
Some tactic of Proteus' son. He's utterly
Without religion or morality, and perfectly capable
Of setting a trap to seize me by force.
Perhaps I should run elegantly back to the tomb
Like a champion filly and hang on tight?
Or howl in ecstasy like one of Bacchus' groupies?
Whoever he is, he's keeping an eye on me.
My God, what a slob! He's utterly uncouth!
MENELAUS. Hey, you. . . !

*All long hair, seaweed and sailcoth, he comes out from
behind the tree towards her, between her and the tomb, but
after a little feinting back and forth she manages to get
past him and back to the tomb.*

MENELAUS.   Now that you've managed to reach
The bottom steps of the tomb, there's no need to hang on
To those soot stained pillars like that. Stay there
If you like. But don't run away . . . Good heavens,
Now I can see you properly, I'm speechless!
HELEN. Help, sisters, I'm about to be raped, this man
Is trying to drag me out of sanctuary
To force me to marry his master, the tyrant
I came here to escape from in the first place!
MENELAUS. No I'm not, I haven't touched you! And I'm
nobody's thug!
HELEN. Only a savage would dress so appallingly!
MENELAUS. There's no need to panic, so don't run away . . .
HELEN. I won't run. But I'll hang on tight to this tomb.

He comes close and peers into her face.

MENELAUS. Who are you madam? I'm sure I know that face.

HELEN. And who are you? I could ask the same question.

MENELAUS. I never saw anyone so exactly alike . . .

HELEN. Oh you gods! Recognition's your greatest gift. . . !

MENELAUS. Are you a Greek woman? Or were you born here?

HELEN. I'm Greek. What about you? Where do you come from?

MENELAUS. You know, you do look exactly like Helen.

HELEN. And you, like Menelaus. I don't know what to say.

MENELAUS. But I *am* Menelaus! You're right! I've been through
hell!

HELEN. Darling, at last! Come to your wife's arms!

MENELAUS. Wife? What wife? Take your hands off my clothes!

HELEN. The wife my father Tyndareus gave you.

MENELAUS. Queen Hecate of the nightmares, is this some
dream of yours?

HELEN. Oh no, I'm no dream: and certainly not a nightmare.

MENELAUS. There's just one of me, I can't be two women's
husband.

HELEN. So who is this other wife that you've married?

MENELAUS. Her in the cave! The one I'm bringing from Troy!

HELEN. You have no other wife except me!

MENELAUS. I don't think I'm mad. I must be seeing things!

HELEN. Now look at me! Don't you *feel* I'm your wife?

MENELAUS. Physically, you're her double. It's uncanny. I'm
baffled!

HELEN. Is anything missing? You ought to know.

MENELAUS. I can't deny it. You're exactly like her!

HELEN. What evidence do you need, beyond your own eyes?

MENELAUS. The trouble is . . . I have another wife.

HELEN. I didn't go to Troy. She was a phantom!

MENELAUS. A phantom? Who makes phantoms with such living
bodies?

HELEN. The gods. From thin air. Which is what she was made
of.

MENELAUS. What god could do that! Really, it's ridiculous!

HELEN. Hera, as my stand in. So that Paris shouldn't have me.

MENELAUS. So how come you were here, *and* at Troy?

HELEN. My name can go anywhere: but not my body!

MENELAUS. Hands off! I'm in enough trouble already.
HELEN. Could you possibly leave me, for an imitation wife?
MENELAUS. Oh yes! You're *exactly* like Helen! Excuse me. . . !
HELEN. Oh how ghastly, I've only just got you back and you're
                              going!
MENELAUS. If my sufferings at Troy were real, you can't be!
HELEN. Oh my God, how dreadful! What woman could possibly
   Suffer more than I do! My darling walks out on me,
   And I shall never see a Greek again, or my home!

Another shipwrecked SAILOR, *pretty near as ragged and*
desperate as MENELAUS, *staggers across the sand dunes.*

SAILOR. Menelaus! At last! I've been looking for you
   All over the place, had a hell of a job
   Finding you in this god-forsaken country!
   The others, your shipmates, sent me to search.
MENELAUS. Why? Have these damned foreigners tried to rob
                               you?
SAILOR. It's a miracle! There's no words to describe what
                           happened.
MENENLAUS. Well say something! It must be, to need all this
                             fuss!
MESSENGER Everything you've suffered, it was all for nothing!
MENELAUS. I know *that*! That's history! Tell me something
                             new.
SAILOR. She's gone! Your wife! Just rose up and evaporated
   Into some fold or crease in the atmosphere!
   Conpletely vanished! She must be hiding somewhere
   Up there, in the sky! She's certainly left
   That weird cave with the eerie atmosphere
   Where we were guarding her. Just before she went
   She said, 'Oh, those poor Phrygians, and all
   The poor Achaeans too, who kept on dying
   On the banks of the Scamander because of me
   Through the machinations of Hera! You all thought
   That Paris had taken possession of me, and moved in,
   But he hadn't at all! And I, having achieved

What I was created for, have stayed long enough,
And must now return to my natural element,
Thin air! And that poor daughter of Tyndareus,
Has acquired her dreadful reputation
For no reason at all! She's completely innocent!'

He turns to impress everyone with this statement, and sees
HELEN *standing in front of him.*

Oh. Hallo, Daughter of Leda.
So here you are, after all. And I've just been telling
Everyone you've been launched into orbit
In one of the remoter constellations of the stars.
That levitation trick of yours was jolly clever.
I didn't know you could do that sort of thing.
But we've had more than enough of your games by now,
We don't want a second helping, thank you!
Your husband and his comrades had quite enough trouble
From you, when we were all at Troy.
MENELAUS. But that's exactly what *she* said! Her story fits
                                                          yours
Exactly. So it *must* be true! This is the day
I've waited for so long, when I hold you in my arms.

*What follows is a kind of love duet, very much what you
would expect from Tosca and Cavaradossi, or Violetta and Alfredo.
The two actors are not singing, but they might just as well be.*

HELEN. Menelaus, my dearest! I've waited so long, but this
    Is my moment of joy!
    My darlings, my husband is in my arms!
    Once again, my embrace
    Enfolds him. After so many dreams
    And sunless mornings, this is my sunlit day!
MENELAUS. And my wife is in mine! With a story like this,
    Where can I begin, at such a moment of bliss?
HELEN. This feels wonderful! My hair's standing on end,
    My eyes are overflowing with tears!

162

How wonderful it feels
To throw your arms right round
Your husband's back, and squeeze!

MENELAUS. You look as marvellous as ever! I don't care what
you've done,
You're my wife, Daughter of Leda and Zeus, and you're
all mine!

Your brothers on white horses by torchlight
Blessed and enriched our wedding night
So long ago. Then the gods robbed my home of its prize!
But now the same immortal power drives
Us both from this happy day
To even greater happiness!
Evil mysteriously
Becomes good, and has brought us together!
We waited so long, but finally
Our bad luck changed. Now may the gods bless
Me with my dear wife's love forever!

CHORUS. May the gods bless you both! I'll join you in that
prayer,
Neither one has suffered more nor less than the other!

HELEN. Dear ones, my friends,
The past is over, sorrow ends,
The tears and the pain are gone.
My beloved is mine, is mine,
And in my arms. All the long years
I have waited for him, and waited
For the return from Troy, so long expected!

MENELAUS. Yes, yes, I'm yours, and you are mine. Confusion,
And years of agony, before I saw through the goddess's
illusion!

These tears are tears of happiness,
I'm crying for joy, not depression
At the years of pain and bitterness,
Those tedious years at Troy, when I believed
That I, of all men, was the most deceived!

HELEN. What can I say? What mortal could ever have hoped
For the bliss of this unexpected embrace?

MENELAUS. I feel just the same! It seemed I had lost you for
ever,
  To the shadows of Mount Ida, and the gloomy battlements
of Troy.
  Tell me, for God's sake, how were you spirited away?

HELEN. Ah no, you touch the beginning of my disgrace!
  Ah no, so bitter to tell, or even remember!

MENELAUS. If it's the gods'. work, you must tell it, I must
hear it all!

HELEN. The words stick in my throat:
  To speak them would be too awful!

MENELAUS. Oh please! Other people's tragedies are a source of
endless delight!

HELEN. It was no throbbing lust
  For strong young limbs in the marriage bed
  Of a sexy barbarian, nor the powerful thrust
  Of banks of oars that sped
  Me towards adultery so fast.

MENELAUS. It wasn't? Then what god or fate plundered my
home?

HELEN. None other than Zeus' own son,
  Hermes the deliverer, who brought me to the stream
  Of the Nile, and left me here alone!

MENELAUS. Unbelievable! Who sent him? What an utterly
frightful story!

HELEN. Oh, how I cried at that time,
  And those tears are still flowing today!
  The consort of Zeus, the sublime
  Hera, is my enemy!

MENELAUS. Hera? But what on earth have we done to anger
her?

HELEN. Ah God, that crystalline spring,
  That glittering bath, remember,
  Where three goddesses to adorn their loveliness, striving
  To be ever more lovely, came together
  To Paris, for the fatal judging!

MENELAUS. I don't understand. Why should Hera, for that
judgement, punish you?

HELEN. To rob Paris of his prize!
MENELAUS.   How? I haven't a clue.
HELEN. Me, promised by Aphrodite!
MENELAUS.   My poor darling! Is that true?
HELEN. Poor me indeed! Dumped in Egypt that way!
MENELAUS. And that's when phantom Helen took your place,
                                        you say?
HELEN. But, ah God, at home, what suffering
  My poor mother had to endure,
  What pain!
MENELAUS.   I don't understand a thing!
HELEN. My mother is dead! She's gone forever!
  My shame tied the noose for her hanging!
MENELAUS. And our daughter, poor Hermione, what's happened
                                        to her?
HELEN. No marriage, no children, don't ask! Husbandless,
  She blames my marriage that was no marriage for her
                                        distress.
MENELAUS. Paris, you destroyed my family, ransacked my
                                        home!
  Now you are destroyed in turn,
  And an army of bronze-clad Greeks shares your funeral urn.
HELEN. And I have been driven from my homeland,
  Cursed by bad luck, and the curse
  Of the goddess – what could be worse?
  Deprived of both city and husband,
  Because I left – but of course, I didn't leave
  At all, it isn't true – my marriage bed
  For a sordid foreign adventure, and an adulterous love!

The love duet comes to an end.

CHORUS. If the future is going to be as happy as this,
  It will make up for all the sufferings of the past!
SAILOR. Menelaus. I'd be glad to join in your rejoicing
  If I understood a word of it. But I don't.
MENELAUS. My dear old chap, of course! We'll share the whole
                                        story!

SAILOR. Didn't this one cause all the trouble at Troy?
MENELAUS. In fact, no, she didn't. The gods deceived me.
  The woman I embraced was a ghost, made of . . . clouds.
SAILOR. What! Are you telling me
  We suffered all that agony for the sake of a cloud?
MENELAUS. Actually, it was Hera's fault. Those goddesses!
                                                    Jealousy!
SAILOR. And this one is a real one. Your actual wife.
MENELAUS. Yes, this one. Definitely. You can take my word for
                                                          it.
SAILOR. Well, young lady, gods are crafty devils
  By nature, so that it's difficult to know
  What they're doing half the time. It's amazing
  How suddenly they turn everything upside down
  And inside out, so that the whole situation
  Is quite different from what you thought it was.
  One man has a hard life, slaves away for years,
  And another does nothing but laze about,
  But then, he dies a horrible death! So there you are!
  You can never tell from one day to the next
  What's going to happen. And good luck never lasts.
  Now, you and your husband, for instance, you've both
  Had your share of troubles, you with your reputation
  Being so terrible, and him, non-stop fighting.
  And what did he get for it, from all those battles?
  He got nothing! And now, when he's more or less
  Given up hoping for anything but survival,
  He suddenly gets the most amazing piece of luck!
  So. You didn't disgrace your old father
  And the heavenly twins after all then, eh?
  And all those things people gossip about,
  It turns out you didn't do any of them. Well!
  I'll tell you one thing. I'll never forget
  Your wedding night, me running alongside
  The four in hand, carrying the wedding torches
  Flaming in my fists! And you up there
  With this chap, in a chariot made for two,
  As you drove away together from your father's mansion

As his wife! It's no sort of a fellow
Who isn't involved in his master's business,
Sharing his happiness in the good times,
And his misery in the bad. I was born a slave,
But I don't have a slave's mentality, I'm conscious
Of my own dignity, and although technically
I can't call myself free, in my mind
I think myself as free as the next man.
That's the best way, otherwise you suffer
Twice over, feeling a slave in your heart
As well as actually being one, someone else's property.

MENELAUS. My dear old comrade, you've had some hard times
Doing your bit for me in the war,
So now, take your share of my good luck too!
You go back to all our friends who were left behind,
And tell them how things stand here, and how
The situation's turned in our favour. Tell them
To stay there on the shore, in a state of readiness,
Because I expect some trouble here, and may well
Have to fight my way out: and that in case
I can work out some method of smuggling my wife
Out of this country, they must stay on their guard,
So that we can combine our forces, and save
Ourselves, if possible, from these uncivilised people.

SAILOR. I'll do just what you say sir . . .

*He begins to walk away, then turns back, almost without
any pause.*

                                        You know, I've been thinking
About this whole business of prophecy,
What a load of rubbish it is! A pack of lies,
The whole lot of it! All that palaver
About the flames from burning meat,
And the meaning of bird cries in flight, there was nothing
In any of that. And frankly, you must be
Simple minded to think that birds
Can help men do or understand anything!

Calchas, for instance. He didn't say,
He didn't even hint, that he understood
That all our friends were giving up their lives
For the sake of a cloud, did he? And neither
Did Helenus say anything of the sort to the Trojans.
But a whole city was put to the sword, and sacked,
For nothing. You could say, I suppose, that the gods
Didn't want us to know what was going on.
But in that case, what use are priests,
Or any of those future-mongers? You might just as well
Say your prayers to the gods, and hope for the best,
And leave all fortune telling out of it.
If you ask me, it's all a con,
Thought up to make money out of gullible people.
No one lazy ever got rich
By burning animals. Intelligence
And common sense forecast the future
Better than any prophet can.

CHORUS. I'm inclined to agree with this old man.
However, a person who has the gods on his side,
Has the best possible insurance policy for the future!

HELEN *hurries the* SAILOR *out.*

HELEN. Yes, well that's enough of all that. So far
Everything's going well. But you must tell me
How you survived, and all your troubles and tribulations
Since you left Troy. Of course, it's pointless,
I know, but, darling, people in love
Adore to know all their lover's sufferings!

MENELAUS. That really is a whole lot of questions
Rolled into one! What's the point of telling you
About all the shipwrecks in the Aegean, and how Nauplius
Lit the beacons on Euboea? No point in describing
Crete, and all the cities in North Africa
Where my ship cast anchor, or the watch tower
Perseus built at the Delta of the Nile.
No point at all. You wouldn't find my stories

At all satisfying: and if I were to tell you
All you want to know, telling it would be like
Living it all over again, I'd be worn out
With suffering and pain twice over!

HELEN. Of course, you're right! My question was silly.
Just tell me one thing. How long were you wandering
On the bumpy back of the salty sea?

MENELAUS. On board ship – as well as the ten years at Troy –
I've seen seven years come and go.

HELEN. What a long time. My poor darling, how dreary for
you!
You escaped all that, and now you face death here!

MENELAUS. What? What are you talking about? You'll be the
ruin of me!

HELEN. He'll kill you, the man who owns this place.

MENELAUS. Why? What have I done to deserve such a thing?

HELEN. You've arrived. Unexpectedly. It'll stop him marrying
me.

MENELAUS. You mean, someone wants to marry my wife?

HELEN. He's prepared to use force. But I've stood up to him,
so far!

MENELAUS. Is he a man with some influence. . . ? Or is he
the King?

HELEN. He's the King, of the whole country. The son of
Proteus.

MENELAUS. That old door woman's riddles suddenly make
sense.

HELEN. What door woman? Did you knock at somebody's
door? Which one?

MENELAUS. This one, and she kicked me out like a beggar!

HELEN. Oh my God! You weren't begging, were you? Asking
for food?

MENELAUS. Well, yes, I was, actually. I didn't *say* I was a
beggar.

HELEN. Then you must know all about my prospective marriage?

MENELAUS. Yes. What I don't know, is if it's been
consummated.

HELEN. Of course not! I've kept myself quite pure. For you!

MENELAUS. I'm very glad to hear it. Have you got any
                                                    proof. . . ?
HELEN. Proof! Look, I've been camping out at this tomb!
MENELAUS. I can see an old mattress. What's that got to do
                                                    with it?
HELEN. *I've* been begging too: to escape this ghastly marriage!
MENELAUS. There's no proper altar. Do the Egyptians worship
                                                    tombs?
HELEN. Yes. I'm protected here as much as in any temple.
MENELAUS. So you mean . . . I can't take you in a ship back
                                                    home?
HELEN. They won't let you touch me. They'll stick a sword in
                                                    your guts!
MENELAUS. That would be ghastly. Dreadfully bad luck!
HELEN. So, don't be ashamed, leave the country, fast!
MENELAUS. Leave you! I destroyed Troy for your sake!
HELEN. Better to go than to stay with me and die.
MENELAUS. No, that's cowards' talk. I'm the man who took
                                                    Troy!
HELEN. You can't kill this King, if that's what you're thinking.
MENELAUS. Why? Is his flesh too tough for cold steel?
HELEN. You'll find out. Wise men don't attempt the impossible.
MENELAUS. So, what shall I do then? Hold my hands out for
                                                    the rope?
HELEN. We're in a tight corner. We must think of some way
                                                    out.
MENELAUS. I would rather die in action than sit and do
                                                    nothing.
HELEN. There's a glimmer of hope . . . just one . . . that might
                                                    save us.
MENELAUS. Is it bribery? Or bravery? Or persuasion?
HELEN. If the King never knows you've come here at all. . . ?
MENELAUS. Who'll tell him I have? He won't know who I am.
HELEN. He has an ally in there, knows as much as a god.
MENELAUS. What, an oracle? A voice from a dark corner?
HELEN. No, his sister. But her name's Theonoe.
MENELAUS. Good name for an oracle! What does she
                                                    do?

170

HELEN. She knows absolutely everything. She'll tell her brother
you're here.

MENELAUS. That means I can't hide. And we'll both be killed!

HELEN. I suppose we might persuade her, if we both begged
her help . . .

MENELAUS. Persuade her about what? Don't delude me with
false hopes.

HELEN. I told you. Not to tell her brother we're here.

MENELAUS. If we could persuade her, it's off, across the border!

HELEN. If she agrees, it will be child's play. But in secret . . .
not possible.

MENELAUS. I think you should do it. Woman to woman.

HELEN. Don't worry, I'll go down on my knees if I have to.

MENELAUS. But supposing she says no? What do we do then?

HELEN. You die. And I, God help me, am forced to get
married.

MENELAUS. Betrayer! You're looking forward to it! The violence
is just an excuse!

HELEN. Not at all! I hereby swear by my husband's life . . .

MENELAUS. Let's get it quite clear! You'll die rather than desert
me.

HELEN. Of course darling, with the same sword, right beside
you!

MENELAUS. Right. Now then, let's shake hands on it.

HELEN. Certainly. If you die, I kiss the daylight goodbye!

MENELAUS. Me too. Without you, my life will end!

HELEN. How though? To show us in the best possible light?

MENELAUS. Oh, I'll kill you on top of the tomb, and then
I'll kill myself. But before that,
I shall put up a hell of a fight
For you, my darling! Let them all come,
I won't tarnish the glorious name
I won at Troy! I won't go back to Greece
To get jeered at and hooted at by the whole nation:
I, who robbed Thetis of her son, Achilles,
Who stood by and watched while Ajax, son of Telamon
Committed suicide, and saw Nestor, son of Neleus
Made childless by the hand of war!

Shall I not be man enough, having seen all these things,
To die myself, for the sake of my wife!
Of course I will! The gods, if they've any judgement at all,
Cause the shroud of earth to lie light on the tomb
Of the courageous man who dies in battle
At the hands of his enemies! Cowards they cast out
On the nearest bare rock, and leave them there!

CHORUS. Oh gods, it's about time the family of Tantalus
Had some luck, and an end to all their sufferings!

HELEN. Oh no, here we go again. This is just my luck!
Menelaus, we've had it! She's coming out here,
Theonoe, the clairvoyante. The house is positively
Reverberating with the sound of doors being unbolted.
Come on, run . . . but what's the point? Whether she's
                                                        in there
Or out here, wherever she is, she still knows
That you've arrived. This really is too much.
I'm permanently in trouble! And you survived Troy
And managed to escape from all sorts of barbarians,
Only to die by barbarians' swords here, after all!

THEONOE *enters, accompanied by half a dozen female
acolytes, who carry incense burners, aromatic torches and
joss sticks.*

THEONOE. Keep in front of me, my dears, hold the aromatic
                                                        torches
Well up, and make sure the smoke from the joss sticks
Circulates and permeates everywhere,
As our ritual demands, so that we may breathe
The open air of heaven with absolute purity.
And you, girl, just in case some man
Has been walking this way, and has polluted the path
With his presence, wave those joss sticks about
And strike the ground in front of me with the torch,
So that I may pass along completely unsullied!
Then, when you've made my customary obeisances
To the god, you can take the sacred flame

Back into my seance room. Well Helen?
What do you think of my prophecies now?
Pretty good eh? Your husband has come.
Menelaus. That's him, standing beside you.
He's lost both his ship and his imitation you
And has escaped from every imaginable danger
To get here. And he still doesn't know
Whether he will get home, or stay here for good.
In fact, there is going to be an argument
On Olympus among the gods this very day,
A specially convened conference sitting
To advise Zeus on that very subject.
Hera, on the one hand, formerly your enemy,
Is now on your side, and is keen to see you
Return to your fatherland with this woman,
So that the whole of Hellas may know
That Aphrodite's prize, the marriage with Paris,
Was an empty illusion. Aphrodite, on the other hand,
Wishes to rain down destruction on your return
Journey, so that she shall not publicly
Be demonstrated to have corruptly fixed
The beauty contest by using Helen
As a bribe, with all the disasters that followed
For just about everybody from that marriage. In fact,
In the end, it's up to me, whether, as Aphrodite
Wishes, I tell my brother you are here,
And so destroy you, or rather, adopt the policy
Of Hera, and save your life, by concealing
This news from my brother, whose standing orders
Are to tell him everything, and particularly
If you should happen to turn up here.
So . . . one of you had better go to my brother
And tell him that this man has come. I owe him that,
And from my point of view, it's the safer course . . .

She begins to go towards the tomb. HELEN *throws herself
on her knees in front of her.*

173

HELEN. Dear madam, consecrated virgin as you are –
 Let me fall on my knees at your feet! Not a posture
 Particularly fetching, and not one I adopt willingly,
 But for the sake of this man, who, the very moment
 I've finally got him back, is on the point of being killed!
 Do not, I beg you, denounce my husband –
 Who has only just this moment returned to my arms –
 To your brother, but spare him, I implore you!
 Don't betray your own integrity
 And sense of what's right, currying favour with him
 By actions which you know to be evil, and at the expense
 Of your own self respect. The gods loathe violence,
 They encourage people to make money honestly,
 Not by robbery and pillage. The sky
 Is our common property, the earth a treasury
 From which we may all fill our houses
 Without stealing what belongs to others,
 Or seizing it by force. I was brought here
 At the direct instigation of the gods –
 Misery though it was for me – Hermes himself
 Gave me to your father to keep safe for my husband,
 Who has now come, and wishes to claim me back.
 But he can hardly take me back home if he's dead,
 Nor could your father ever have returned
 A living being to a dead one!
 Consider for a moment the gods' intentions,
 And your father's too. Would the immortals,
 Would your father, of blessed memory,
 Want you to give back their neighbour's property
 Or not? I think they would. You ought not
 To defer to the wishes of a notoriously irreligious
 Brother, rather than a sainted father.
 If you, as a confidante of the spirit world
 And prophet of the divine order, should overturn
 You father's good intentions in the interest
 Of a corrupt and lascivious brother, it would be
 A scandal, that you, who claim to know
 All the secrets of the gods, present and future,

Should not know the difference between right and wrong!
Menelaus has suffered enough. Spare him the final misery;
And you can see the state that I'm in! So take my side,
And let us both enjoy a bit of luck for a change!
I don't think there's one person on earth
Who doesn't hate Helen. Everyone in Hellas
Takes it for granted I did the dirty on my husband
And went to live a life of unimaginable luxury
In Troy. But if I manage to get back
To Greece, and eventually to Sparta, when they hear
And see, with their own eyes that it was crafty trickery
By the gods that cost so many of their lives,
And that I wasn't the woman who betrayed my family,
At all, they will readmit me to the ranks of the respectable,
And I shall be able to arrange a marriage
For my daughter, whom at the moment no one
Will touch with a bargepole. And finally,
I shall say goodbye to this place of my exile
For the pleasures and treasures of my own home.
Even if my husband had died and been burned
On a funeral pyre in a distant land
I would honour his memory with my tears.
But he's alive, he's here with me, he's survived
All that! You can't tear him away from me now!
You can't do that, prophetic virgin, I beg you,
Don't do that to me! Grant me this favour,
Follow in the footsteps of your father, who was famous
For his sense of justice! There can be no greater praise
Of a child whose father was remarkable for his goodness
Than to say, 'She's keeping up her dad's good work!'
THEONOE. Yes. It's very sad. A very moving speech.
  You deserve to be pitied. But I'm very keen
  To hear Menelaus pleading for his life.
MENELAUS. Well. I'm certainly not going to grovel in front
                                                    of you,
  Or burst into tears! If I did that,
  If I crawled before you like a coward,
  Troy would be ashamed of the man who conquered her!

I'm not denying that it is quite good form
For a well born gentleman to shed a tear
Or two, at the right time, a disaster, for instance.
For my part, I prefer naked courage
To that sort of gentlemanly behaviour,
If that is what it is. So if you want
To help someone who is your guest – as you should –
Who wishes to assert his unquestioned claim
To take back his wife, simply hand her over,
And take the credit for helping both of us.
If you don't want to, it won't be the first time
I've been in a tight spot, and you will have demonstrated
Quite openly to everyone that you're an evil woman!
Meanwhile, I shall say something worthy of both of us,
And just, and most likely to arouse
Your sympathy, in reverent prayer
Here at your father's grave, wishing he
Were here to hear me himself. Old man,
This stone tomb is your home now.
Give her back to me. I now reclaim
My wife at your hands, whom Zeus gave you
To keep in trust for my return.
I know you can't return her to me
Personally, because you're dead. But this woman,
I'm sure, will hardly think it suitable
That her father, whose reputation during his life
Was so unimpeachable, should be summoned from the dead
And cursed as a promise breaker. Well. It's up to her.
Her decision now. King of the Underworld,
Let me enlist you on my side.
You've had a good many dead bodies
Despatched to your kingdom by my sword
For this woman's sake, you've had your cut,
You've been paid in full! So now, you can either
Bring all those dead men back to life,
Or compel this woman to live up to the example
Of her godfearing father, by giving back my wife . . .
However, if you intend to rob me of the woman

I married, let me tell you what she left out
Of her little speech. Get this clear, virgin,
That I have sworn a solemn oath
First, to fight your brother. Either he
Or I must die, it's as simple as that!
But if he refuses to take me on
In single handed combat, but decides
To starve us out as we take sanctuary
At this tomb, I am quite determined
To kill her, and then drive this two edged sword
Into my own guts, right here, on top of the tomb.
So that rivers of blood will gush down all over
Your father's grave! And we shall both of us lie,
Two corpses, side by side
On this polished slab, something you will remember
With agony for the rest of your life, which will be
A permanent insult to your father's memory!
No one is going to marry this woman, not your brother
Nor anyone else! I shall either take her home,
Or if I can't do that, take her to the dead!
That's not a sob in my voice, don't think it is!
If I were to burst into tears now
I'd be pathetic, and I'm not, I'm a hero!
Go on, kill me if you like,
You won't be killing a nobody, oh no,
You'll be killing somebody really famous!
But listen. It would actually be very much better
If I could persuade you to do what I say.
Then you'd be in the right. And I'd have my wife.

CHORUS. Madam, in this case you are the judge.
It'd be nice if your verdict could please everyone.

THEONOE. Both by instinct and by preference
I revere the gods, and I have a particular concern
For the purity of my own soul. I would never
Do anything to injure my father's reputation,
Nor can I indulge my brother in anything
That will bring him into disrepute. At the very
Centre of my being there stands a great temple

Of righteousness, inherited, no doubt,
From my immortal grandfather, Nereus.
So. I will try to save Menelaus' life.
I will cast my vote with Hera, since she
Wishes to protect you. As for Aphrodite –
May she be gracious to me, of course –
But I have had absolutely nothing to do with her
So far, and don't intend to start now.
I am virgin, and will attempt to remain so.
For your implied strictures on my father's honour
Spoken over his tomb – my own position
Is very much the same, namely that I should
Consider myself in the wrong not to give her back.
My father too, I'm quite sure, if he had lived,
Would have returned her to you, and you to her,
For both good and evil actions have their reward
In the underworld, just as they do on earth.
The dead may have no personal consciousness,
But they become eternally aware when they become

one

With the greater consciousness of the everlasting cosmos!
So, to bring this little homily to an end,
I shall keep my mouth shut, as you asked me to,
And not aid and abet my brother's immorality.
In fact, I'm doing him a good turn, though it may
Appear otherwise, if I turn him from degraded behaviour
Towards some sort of moral and spiritual feeling.
You must work out some way to escape
For yourselves. I shall keep out of the way
And say nothing at all. I advise you to begin
By praying to the gods, to Aphrodite, first of all,
To allow you to get back home, and then
To Hera, who at the moment supports you and your

husband,

That she should not change her mind. And to you,
My dear dead father, I say that to the limit
Of my strength I shall defend your good name
And the memory of your goodness from all detractors.

HELEN

She makes an obeisance to the tomb, then goes in a
dignified manner back into the palace.

CHORUS. The wicked have never prospered. But the righteous
                                                        can hope
  That their honesty will eventually be rewarded.
HELEN. Listen Menelaus, we have nothing to fear
  From the virgin anymore. From now on, you
  Must take over, and make a plan for our salvation.
MENELAUS. Ah, yes. Right. Listen. You've been here a long
                                                        time,
  Been quite friendly with all the King's servants, eh?
HELEN. What d'you mean by that? Can I really hope
  You've got a plan that might work, for both of us?
MENELAUS. Could you persuade one of the grooms
  To give us a chariot and four good horses?
HELEN. It's possible. But pointless. How could we escape?
  We know nothing of the country, and it's full of Egyptians!
MENELAUS. Hadn't thought of that. You're right. It's hopeless.
  I could hide in the house, kill the King with my sword!
HELEN. She's his sister! She would hardly keep quiet
  About a man who intended to murder her brother!
MENELAUS. But I haven't got a ship to get away in.
  The one I had's at the bottom of the sea.
HELEN. Listen, for a minute, to a woman's plan.
  Do you mind if I tell them you're dead, when you're not?
MENELAUS. It's bad luck to do that. Still, if it will work
  I'm quite willing, so long as I'm not actually dead.
HELEN. And then, you see, I can appear before that monster
  With my hair cut off, wailing and weeping . . .
MENELAUS. How will that help, or make us any safer?
  Anyway, it's not original, I've seen it in a play.
HELEN. I'll ask the tyrant if I can conduct
  Your funeral at sea, as if you'd been drowned!
MENELAUS. So what? We still haven't got a ship.
  How can we escape by faking my funeral?
HELEN. I'll ask him to *give* me a ship, from which
  I can cast your funeral offerings into the arms of the sea!

179

MENELAUS. That's a brilliant idea! But supposing he tells you
    To hold my funeral on land? That'll wreck the whole plan!
HELEN. But I'll tell him it's our custom, that we Greeks never
                                                            bury
    Someone who died at sea on land!
MENELAUS. I hope you can pull it off. Then I can come aboard
    And help with the ceremony. In the same boat. Eh?
HELEN. You've got it in one! It's essential you're there,
    And all your sailors who escaped from the wreck.
MENELAUS. Just find me a ship riding at anchor
    And all my boys will be there, swords in hand!
HELEN. Of course, you must take command. Then all we need
    Is a following wind and a fast moving ship.
MENELAUS. And we'll get them! The Gods are on our side!
    One thing. Who will you say told you I was dead?
HELEN. You, you dimwit! You sailed with Atreus' son!
    You're the only survivor! You saw him die!
MENELAUS. Of course! And these bits of sail round my body
    Will be proof that I've just survived a shipwreck.
HELEN. That's right, very handy. Bad luck at the time,
    But it may prove to be very useful in the end.
MENELAUS. Right! Do I come with you into the palace,
    Or sit here by the tomb twiddling my fingers?
HELEN. You stay here. If he tries anything on,
    The tomb gives you sanctuary, and of course, you have
                                                    your sword!
    I'll go inside and cut off my hair,
    Take this white dress off and put on my black,
    And give my cheeks a going over with blood-red fingernails!
    We're playing for high stakes in this game, and there's only
    Two possible results. Either I'm found out,
    And die, or I save your life, and see
    The shores of my homeland once again!
    Great Queen, you who go to bed with Zeus,
    Hera, give some peace to two tired people
    Who've suffered too much. This is our prayer,
    Stretching our hands up towards the heavens
    Where you live among the intricate patterns of the stars.

And you, Aphrodite, who won the prize for beauty
By using marriage with me as a bribe:
Daughter of Dione, don't destroy me for it.
You've done enough damage to me already
Making use of my name, though not my body,
Among the barbarians. If you're determined to kill me
Let me die, if I must, at home, among
My father's people. Are you never satisfied
At the sufferings you inflict on human beings?
Your weapons are lust, and deceit, every sort
Of intrigue and manipulation, even potions and poison
And bloodshed within families. If only your power
Could be restrained! For what other goddess
Has given mankind gifts as sweet as yours!
What I say is the truth. I can't be more sincere.

She goes into the palace, and MENELAUS, *distinctly nervous,
climbs up onto the tomb and crouches down behind it. The*
CHORUS' *ode that follows is the first to be entirely
serious, without a hint of parody.*

CHORUS. Master singer of the Muses' concert hall,
   The tree-columned forest, where, under the leaves' green
                               shroud,
  Melancholy nightingale,
  Virtuoso of the melodious lambent, you enthrall
  Men's ears with your sad vibrato, come with your art to aid
  My threnody for Helen's suffering
  And the Trojan nation's measureless weeping,
  As under the spears they fell
  Of the remorseless Greeks! Their fate was sealed
  When over the foaming plain of ocean
  With his barbarian oarsmen, Paris arrived,
  Bringing to the sons of Priam from Lacedaemon
  The phantom Helen, his fatal dream
  Of a bride, that would bring them all to destruction –
  And Aphrodite at the helm!

How many thousands of Greeks, by sling-shot or spear
Gasped out their breath and died, and entered the ever-open
                                                    door
Of eternity! Their widows
Shave their heads for grief, and howl in their despair
At their empty bedrooms. And how many thousands more
Nauplius, who sailed alone, destroyed
When he fired a beacon on the sea-hammered
Coast of Euboea, so that those
Who saw his signal, like a deceptive star,
Were lured to their deaths, on the cliffs of Cape
Caphereus, or on some rocky shore
Of the windswept Aegean! Menelaus had no hope
Of a harbour in mountainous Malea, driven
Far from home, with his meaningless prize, the ghost that
                                        made all Greece weep,
Hera's holy illusion!

What man can claim to understand
The manifestations of God, or his absence,
Or even the passing shadow of his hand
In human affairs, in the quest
For the deepest truths of human existence?
We see only contradictions, the last
Immortal decree overturning the first,
Without pattern, so that luck good or bad, mere chance,
Seems the only constant. Helen, you were blessed
With Zeus as a father. Swan wings
Disguised him as he conceived you in Leda's embrace.
Now all Greece reviles you as treacherous, faithless, wicked,
                                the most godless of things,
So where on earth can the truth be found? I place
My trust in the word of the gods, at last.

Lunatics, all of you, who see it as an instance
Of your manhood, with spear thrust or sword cuts
To end some poor devil's life, what ignorance,
What savagery! If bloodshed

Is to be the only arbiter of the rights
Of human conflict, mankind
Will never see an end to war, or cities at peace.
The Trojans went to grave chambers in their native earth
Helen, because of you, when without loss
Of manhood, by holding talks
They could have ended the war! Now the kingdom of death
Is their only country, and flame, like Zeus' merciless
thunderbolt strikes
Their walls to ashes. Helen's suffering, in plain truth,
Breeds dead men, broken families, universal distress.

The King, THEOCLYMENUS, *enters from his hunting party,
accompanied by hounds, huntsmen and dog handlers, equipped
with nets, and carrying some slaughtered game.*

THEOCLYMENUS. All honour to the tomb of my father! I
buried you,
Proteus, outside my front door
So that I, Theoclymenus, your son,
Could pay my respects both entering and leaving
My house with the least possible inconvenience.
All right then, you men, take the hounds and hunting nets
To the royal kennels behind the palace.

*All the huntsmen, dogs, beaters, and other attendants go
off into the palace.*

I'm a fool, of course, over and over again
I say to myself, 'You're far too kind hearted,
You should hand down a good many more death sentences
Than you do.' And now, you see, as a result,
I hear that some Greek is at large in the country,
Having slipped past the coastguards and frontier posts
Without being spotted. He's either a spy,
Or some kind of bounty hunter or mercenary
Who's after Helen, to filch her from under
My nose! If we take him, he'll die, that's for sure.

He looks up at the tomb, and notices that HELEN'*s mattress
is empty.*

> Hallo . . . What's this. . . ?
> It looks as if the whole thing's already
> Over and done with! The Tyndareus girl
> Has gone, there's her mattress by the tomb,
> Completely empty, and she is probably
> On her way out of the country by now!
> Hey you people over there, unbolt the gates,
> Get the horses – where are the guards? –
> Bring the chariots out from the coach house,
> If she gets clear over the frontier
> It won't be because of any lack of effort
> On my part! I want that woman for my wife!

Suddenly, he sees HELEN *re-entering from the palace, dressed in
black, with her hair savagely cut off.*

> Hold on a minute, everybody, stop!
> The woman we're after . . . is still here in the palace,
> She hasn't escaped at all. There she is!
> Well . . . Why have you put on that black dress
> Instead of your white? And why have you carved
> Your hair off so crudely with a kitchen knife
> From that magnificent head? Your cheeks are wet
> With tears. Real ones. Have you put on
> This display of mourning because of some prophetic dream
> Or nightmare? Or have you had some bad news
> From home that leaves you in such an emotional state?

HELEN. Lord and Master! that's the name I must call you
> > by now!

> I'm ruined, finished. All my hopes are gone!

THEOCLYMENUS. Really? Has there been some disaster? What's
> > happened?

HELEN. Menelaus . . . how can I say it? I've lost him! He's
> > . . . dead!

THEOCLYMENUS. I don't rejoice at the news. But it's a bit of
luck for me.
HELEN. I shall never be happy again . . . or not yet.
THEOCLYMENUS. How do you know? Did Theonoe tell you?
HELEN. Yes, she did . . . and the man who was with him when
he died.
THEOCLYMENUS. What? Is there someone who can actually
confirm it?
HELEN. Yes, he's here. If I had my way, I'd wish him
elsewhere!
THEOCLYMENUS. Who is he, where? I must find out for sure.

In response to HELEN's *frantic gestures,* MENELAUS *peeps out
nervously from behind the tomb.*

HELEN. That's the one, sitting there. Cowering by the tomb.
THEOCLYMENUS. Good God! What a scruff! His suit suits him!
HELEN. Ah, heavens, my poor husband must look just like
him now!
THEOCLYMENUS. From what country? And how did his journey
bring him here?
HELEN. He's a Greek, an Achaean. One of my husband's
shipmates.
THEOCLYMENUS. And how does he say Menelaus died?
HELEN. It's heartbreaking! In the watery waves of the salt sea!
THEOCLYMENUS. What foreign waters was he sailing in at the
time?
HELEN. Wrecked on the inhospitable coast of Africa!
THEOCLYMENUS. How come he didn't die? If he was in the
same ship. . . ?
HELEN. The lower classes have all the luck . . . never the
nobility.
THEOCLYMENUS. Where did he leave the wreck, before he
turned up here?
HELEN. Where I hope he'll die horribly. . . !

Half to herself, to ward off bad luck.

185

                                          But not Menelaus!

THEOCLYMENUS. Menelaus is dead already. What ship did this
                                          man come in?

HELEN. Sailors spotted him, and picked him up, he says.

THEOCLYMENUS. And where's the deadly creature sent to Troy
                                          in your place?

HELEN. You mean the phantom, made of clouds? Vanished,
                                          into thin air!

THEOCLYMENUS. Oh Paris, the whole nation of Troy: destroyed
                                          for nothing!

HELEN. And I too shared the bleak fate of Priam's children.

THEOCLYMENUS. Was your husband left unburied? Or did
                                          someone cover him up?

HELEN. Oh God, unburied! That's my worst suffering yet!

THEOCLYMENUS. And is that why you've cut off your beautiful
                                          blonde hair?

HELEN. Yes, I love him, I mean, I did! Here, or wherever!

THEOCLYMENUS. Are you sure all this is true? Are your tears
                                          genuine?

HELEN. I could hardly deceive your sister, could I?

THEOCLYMENUS. You could not! So what now? You won't stay
                                          at that tomb?

HELEN. I have to keep my distance, to stay loyal to my
                                          husband.

THEOCLYMENUS. You're very tantalising! Let the dead rot in
                                          peace!

HELEN. All right then. Let's get married. Say when.

THEOCLYMENUS. At last, but worth waiting for! My darling,
                                          thank you!

HELEN. And for your side of the bargain . . . we'll forget the
                                          past!

THEOCLYMENUS. Yes yes, state your terms. One good turn
                                          deserves another.

HELEN. We'll make a peace treaty. And you'll forgive me
                                          everything!

THEOCLYMENUS. No more quarrelling. All gone! Little bird,
                                          fly away!

HELEN. Then if you really love me, I beg you, on my
knees . . .
THEOCLYMENUS. Just say what you want darling, there's no
need to beg.
HELEN. To give my dead husband a proper funeral.
THEOCLYMENUS. You can't bury someone missing. Unless you
bury a ghost.
HELEN. But we Greeks have a custom, when someone's lost at
sea . . .
THEOCLYMENUS. What happens? Pelops' family, of course,
knows about such things.
HELEN. We bury an empty shroud, with no body in it.
THEOCLYMENUS. Build a tomb then, do what's required –
anywhere in my land!
HELEN. Oh no! Sailors lost at sea are never buried like
that!
THEOCLYMENUS. How then? I know nothing about your Greek
customs.
HELEN. We take all the offerings for the dead out to sea . . .
THEOCLYMENUS. And what offerings do you require for the
deceased?
HELEN. He knows! I've had no experience of funerals,
fortunately!

She beckons MENELAUS *forward.*

THEOCLYMENUS. Well, stranger, you've brought me some very
good news!
MENELAUS. It's not good news for me. Or the poor chap who's
dead.
THEOCLYMENUS. Well then, how do you bury men who died at
sea?
MENELAUS. That depends on how well off you are at the time.
THEOCLYMENUS. Money's no object. For her sake, ask for
anything.
MENELAUS. There's a blood sacrifice first, to the spirits of
the dead.
THEOCLYMENUS. What do you sacrifice? Tell me what you want.

MENELAUS. Well, what have you got? What you suggest will
be fine.

THEOCLYMENUS. We usually sacrifice a horse, or a bull.

MENELAUS. Whatever you give, it's got to be the best.

THEOCLYMENUS. I always have the best. My herds are
incomparable.

MENELAUS. A properly laid out bier . . . with no body, of
course!

THEOCLYMENUS. That's no problem. Is anything else customary?

MENELAUS. Top quality bronze weapons. He always liked a
good spear . . .

THEOCLYMENUS. What I give will be worthy of Pelops'
descendants.

MENELAUS. And of course, the best quality produce from your
farms.

THEOCLYMENUS. But how do you throw all this into the sea?

MENELAUS. You need a ship. And men to row it.

THEOCLYMENUS. And how far out from land must this ship go?

MENELAUS. Till the waves from her wake are barely visible
from the shore.

THEOCLYMENUS. So far? Really! Why do the Greeks do that?

MENELAUS. So that the waves won't wash up our offerings on
the beach.

THEOCLYMENUS. You shall have a Phoenecian ship. They're
very fast.

MENELAUS. That sounds great . . . I mean . . . Menelaus will
like it.

THEOCLYMENUS. Can't *you* do all this, without her?

MENELAUS. On no! It must be mother, wife or child.

THEOCLYMENUS. So you say it's her job, to bury her husband.

MENELAUS. Yes, the dead must have their due. It's only decent.

THEOCLYMENUS. Then she must do it. It's in my interest to
encourage

My wife to take religion seriously.
Go inside and select what ornaments and gifts
For the corpse you think suitable.
And you, since you have been so helpful
And pleased me so much, I don't intend

188

To send you away empty handed.
You really are the most appalling scruff,
But since you brought me such very good news,
You shall have some decent clothes, instead of these rags,
And plenty of food to get you back home
To your native country. And you, my poor girl,
There's no point in exhausting yourself
With weeping to no purpose. The fact is,
Menelaus has had his lot. You will never
See him alive again. He's dead.

MENELAUS. Young lady, your duty is plain. You must accept
Your present husband, the one who stands before you,
And forget the one who no longer has any
Claim on you at all. That's the best way out
In your current situation. And if I get back to Greece,
In safety, I'll tell them that all those stories
About you are libellous nonsense! Provided,
That is, that you act the way a good wife
Ought to act, towards her husband.

HELEN. Oh, I shall, don't you worry, my husband
Won't have the slightest cause to complain
At my behaviour. Well, you'll be there,
Won't you, so you'll see for yourself!
But now, you, my poor chap, go inside,
Have a lovely bath, and get those dreadful clothes off!
And then, at once, I shall give you your reward,
Because you deserve it! I'd take it as a great
Favour if you'd behave exactly towards me
As my husband would, as though you really were
My beloved Menelaus, paying due honour
To his memory. And in return,
I shall certainly behave towards you
Exactly as a wife behaves towards her husband!

HELEN *and* MENELAUS *rush into the palace together, barely
able to restrain themselves one moment longer.*

THEOCLYMENUS *follows them, with as much dignity as he can
manage, beaming round to everyone that he is in charge.*

CHORUS. There was a time when the Great Mother,
   Goddess of the Mountains, ran
   Like a madwoman through the green
   Shadows of the deepest forest, and under
   The flooding river water, down
   Below the echoing thunder of the salt sea,
   Searching, in an ecstasy of pain,
   For her lost daughter, whose name is a mystery
   Never to be spoken. In her despair
   She invoked the cymbals and gongs
   Of Bacchus, whose deep voiced songs
   Tranced the most savage animals to draw
   Her chariot. Artemis, like a tornado, swept
   Along at her side, to find the child, kidnapped
   From the girls' dancing circle, her bow
   Taut and arrows invincible, and Athene stepped
   Pace for powerful pace with them, with her armour and

                                      spear.
   But Zeus, whose keen eyes from heaven see everything clear,
   Had another ending in view.

   So when the Great Mother, in despair, and worn out
   With her endless search, and the emotion
   Of her daughter's mysterious abduction,
   Came to the summit of Ida, the snowy lookout
   Where the nymphs of the mountain keep guard, she threw
   Herself down in a snowdrift between thickets and rocks

                                in her grief –
   And the green pastures below
   Withered, the fruit and cornfields that sustain the life
   Of man, died, famine wasted a generation,
   The livestock grew thin, no leaves,
   Green and succulent, no grass,
   No tender vine shoots to prevent the starvation.
   The economy of the cities, and all commerce, died,
   The temples stood empty, the gods denied
   Their rituals of sacrifice;
   No altars smoked with incense, no offerings glowed

With the flame of holy oil. Even the fountain
Of pure spring water that gushes from the mountain
In her terrible grief, she froze.

Not only were the race of men starving,
She had brought to an end the Olympian suppers
Of the gods themselves. So Zeus, hoping
To placate the furious grief of the sponsor
Of all growing things said, 'Go, you harbingers
Of Spring, the three Graces, go to angry Demeter
Still weeping the tears of a mother
For her dead child, and with your soothing voices
Lessen her pain: go too, you Muses, bring her dancing
And songs.' And supreme Aphrodite, who embraces
Everything that grows or is born, most beautiful
Of the Immortals, took the powerful
Bronze gongs that speak from the profoundest earth,
And the taut-skinned drum. Smiling,
Demeter acquiesced, took up the sweet-singing
Oboe, and joined the dance of rebirth.

You, Princess Helen, made no sacrifice,
According to ancient rite
In the secret chamber of the great goddess
To calm the frenzy of her anger.
Dear child, you lived unaware of the yearly debt
We all owe to the Great Mother.
No one doubts the anarchic power
Of the instruments of Bacchus, the dappled fawnskin
Cloak, the sacred reed, wound with ivy like a sceptre,
The bull-roarer, with its vibrating whine
As it whirls in the air, and the crazed Maenads screaming
With their loosed hair wild and streaming
For Bacchus at the night-long orgy
Of Demeter. But Helen too has a power
That soothes gods and remedies disaster:
The mystery of her unearthly beauty.

Enter HELEN *from the palace, even more radiant than usual.*

HELEN. Oh, that's better! Everything in the Palace,
    My dears, is going swimmingly.
    The daughter of Proteus, who is, of course,
    Part of the escape plan, has been interrogated
    By her brother, but has said not a word about
    My husband being here. She told him he's gone
    Below, to the country of eternal darkness –
    Out of pure kindness to me she did it,
    No other reason. My husband's been lucky
    Too, he's managed to get his hands on
    Some first rate equipment. All the military gear
    That was supposed to be part of the offering to the sea,
    He's armed himself with, sliding his left arm
    Into the shield grip, and grabbing the spear
    With his right, pretending he's part of the ritual
    Of honouring the drowned man! He's managed to get
    Some body armour too, so he's well protected.
    As soon as we get on board the ship
    And the oars get moving, he intends to give
    Any number of those Egyptians one hell of a pasting!
    I've managed to get him a change of clothes
    Instead of those appalling rags from the shipwreck.
    And at last, and, I can tell you, not before time,
    I got him into the bath and gave him a wash
    In clean water. God knows how many years
    Since that last happened! Oh look, he's coming out
    Of the house . . . the man who thinks he has marriage
    With me neatly in the palm of his hand!
    So I'd better shut up. And you, my dear girls,
    If you're really our friends, as you say you are,
    Be discreet, and keep your mouths shut!
    Perhaps, if we can make it, with a bit of luck,
    We can help you to escape too, one day!

Enter THEOCLYMENUS, *with* MENELAUS *dressed and armoured,
and followed by a huge train of attendants carrying his gifts for the*

funeral, including food, clothing, jewellery and gifts, and animals,
not unlike the Grand March in Aida.

THEOCLYMENUS. Everybody keep in line! All you slaves
   Carrying the funeral offerings to be thrown into the sea,
   You must do exactly what this foreigner said!
   Look, Helen, I don't want to speak out of turn,
   But why don't you take my advice? Stay here.
   You will show just as much respect for your husband
   Whether you're there in person or not.
   The fact is, I'm terribly afraid
   You might be overwhelmed by some neurotic desire
   To throw yourself into the sea, overcome
   With devotion to your former husband!
   You're making an excessive fuss about him,
   Considering he's not here, not even his body!
HELEN. My dear, very soon to be my husband,
   It's a matter of the respect a wife has for her spouse,
   And my gratitude for the partnership we shared together
   That I should honour his memory. I loved him quite enough
   To die with him, as a matter of fact. But really,
   What's the point? It can give him no pleasure
   That I should join him among the dead. No.
   I must go, in person, to honour the dead man
   With my gifts at his funeral. And may the gods
   Give you exactly what I wish for you,
   And to this stranger as well, since he
   Has been so helpful in everything I'm doing.
   I shall be exactly the sort of wife to you
   You deserve to have in a house like this,
   Because you've been very kind to Menelaus,
   And to me. Don't worry. There's going to be
   A happy ending, I'm quite sure of that.
   Now, just to put the cherry on top of the cake
   Of your generosity towards me, order someone
   To give us the ship . . . to carry all this stuff.
THEOCLYMENUS. You, go and commandeer one of the ships
                             built at Sidon,

The fifty-oared jobs, and the rowers to man it!

HELEN. He's in charge of the funeral, so he'd better command
it.

THEOCLYMENUS. Yes, of course. Tell the sailors he's in
command.

HELEN. Say it again, to make it clear. So there's no
misunderstanding.

THEOCLYMENUS. He's the captain. That's twice. Shall I say it a
third time?

HELEN. No, blessings upon you . . . and on my plan too!

THEOCLYMENUS. Now, don't spoil that beauty with too much
crying.

HELEN. Today will show you just how grateful I am.

THEOCLYMENUS. Why bother with the dead? It's a
waste of time.

HELEN. There are two sorts of truth you know. A dead one,
and a living.

THEOCLYMENUS. I shall be just as good a husband to you as
Menelaus.

HELEN. I can't find fault with you at all. All I need is good
luck.

THEOCLYMENUS. That's up to you. If you give me all your
love . . .

HELEN. I don't need lessons in loving people I love.

THEOCLYMENUS. Why don't I come with you, to look after you,
and to help!

HELEN. No, no, it's all right! I'm your slave, not you mine.

THEOCLYMENUS. Carry on then! I don't need to bother
With all this Pelopid ritual. Menelaus certainly
Didn't die here, my house is quite clean,
And no purification is necessary.
You, go and tell all the top people
To bring their wedding presents into my house.
And tell them I expect to hear
Music in celebration of my wedding
In every corner of the land, nuptial odes
And ballads, all that sort of thing,
And that they must put on such a show to commemorate

My marriage to Helen, that everyone else
Will be green with envy! And you, foreigner,
Take all the gifts and offerings in honour
Of her first husband, and see them all consigned
Into the bosom of the deep! And then come back here
With my wife as quickly as you possibly can.
And after that, when you have had your share
Of the wedding banquet, you can go home,
Or live happily here, just as you please.

THEOCLYMENUS *goes into the palace. The huge procession is*
already on the way out.

MENELAUS. Oh Zeus, wise god as you are, and Father
Of all things, look after us now, and keep us
Out of trouble! We're like two yoked mules
Carrying the pack of our misfortunes
To the top of a mountain: we could do with some help!
Just one touch with your fingertip is all we need
To get us safe to the top. We've had
More than our share of disasters already,
And I've called you plenty of names in the past,
Gods, complimentary, and not so complimentary,
But I don't deserve bad luck all the time,
Surely I ought to be given some chance
To get back on my feet again? One favour
Is all I need now! If you give me that,
I shall live in happiness for the rest of my life!

Exit HELEN *and* MENELAUS.

CHORUS. Racing Phoenecian galley
From Sidon, your bow cuts through the waves
In a leaping flurry
Of foam, your incomparable rowing drives
You onward like the leader of a chorus of silvery
Dolphins, whenever the sea
Is flat and unruffled by the lazy breeze,

And in drowsy tranquillity
The nymph of the doldrums, Pontus' daughter,
Whispers across the grey-blue water,
'Spread your sails, sailors, to catch the gentlest breath,
Take your pine blades in hand
And row Helen back to the land
Of sheltered harbours, and Perseus' city, her native hearth.'

When you reach the flood waters
Of the river Eurotas, you will surely see
The water-nymph daughters
Of Leucippus, or, at the Temple of Athene,
Join the revels for the death of Hyacinthus, laughter
And dancing, all night till dawn:
Hyacinthus, so much loved by Apollo, accidentally
Killed by a discus, thrown
By the god himself, as they competed together.
That day was sanctified in Sparta for ever
By the son of Zeus, to bring bulls to the slaughter,
And for feasting. Perhaps you will see
The child you left, Hermione.
No marriage torches have yet been lit for her.

Oh for wings to fly
In a squadron across the sky
Like the African cranes,
Who, leaving winter and foul weather
Behind them, flock to the cry of their leader
Across the waterless plains
To a valley of corn and vines,
Following his voice in strict formation.
You long-necked sprinters, whose soaring
Wings beat in well-matched competition
With the racing clouds, swoop under the Pleiades,
Riding at the zenith in the dark skies
Of Orion's nocturnal hunting:
Like a messenger with good news, landing
On the banks of the Eurotas, proclaim

That Menelaus has taken Troy, he still lives,
And is finally coming home!

And you on your stallions galloping
Above the clouds, in a glittering
Hailstorm of stars,
You Heavenly Twins, who in Immortal company
Inhabit the eternal mansions of the sky,
At long last, Helen's saviours,
Skimming the blue-grey waters,
Come to her aid, where the breakers foam grey
On the dark blue skin of the sea.
Bring breezes to speed her on her way,
Fresh from the hand of Zeus. And purify
Your sister's reputation, the ignominy
Of bedding with a barbarian, which she
Endured through the jealousy
Of three goddesses on Ida. In a word,
She never set eyes on Troy, or the towers so magnificently
Built by Apollo the god!

A MESSENGER *comes running in from the direction of the
sea. He is one of* THEOCLYMENUS' *sailors, with his clothing
torn as though in a fight, and soaking wet from the sea.
He shouts towards the palace.*

MESSENGER. My Lord! This is terrible!

He turns to the CHORUS.

                        Has he gone into the house?

The door opens, and THEOCLYMENUS *appears.*

  Prepare for a shock, sir. I've got very bad news.
THEOCLYMENUS. What news?
MESSENGER.   You're going to have to find another wife,
Because Helen has gone. She's left the country.

THEOCLYMENUS. How? She can't fly! Not by land, I'm sure
                                                    of that!
MESSENGER. Menelaus has quite simply sailed away with her.
   He came here himself, and told you he was dead!
THEOCLYMENUS. No, that's outrageous! Where did they get
                                                    a ship
   To sail away in? I don't believe it!
MESSENGER. You gave him one. That foreigner. You remember.
   And a first rate crew. That question's soon answered!
THEOCLYMENUS. But how on earth did they do it? I've got
                                                    to know!
   I could never have imagined that one man
   Could overpower so many – you among them!
MESSENGER. Well sir, as soon as we left the Royal Palace,
   The daughter of Zeus led the procession
   Down to the sea, moving in step
   With the funeral march so elegantly,
   And with such a pretty little foot, all the time
   Howling and keening for her dead husband,
   Who was there beside her all the time,
   Not dead at all. So, when we got
   To the dock gates, we went into the shipyard
   And dragged down a ship, the latest Sidon model,
   And launched her – it was her maiden voyage.
   And she was a beauty, with fifty oars
   And fitted rowing benches. So everyone
   Got moving on all the preparations
   For sailing, one group stepped the mast,
   Another set out the banks of oars
   Into the rowlocks, and roped the white sails
   Onto the spars, and reefed them, and lowered
   The twin rudders over the sides, and lashed them
   To the crossbars. Anyway, while we were doing,
   All this – they were watching for the most opportune time
   Of course – a crowd of Greeks, Menelaus' shipmates,
   Came crunching down the shingle, all dressed in rags
   From the shipwreck, but a fine body of men,
   However scruffy they looked. The son of Atreus,

When he saw them, made a heart rending speech,
A really meretricious performance it was too,
With a little sob in his voice, 'Oh, you poor devils,'
He said, 'what Greek ship has gone to the bottom
To bring you here in this state? Have you come
To join in the funeral ceremonies for the drowned
Son of Atreus, with this girl of Tyndareus'
Family, performing, because the poor man is not here,
The ritual of the empty shroud?'
And they, of course, put on a great show,
Crying their eyes out, and clambering aboard
Carrying their sea offerings for Menelaus.
We started to get a bit suspicious
At this, muttering together and grumbling
That it was a hell of a lot of extra passengers
For one ship. But when it came to it,
Remembering what you said, we kept our mouths shut.
Your orders were quite clear, that the stranger was in
command.
That was the main cause of the disaster that followed.
We got all the other stuff on board ship
Easily enough, as it was all pretty light,
But the bull planted his feet on the gangplank,
And he wouldn't budge, he kept on bellowing
And rolling his eyes, and hunching his back,
And lowering his head and glaring at us
Along his horns, so we didn't dare
Lay a finger on him. But then Helen's husband
Shouted out, 'Come on chaps, you sacked
The city of Ilium, so you can show them how the Greeks
Handle a recalcitrant bull! Now, get
Your young shoulders under his belly and lift
Him bodily up onto the bow deck,
Where my sword will be ready when the time comes
For the sacrifice!' And as soon as he had said it,
They grabbed hold of the bull and hoisted it up
And manhandled it on to the forrard deck!
There Menelaus calmed it down – like you would

A nervous horse without a yoke fellow –
By stroking its neck. Eventually,
When everything was loaded on board ship,
Helen climbed up the ladder – we caught a flash
Of her beautiful ankles too – and seated herself
In the middle of the poop deck: and Menelaus,
Who, theoretically at least, was supposed to be dead,
Sat down beside her. All the rest of the Greeks
Sat equally along the port and starboard side,
Each man sitting next to a rower,
And with a sword well hidden inside his rags!
And then, the bosun gave the note,
And the sound of our rowing song rolled across the waves
As we pulled out to sea. When we'd gone some distance,
Not too far from land, but not too close either,
The helmsman asked, 'How much farther
Stranger? Is this far enough? Or shall we pull out
A bit farther yet? You're in command.'
And Menelaus said, 'This is quite far enough
As far as I'm concerned.' And drawing his sword
In his right hand, he made his way
To the deck forrard, and got into a good position
To sacrifice the bull. And as he cut its throat,
He didn't even mention the dead man's name
But said this prayer, 'Poseidon, God of the Ocean,
You who live in the salty depths of the sea,
And you immortal sea-nymphs, daughters of Nereus,
Help me to reach the cliffs of Nauplion
In safety, together with my wife,
And get us away from this land unmolested!'
And the blood spurted out in an uninterrupted stream
From the bull's throat, straight into the sea,
A very good omen for the foreigner,
We all thought. Then one of our men
Suddenly shouted, 'There's something fishy here,
We're being taken for a ride! Turn back to land,
Tell the starboard bank of oars to pull us round,
And you, push the tiller hard over!' But the son

Of Atreus, jumping up on the dead bull's carcass,
Shouted out to his comrades, 'What are you waiting for
Lads, you're the flower of Greek manhood,
Kill these lousy barbarians and chuck them
Into the sea!' And our bosun shouted
To all our crew, in defiance of him,
'Come on boys, grab hold of a spar,
Rip up the rowing benches, drag the oars
Out of the rowlocks, and smash the heads
Of these foreign enemies into a bloody pulp!'
And at that, everybody was on their feet,
Our side armed with bits of wood
From all over the ship, and the others with swords!
The deck was soon slippery with blood, and Helen
Shouted encouragement from the stern, 'Live up
To your glorious Trojan reputation, my lads,
Show these barbarian layabouts what's what!'
Then the fighting was fast and furious,
Some men beaten to their knees, others keeping their feet
Somehow, and some already stretched dead
On the boards. And Menelaus, well armed as he was,
Spotted where his comrades were up against it
And waded in with that strong right arm of his,
So that a good many of them took a header
Into the sea, and it wasn't long before there wasn't
A single one of your crew left on the rowing benches.
Then Menelaus stood over the helmsman and made him
Set course for Greece. His Greek crew
Hoisted the sail, and almost at once
The wind set fair behind them. So,
There it is, they've gone. I escaped the slaughter
By shinning down the anchor rope into the sea.
I was pretty well all in when a fisherman
Picked me up and brought me ashore
So I could bring you the news, and tell you how it happened.
And the moral of the story, I reckon is this:
Always be moderately suspicious of everyone
And never give complete trust to anybody.

CHORUS. Who would have thought that Menelaus
  Could deceive a man like you? Yet he was here all the time.
THEOCLYMENUS. Oh God, how humiliating, to be taken

                                   in

  And made a fool of by a woman!
  My bride, the one I selected to be my wife,
  She's got clean away! If there were any chance
  Of catching that ship, I'd be after them,
  Just to get my hands on those foreigners!
  But since I can't do that, I'll punish my sister instead!
  She betrayed me! She saw Menelaus in the house
  And didn't tell me one word about it!
  That's the last time she'll deceive a man with her prophecies!

He grabs a sword from one of his guards. The CHORUS *(See
Introduction) rushes to bar his way into the house. The following
lines being taken severally by different members, or in groups.*

CHORUS. No master, where are you going? Not to kill her!
                                        You can't!
THEOCLYMENUS. To execute justice! So get out of my way!
CHORUS. I'll hang on to your clothes! What you're doing is
                                    wicked!
THEOCLYMENUS. You can't stop me, you're a slave!
CHORUS.   I can when I'm in the right!
THEOCLYMENUS. No you're not. If you prevent me . . .
CHORUS.   I won't let you go. . . !
THEOCLYMENUS. From killing my bitch of a sister . . .
CHORUS.   Your god-fearing sister, you mean!
THEOCLYMENUS. Who betrayed me.
CHORUS.   That was the honourable thing to do.
THEOCLYMENUS. She gave my wife to someone else!
CHORUS.   She belonged to him already.
THEOCLYMENUS. Who can own my property!
CHORUS.   The man who got her from her father!
THEOCLYMENUS. Chance gave her to me!
CHORUS.   And morality took her back!
THEOCLYMENUS. It's my business. You're no judge.

CHORUS.   But I have the better case.
THEOCLYMENUS. Am I a subject, or a King?
CHORUS.   A true King's just, not wicked.
THEOCLYMENUS. You must want to die!
CHORUS.   Yes, kill me if you want to!
  But I won't stand by and watch you murder your sister!
  It's the noblest thing a slave can do, to die for his master!

In the heavens, the Dioscuri, the Heavenly Twins, appear,
each one an exact mirror image of the other.

DIOSCURI. Control your anger, Theoclymenus,
  King of Egypt, before it drives you
  To do something unjust! We,
  The Heavenly Twins, whom Leda bore,
  Together with Helen, who has just escaped
  From this country, we call upon you by name!
  You are in this murderous fury about a marriage
  That was emphatically not made in heaven.
  Nor did your sister, the virgin Theonoe,
  The daughter of the immortal sea-nymph,
  Wrong you in any way. On the contrary,
  She carried out the wishes of the gods
  And honoured the intentions of your father.
  It was always a part of the gods' plan
  That Helen should live here in your house
  Up to this present moment. But now
  That the very foundations of Troy are destroyed,
  And the name of Helen, which she lent to the gods,
  Is no longer required, it is right and proper
  That the old marriage bond should be re-asserted
  And that she should return home to live with her husband.
  So put that ominous sword back into its scabbard,
  Cease to threaten your sister, and acknowledge
  That she has acted with great wisdom. In fact,
  We would have helped our sister long ago –
  We did become gods, as you see, thanks to Zeus –
  But we were not strong enough to change

The preordained pattern of events,
Nor to influence the powerful cabal of gods
Who had stitched up the whole business to turn out like this.
That is our message to you, Theoclymenus.
To our sister we say, enjoy the trip
With your husband! You shall have a following wind
All the way home, and we, your twin brothers
And true saviours, will ride the white horses of the sea
Alongside your ship till you reach home port.
And when the time comes for the last lap
And you breast the tape in the race of life,
You, too, will become divine,
And along with us, the Heavenly Twins,
Receive prayers and sacrifices from the human race!
Zeus has it all planned. And the first spot
Where Maia's son, Hermes, rested for a breather
In his mad dash across the sky after snatching you from
                                                                Sparta
So that Paris shouldn't have you, I mean the island
Of Acte, close to the coast of Attica,
That spot will always be called 'Helena'
Because when you were whisked away from your home,
It afforded you some rest. Menelaus, the wanderer,
Will eventually reach the Islands of the Blessed.
We gods, you know, are always biased
In favour of the upper classes. The nastiest
Sufferings are always reserved for the masses.

THEOCLYMENUS. Sons of Leda and Zeus, I certainly withdraw
All my claim on your sister, and apologise for my anger.
Of course I won't kill Theonoe! And let Helen
Go back to her home by all means,
If that's what the gods want. And let me tell you,
That you have a very wonderful sister,
An absolute model of chastity, as you would expect
Being of the same blood as yourselves!
All hail to you, and to the astonishing intellect
And imperishable nobility of Helen, qualities
Seen in very few other women . . . if any.

HELEN

The Dioscuri fade away, and the sky returns to unsullied Egyptian blue. THEOCLYMENUS *moves into his palace with as much dignity as he can manage in the circumstances.*

CHORUS. The gods take many different shapes.
  By contraries and opposites they have their way.
  They disappoint expectation, frustrate hopes,
  And write unexpected endings to the play.
  We have seen them in action, in this story, today.